AS-Level Sociology

The Revision Guide

Editors:
Gemma Hallam, Katherine Reed

Contributors:

Charley Darbishire, Anna Hazeldene, Neil Renton, Frances Rippon, Claire Thompson, Julie Wakeling, Andrew Walker

Proofreaders:

Kate Houghton, Kate Manson, Lee Murray, Sarah Acford-Palmer, Kate Redmond, Jennifer Underwood

Published by Coordination Group Publications Ltd.

This book is suitable for:

AQA and OCR.

There are notes at the tops of double pages to tell you if there's a bit you can ignore for your syllabus.

ISBN: 1 84146 977 7
Groovy website: www.cgpbooks.co.uk
Jolly bits of clipart from CorelDRAW
Printed by Elanders Hindson, Newcastle upon Tyne.

Nature and Role of Family in Society

Marxists See the **Family** as Meeting the **Needs** of the **Capitalist System**

Like functionalists, Marxists view the family as performing **essential functions** for modern industrial society. The key difference is that **Marxists** argue that the family **benefits** the minority **in power** (called the "**bourgeoisie**") and the economy, but **disadvantages** the **working class** majority (called the "**proletariat**").

1) **Engels (1884)** said the family had an **economic function** of keeping wealth within the **bourgeoisie** by passing it on to the next generation as **inheritance**. In other words, when a **rich person dies**, their **kids get their money**.
2) **Zaretsky (1976)** focused on how the family helped the capitalist economy. He argued that the family is one place in society where the **proletariat** can have **power** and **control**. When the **working man** gets home, he's **king of his own castle**. This relieves some of the **frustration** workers feel about their low status, which helps them to **accept** their **oppression** and exploitation as workers.
3) The role of women in the family in capitalist society as "**housewife**" means workers are **cared for** and **healthy**. This makes them **more productive** — a great benefit that the capitalist class (the employers) get for **free**.
4) The **family household** is a unit with the **desire** to **buy** the **goods** produced by capitalist industry, e.g. washing machines, cars, fridges. The family is a **unit of consumption**. The family buys the goods for more than they cost to produce and the **bourgeoisie get the profit**.

All in all, Marxists argue the family is a **very useful tool of capitalism**.

The **Marxist** View is **Criticised** for being too **Negative**

The Marxist view of the family is all about it being a **tool of capitalist oppression**, and **never mentions nice things**, like bedtime stories for the kids, or trips to the zoo.

Criticisms of the Marxist view of the family

1) Marxist sociology is entirely focused on **benefits to the economy**, and benefits to the working man's **boss**. It **ignores other benefits** to individuals and society.
2) Traditional Marxist sociology **assumes** that the worker is **male**, and that women are **housewives**.
3) There is **no Marxist explanation** for why the family flourishes as an institution in **non-capitalist** or **communist** societies and there is little Marxist research on **alternatives** to the family.

Functionalist and Marxists both see the family having a **key role** in society in **reproducing social structure and order**. The **key sociological debate** between them is whether this is **positive** or **negative** and **who benefits**.

Practice Questions

Q1 What do sociologists define as a household?

Q2 What are the key functions of the family according to Parsons?

Q3 Explain the ways in which Functionalist and Marxist perspectives on the role of the family are similar.

Q4 Explain the ways in which Functionalist and Marxist perspectives on the role of the family are different.

Exam Questions

Q1 "The nuclear family is universal and inevitable." Discuss. (15 marks)

Q2 Examine the view that the family performs the vital function of maintaining the 'status-quo' in society. (20 marks)

Cog in society's machine or tool of capitalist oppression — you decide...

If you're comparing Functionalist and Marxist perspectives about the role of the family, make sure you cover the pros and cons of each view — and most importantly make sure you answer the question. Remember, Functionalists believe that the family is there to keep society chugging along smoothly, and Marxists believe it's there to help exploit the common worker.

Nature and Role of Family in Society

There's a lot of different feminist theory about the family — it's generally left wing and anti-traditional. But it's worth looking at recent right wing pro-traditional ideas as well. And at the postmodernists — who say everyone can do what they like. Hooray.

*Most **Feminists** Believe the **Family Exploits** and **Oppresses Women***

1) From a **feminist perspective**, the **family** helps to **maintain the existing social order**. (If that sounds familiar, it's because Functionalists and Marxists also talk about keeping up the existing social order.)
2) Feminists call the existing social order **patriarchy**. Patriarchy is the **combination of systems, ideologies and cultural practices** which make sure that **men** have power.
3) Feminist theory argues that the family **supports** and reproduces **inequalities** between men and women.
4) The idea is that women are **oppressed** because they're **socialised** to be **dependent** on men — and to put themselves in second place to men. The **family** has a central role in this socialisation — **male and female roles** and **expectations** are **formed in the family** and then **carried on into wider society**.
5) Feminist sociologists say that there's an **ideology** about men's **roles** and women's **roles** in the family.

An ideology is a set of ideas about the way things are and the way things ought to be.

*There are **Three Main Strands** of **Feminist Thought** on the **Family***

The three strands of feminist thought are **radical feminism**, **Marxist feminism** and **liberal feminism**.

The distinction between the three theories comes from what they see as the **root cause of patriarchy**. For radical feminists it's the **power dominance of men**, for Marxist feminists it's the **capitalist system** and for liberal feminists it's **cultural attitudes** and laws that allow **discrimination**.

All these theories generalise quite a bit.

Marxist feminism — key points

Marxist feminism sees the **exploitation of women** as essential to the success of **capitalism**. The family produces and cares for the next generation of workers for society at almost **no cost** to the capitalist system. It's cost-free because society accepts that **housework** should be **unpaid.** Men are paid for work outside the home, but **women aren't paid** for work **inside** the home. If this sounds out-dated, remember evidence shows that even when women work outside the home they still do **most** of domestic labour (see p.20-21). **Benston (1969)** points out that if housework were paid even at **minimum wage** levels it would **damage capitalist profits** hugely. **Ansley (1972)** thinks that men take out their frustration and stress from work on women, instead of challenging the capitalist system.

Radical feminism — key points

Radical feminist theory also highlights **housework** as an area of **exploitation of women** but... and it's a big but... radical feminists don't see this as the fault of the capitalist system. Radical feminists see exploitation of women as being down to the **domination of men in society**. Radical feminism believes that **men will always oppress women**. **Delphy and Leonard (1992)** are radical feminists who see the family as a patriarchal institution in which **women do most of the work** and **men get most of the benefit**.

Liberal feminism — key points

Liberal feminists emphasise the **cultural norms** and **values** which are reinforced by the family and by other institutions in society. The family is only sexist because it **supports mainstream culture** which is sexist. Liberal feminists believe **social change is possible**. They try to put pressure on institutions such as the **legal system** and **government** to change laws and social policies which discriminate against women.

*Feminist Theory has been **Criticised***

1) Feminist theory of all strands has been **criticised** for portraying women as **too passive**. It plays down the ability of individual women to **make changes** and **improve** their situation.
2) Feminist sociology **doesn't acknowledge** that **power might be shared** within a family.
3) Some feminist theory has been criticised for **not considering** the households in society which **don't** feature a **man and woman partnership**, e.g. **lesbian** and **gay** relationships and **single-parent** households. The power structures in those families **don't get looked at**.
4) Some **black feminists** have pointed out that a lot of feminist theory doesn't address the fact that women from different **ethnic backgrounds** have different **life experiences**.

Nature and Role of Family in Society

*The **New Right** Believe the **Nuclear Family** is the **Bedrock of Society***

1) **New Right theory** developed in sociology in the **1980s**. It's based on the idea that the **traditional nuclear family** and its **values** (mum, dad and kids, parents married, dad in paid employment) are best for society.
2) New Right theorists reckon that **social policies** on family, children, divorce and welfare have **undermined** the **family**.
3) **Charles Murray** is a New Right sociologist who says the traditional family is under threat. **Murray (1989)** says that **welfare benefits** are **too high** and create a "**culture of dependency**" where an individual finds it easy and acceptable to take benefits rather than work.
4) New Right theorists are particularly concerned about giving lots of **welfare benefits** to **single mothers**. They also think that it's a very **bad idea** to have children brought up in families where adults aren't working.
5) New Right sociologists believe that the increase in **lone-parent** and **reconstituted** (step) families and the easier access to **divorce** have led to a **breakdown in traditional values**. They say that this causes social problems such as **crime** to increase.
6) Some politicians have made use of the new right theory. It's had an influence on **social policy** — making it **harder** for people to **get benefits**.

There's more about the New Right on page 66.

Pine cladding — that's the <u>real</u> bedrock of society

New Right theory has been **criticised** for **"blaming the victim"** for their problems.

Postmodernists** Say **Diversity** in Family Structures is a **Good Thing

1) The **central idea** of **postmodern views of the family** is that there's a much **wider range** of **living options** available these days — because of social and cultural changes. There are traditional nuclear families, stepfamilies, cohabiting unmarried couples, single people flatsharing, more divorced people etc.
2) Postmodern sociologist **Judith Stacey (1990)** reckons there's **such a diversity** of family types, relationships and lifestyles that there'll **never** be **one dominant type** of family in Western culture again. She says that "Western family arrangements are **diverse**, **fluid** and **unresolved**". This means a person can move from one family structure into another, and not get stuck with one fixed family structure.
3) Postmodernists say the **key thing** is the idea that contemporary living is so **flexible** that one individual can experience lots of different types of family in their lifetime. Postmodernists see this **diversity** and **flexibility** as **positive** — because it means individuals can always **choose** from several options depending on what suits their **personal needs** and lifestyle. People aren't hemmed in by tradition.
4) Sociological **criticism** of postmodern theory **questions** whether this "journey through many family types" is really all that typical. **O'Brien and Jones (1996)** concluded from their UK research that there was **less variety** in family types than Stacey reported, and that **most** individuals actually experienced **only one or two** different types of family in their lifetime.

Practice Questions

Q1 Identify three different strands of feminist thought.

Q2 Give two characteristics of patriarchy.

Q3 What does Murray mean by a "culture of dependency"?

Q4 Why do postmodernists think there will never be one dominant type of family in Western culture again?

Exam Question

Q1 Examine the view that the family serves to reproduce the unequal position of women in society. (15 marks)

<u>If this is too difficult to learn, blame your family. Or blame society...</u>

Another couple of pages all about different views of the family. Feminist theory is complicated because there are different varieties of feminism. Which one you go for depends on exactly how unfair you think family life is on women, and exactly whose fault it is. Don't forget to learn the reasons why sociologists say each theory might be wrong, or flawed.

Changes in Family Structure

The average family today doesn't have the same structure as the average family 500 years ago. Sociologists suggest various reasons for this, mostly to do with people moving to cities to work in factories.

Industrialisation *Changed* ***Family Structure***

1) There are **two basic types of family structure** you need to know: **extended** and **nuclear** (see p.12).
2) There are **two basic types of society** you need to know.

Pre-industrial society: This means society before industrialisation. It is largely **agricultural** and work centres on home, **farm**, village and **market**.

Industrial society: This means society during and after **industrialisation**). Work centres on **factories** and production of goods in **cities**.

Industrialisation is the process by which production becomes more mechanical and based outside the home in factories. People travel outside the home to work and urban centres (cities) are formed. Industrialisation in the UK started in the 18th century.

3) What you really, really need to know is **how these two affect each other**.

In **pre-industrial** society the **extended** family is most common. Families **live and work together** producing goods and crops to live from, taking the surplus to market. This is where the term **cottage industry** comes from.

In **industrial** society the **nuclear family** becomes dominant. There is a huge increase in individuals leaving the home to work for a wage. The key social change is that industrialisation **separates home and work**.

Remember — **industrialisation is historical fact** but the **nature** of the **social change** it created is **sociological debate**.

Functionalists *Say* ***Industrialisation*** *Changed the* ***Function*** *of the Family*

American sociologist **Talcott Parsons** studied the **impact of industrialisation** on **family structure** in American and British society. Parsons thought that the dominant family structure changed from extended to nuclear because it was **more useful** for industrial society — i.e. the **nuclear family** is the **best fit** for **industrial society**.

1) Lots of **functions** of the family in **pre-industrial** society are **taken over by the state** in **industrial** society — e.g. policing, healthcare, education.
2) The nuclear family can focus on its function of **socialisation**. The family socialises children into the roles, values and norms of industrialised society.
3) Parsons said the industrial nuclear family is **"isolated"** — meaning it has **few ties** with local **kinship** and economic systems. This means the family can up sticks and **move easily** — ideal for moving to where the work is.

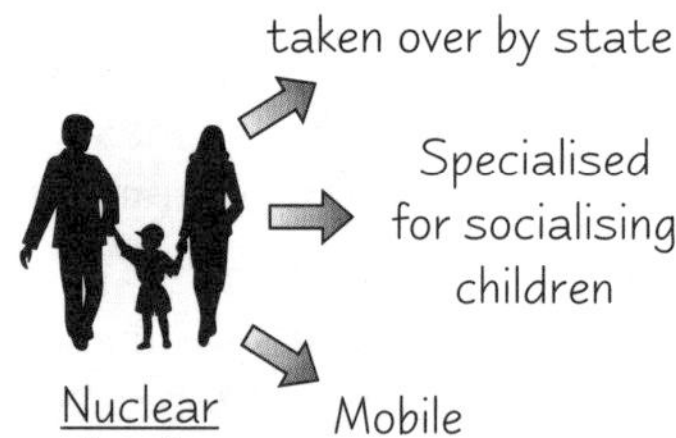

In short, **family structure adapts** to the **needs of society**.

Functionalists *Say* ***Industrialisation*** *Changed* ***Roles*** *and* ***Status*** *in the Family*

Status for an individual in **pre-industrial society** was **ascribed** — decided at birth by the family they were born into. Parsons reckoned that in industrial society an individual's status is **achieved** by his / her success in society **outside their family**.

The idea here is that the **nuclear family** is the **best** for allowing individuals to **achieve status** and position without **conflict**. It's OK for an individual to achieve higher or lower status than previous generations. This allows for greater **social mobility** in society. People can **better themselves**.

Parsons says that **specialised roles** for men and women develop within the family. He thought that men are **instrumental** (practical / planning) leaders and women are **expressive** (emotional) leaders in a family. As a **Functionalist**, Parsons said these roles come about because they're **most effective** for society. **Feminists** and **conflict theorists** disagree — they say these roles come from **ideology** and **power**.

Other Sociologists *say it's all* ***More Complicated***

Functionalists are **criticised** for seeing the modern nuclear family as **superior** — something that societies have to evolve into. They're also criticised for putting forward an **idealised** picture of history. **Historical evidence** suggests there's actually been a **variety** of family forms in the past and now.

Sociologist **Peter Laslett (1972)** reckons that the **nuclear family** was the **most common** structure in Britain even before industrialisation. His evidence comes from **parish records**. Also, **Laslett and Anderson (1971)** say that the **extended family** actually was **significant** in industrial society. Anderson used the **1851 census** for evidence. He said that when people moved to the cities for industrial jobs, they lived with relatives from their extended family.

Changes in Family Structure

Willmott and *Young* Said Families Have *Developed* Through *Three Stages*

British sociologists **Willmott and Young (1960, 1973)** did two important studies looking at family structures in British society in the 1950s to the 1970s. They mainly studied families in different parts of London and Essex. Their work was testing the theory that the nuclear family is the dominant form in modern industrial society.

You need to remember their conclusion, which was that **British families have developed through three stages**. (Initially, they set out four stages, but there wasn't a lot of evidence for the last stage, so they dropped it.)

Stage One: Pre-Industrial	Family works together as **economic production unit**. Work and home are combined.
Stage Two: Early Industrial	Extended family is broken up as individuals (mostly men) leave home to work. Women at home have strong **extended kinship** networks.
Stage Three: Privatised Nuclear	Family based on **consumption**, not **production** — buying things, not making things. Nuclear family is focused on its **personal relationships and lifestyle**. Called "**The Symmetrical Family**" — husband and wife have joint roles.
Stage Four: Asymmetrical	Husband and wife roles become **asymmetrical** as men spent more leisure time **away from the home** — in the pub for example. this stage got dropped

Husband and wife roles are called "conjugal roles" by sociologists

Other Sociologists have *Criticised* Willmott and Young

1) Willmott and Young (and other functionalists) have been criticised for **assuming** that family life has got **better and better** as structure adapts to modern society. They're described as "**march of progress**" theorists, which, I believe, is a bit of an insult in the world of sociology.
2) Wilmott and Young **ignore** the **negative** aspects of the modern nuclear family. Domestic violence, child abuse and lack of care for the elderly and vulnerable are all problems in society today.
3) **Feminist** research suggests **equal roles** in the "Symmetrical Family" don't really exist (see pages 20 and 21).

Different Classes Might Have *Different Family Structures*

Willmott and Young's work in the **1960s** and **1970s** supported the **theory** that **working class** families had **closer extended kinship networks** than middle class families.

To get up to date, the British Social Attitude Surveys of **1986** and **1995** showed that **working class** families have **more frequent contact** and ties outside of their nuclear family.

Recent work by **Willmott (1988)** suggests that **extended family ties** are **still important** to the modern nuclear family but they're **held in reserve** for times of **crisis** rather than being part of everyday life. For example, if your house floods, you might go and stay with your sister, even if you don't usually spend loads of time with her. In Parsons' terminology this makes the modern family "**partially isolated nuclear**".

Practice Questions

Q1 Give an example of social change caused by industrialisation.

Q2 What roles did Parsons believe men and women had within the nuclear family?

Q3 What is meant by the term "The Symmetrical Family"?

Q4 Outline one criticism of Willmott and Young's "march of progress" theory.

Exam Questions

Q1 Evaluate the assertion that the family structure in Britain has adapted to best fit the needs of modern industrial society. (15 marks)

Q2 "The British extended family ended with industrialisation." Discuss. (20 marks)

My mum works at Sellafield — we're a real nuclear family...

OK — here's something where it helps to have a vague idea about history, and about what this "industrialisation" business was. The idea is that when people went to live in cities and work in factories, society changed. Of course, it'd be far too much to expect sociologists to agree about it. Oh no. So you have another couple of pages of sociological debate...

Family Diversity — Changing Family Patterns

These pages are about which family types are getting more common, and which are getting less common.

Social Trends Indicate More Variety of Families and Households

Official **Social Trends** statistics clearly show that the **variety** of family types has **increased** in Britain since the **mid 20th century**. There's now no such thing as "the British family" — there's several kinds of family structure out there.

Look at the evidence:

1) There were **24.4 million** households in the UK in 2002 — up by a third since 1971.
2) The **average size** of household is getting **smaller**. The number of households made up of **5 or more** people has **fallen** from **14%** in 1971 to **7%** in 2002.
3) You might think that more small households means more nuclear families. However, the percentage of households which are **nuclear families** has **fallen** from **33%** in 1971 to **25%** in 2002.
4) Two of the biggest **increases** have been in **single person** households and **lone parent family** households. This explains why the average size of households has got smaller.
5) There's been an increase in the **proportion** of families which are **reconstituted** families — also known as **step-families**. There are **more step-families** now that there's **more divorce**. In 2001-2, **8%** of all households were **reconstituted families**.

These stats are from "Social Trends (2003)"

The two **overall patterns** are:

1) There's been an **increase** in the **diversity** of families in the UK. There are more **different kinds** of family.
2) **Nuclear family** is still the most **common** type of family, even though the **proportion** of nuclear families is going down. In 2002, **78%** of children lived in nuclear families.

Class, Ethnicity and Sexuality Affect Which Types Of Family You Experience

Eversley and Bonnerjea (1982) found **middle class** areas in the UK have a **higher** than average proportion of **nuclear families**. Inner-city **working class areas** are more likely to have a higher proportion of **lone-parent households**.

Lesbian and **gay** families have been hidden from the statistics. The **official definition** of a couple has only included **same-sex couples** since 1998.

The study of **ethnic minorities** by **Modood et al (1997)** found that:

1) Whites and Afro-Caribbeans were most likely to be **divorced**. Indians, Pakistanis, Bangladeshis and African Asians were most likely to be **married**.
2) Caribbean households were the most likely to be **single parent families**.
3) **South Asian** families are traditionally **extended** families, but there are more **nuclear family** households than in the past. **Extended kinship links** stay strong and often reach back to India, Pakistan or Bangladesh.
4) There's **diversity** within each ethnic group though.

Fewer People Marry and More People Live Together Instead

In 2001 the **lowest** number of **marriages** took place in the UK since records began.

This does NOT mean a decline in family life, though:

1) Over the same period of time there's been an **increase** in the number of adults living with a partner (**cohabiting**). In 2001-2 a **quarter** of all non-married adults aged 16-59 were **cohabiting**.
2) **Social trends statistics** show that living with a partner doesn't mean you **won't** get married — it's often just a **delay** in tying the knot. A **third** of people who cohabited with a partner went on to **marry** them.
3) The **majority** of people in the UK do marry but the **proportion** who are **married at any one time** has **fallen**.

You need to know **why** these trends have developed.

1) **Men** tend to **die** before women. **Elderly widows** make up a lot of **single person households**. There are **more old people** these days, so this helps explain why there are so many single person households.
2) **New Right theorists** believe that the decline in marriage means a **decline** in **traditional family values**. However, evidence suggests cohabiting families actually have **similar norms** and **values** to married ones.
3) **Postmodern theorists** say the **role** of intimate relationships has changed — the emphasis is less on having kids and more on self-expression and emotional fulfilment. **Giddens (1992)** says that people are getting more likely to have a **series** of **cohabitations** rather than a **lifelong marriage,** this is known as **serial monogomy**.

Family Diversity — Changing Family Patterns

The UK has one of the **Highest Divorce Rates** in Europe

1) There's been a **steady rise** in the **divorce rate** in most **modern industrial societies**.
2) The **divorce rate** is defined as the **number of people per 1000 of the population** who are **divorced**. In 2000, Britain's divorce rate was **2.6** compared to the European average of **1.9**.
3) **Actual divorces** in the UK rose from **25,000** in **1961** to **146,000** in **1997**.
4) For every **two marriages** in Britain in **1991**, there was **one divorce** (source — Social Trends 1994).
5) The **proportion** of population who were **divorced** at any one time was **1%** in **1971** and **9%** in **2000**.
6) The average **length** of a marriage before it ends in divorce has remained **about the same** — **12 years** in **1963**, **11 years** in **2000** (source — Census 2001 report).
7) Although the divorce rate is increasing, divorced people are **marrying again**. In 2001, **40%** of all marriages were **re-marriages**.

You don't have to learn all of these statistics, but if you can learn some of them off by heart and quote them in your essays, you'll look very bright and shiny.

There are several **social**, **cultural** and **political** factors you **need to know about** when you're explaining why divorce is increasing in the UK.

1) Divorce has become **easier to obtain**.
2) Divorce is more **socially acceptable**.
3) Women may have **higher expectations** of marriage, and **better employment opportunities** may make them less financially dependent on their husbands.
4) Marriages are increasingly focused on **individual emotional fulfilment**.
5) The New Right believe that marriage is **less supported by the state** these days.

Availability and acceptability are the buzz words in the debate on divorce.

Remember — the **link** between divorce and marriage breakdown isn't completely straightforward. Some couples separate but never actually go through with the divorce procedure.

You **can't assume** marriage was **happier** in the past because there were **fewer divorces**. A marriage can break down but the couple still **stays married** and living together. This is called an **empty-shell marriage**.

People are Having **Fewer Children** and Having them **Later In Life**

One very clear change in British family life is the **decrease** in the **average number of children** people have.

1) People are having **fewer children**. The average number of children per family was **2.4** in **1971** compared to **1.63** in **2001** (the lowest ever recorded).
2) Women are having children **later**. The average age of women at the birth of their first child was **24** in **1971** compared to **27** in **2001**.
3) More people are **not having children at all** — **9%** of women born in **1945** were childless at age **45** compared to **15%** of women born in **1955**.

Social changes have influenced these trends. **Contraception** is more readily available and **women's roles are changing**. The emphasis on the **individual in post-industrial society** is a key factor. Children are expensive and time consuming, and couples may choose to spend their time and money in other ways. The **conflict** between wanting a **successful working life** and being a **mum** has made many women **put off having kids until later**.

Practice Questions

Q1 Which household types have increased in the UK in recent years?

Q2 What evidence is there that divorce has increased in the UK in recent times?

Q3 Explain the reasons sociologists have identified for the trend for women to have children at a later age.

Exam Questions

Q1 Identify and examine the overall patterns in family diversity in Britain since 1960s. (15 marks)

Q2 "An increasing divorce rate does not necessarily indicate a decline in the popularity of family life." Discuss. (20 marks)

86% of people get bored of reading about divorce statistics...

Sometimes I wonder what sociologists would do without the Office of National Statistics, and their Social Trends reports. Anyway, jot down your own list of trends in the size of family, the number of single person households, the number of divorces and the number of people cohabiting. You have to know which are going up and which are going down.

Roles and Relationships within the Family

As well as studying the place of the family unit in wider society, sociologists also research what happens within the family. The key focus is on the different roles and expectations of men, women and children within the family.

The Rise of the Nuclear Family led to Joint Conjugal Roles

Conjugal roles are the roles of **husband and wife** (or partner and partner) within the home. **Elizabeth Bott (1957)** studied how **jobs and roles within the family** were **allocated** to **men and women** in modern industrial Britain.

Sure, her study is **old**, but it's a **good foundation** for the debate so don't dismiss it — **learn it**.

Bott (1957) identified two ways household jobs can be shared

Segregated roles	Husbands and wives lead separate lives with clear and **distinct responsibilities** within the family. Man goes out to work and does DIY. Woman stays home, looks after kids and does all the emotional stuff.
Joint roles	Husband and wife roles are **more flexible** and shared with less defined tasks for each. Usually leisure time is shared. Responsibility for making decisions is also shared.

Willmott and Young (1973) studied the changing structure of the British family from extended to nuclear (see p.16-17). They reckoned that the increase in the nuclear family meant that **joint conjugal roles** would develop. They predicted that **equal** and **shared responsibilities** would be the **future norm** in British families.

Willmott and Young's picture of **widespread equality** in marriage was **criticised** as soon as it was published.

Oakley (1974) pointed out that their study only required men to do a **few things round the house** to qualify as having joint roles. Their **methodology** overlooked the **amount of time** spent on housework — making 10 minutes washing up equivalent to an hour's hoovering, an hour's ironing and all the rest of the housework too. Oakley's research found it was **pretty rare** for men to do a lot of housework.

Conjugal Roles are Still Unequal Although Most Women have Paid Jobs

Since the early studies by Bott and Willmott and Young, **new family structures** have developed. There are now lots **more families** where **both partners work outside the home**. Sociological evidence shows that an **equal share** of **paid employment** hasn't led to an **equal share** of **domestic labour**.

1) **Edgell (1980)** tested Willmott and Young's theory and found **none** of his sample families had **joint conjugal roles** in relation to housework. However, he did find **increased sharing of childcare** between men and women.
2) **Oakley (1974)** found that women took on a **double burden** — taking on **paid jobs** and still **keeping** the **traditional responsibilities** for **home** and **children**.
3) **Boulton (1983)** concluded that **men may help out** with specific bits of childcare, like nappy-changing but **women** are still **primarily responsible** for children.
4) **Ferri and Smith (1996)** found that **two thirds** of **full-time working mothers** said they were responsible for **cooking** and **cleaning**. **Four fifths** of the same group said they were responsible for **laundry**.

These are all **small-scale studies** — it's important to look at research of a much **larger sample**. The **British Attitudes Survey 1991** was a **large scale study** of **1,000 married couples.** It showed a very **clear division of labour** — **women** did **most of the housework**. For example, washing and ironing was mainly done by women in 84% of households, shared equally in 12% and mainly done by men in 3%.

Industrialisation led to the Creation of the "Housewife"

1) **Oakley** thinks that the role of the **housewife** was **socially constructed** (see page 24) by the **social changes** of the **Industrial Revolution**, when people started **going to work in factories** instead of working at home.
2) **Married women** were often **not allowed** to work in factories. A new role of **housewife** was created for married women.
3) Middle class households had female **servants** to do domestic work. Working class women did it themselves.
4) The **cultural values** that said women should be in charge of housework were **so dominant** that domestic work came to be seen as "**naturally**" (biologically) the role of women.

Roles and Relationships within the Family

Decision Making and Sharing of Resources can be Unequal

As well as looking at the **division of labour** and tasks in the home, sociologists have researched how **power is shared** in the home. The traditional role of the **man** holding **power to make decisions** was **so widespread** that the phrase "**who wears the trousers**" is often used to mean who's in charge.

Edgell (1980) interviewed middle-class couples

He found that **men** had **decision making control** over things both husband and wife saw as important, whilst women had control over minor decisions. Half of husbands and two thirds of wives expressed a view that sexual **equality** was a **bad thing**.

Alas, no one knows who was wearing these trousers. It's a mystery.

Pahl (1989, 1993) researched money management by 100 dual income couples

He concluded the most common form of financial management was "**husband controlled pooling**" which he defined as: money is shared but husband has the dominant role in how it's spent.

Explanations for Inequality are based on Theories About Power in Society

Guess what? There are **Functionalist**, **Marxist** and **Feminist** theories on power in society.

1) For **Functionalists**, men and women still largely perform **different tasks** and **roles** within the family because it's the **most effective way** of keeping society **running smoothly**.

2) **Marxist** sociologists interpret the fact that men and women have different roles as evidence of the **power of capitalism** to **control** family life. They say women and men have unequal roles because **capitalism works best that way**. Even with more women working outside the home in equal hours to men, the capitalist class needs to **promote women** as "naturally" **caring** and **nurturing** to ensure workers are kept fit, healthy and happy. This role for women is maintained **ideologically** through the **media**, e.g. in adverts.

3) From a **feminist** perspective, inequality in household roles demonstrates **inequality in power** between men and women. A **patriarchal** society will produce **unequal conjugal relationships** because society's **systems** and **values** will **inevitably** benefit men at the expense of women.

So, all explanations of conjugal roles lead back to **different theories** about **power in society**.

These explanations all agree that different roles for men and women in the family help to **maintain the status quo** (keep things the way they are at the moment) in society — the disagreement between them is over **who benefits**.

Practice Questions

Q1 Define the term "conjugal roles".

Q2 Describe the differences between joint and segregated conjugal roles.

Q3 What is meant by the "double-burden" of women in modern society?

Q4 How was the role of "housewife" socially constructed?

Q5 Identify two areas of inequality in conjugal relationships other than household chores.

Exam Questions

Q1 Examine the evidence that conjugal roles are still unequal in modern British society. (15 marks)

Q2 "Power is the key to understanding relationships within the family". Explain and discuss. (20 marks)

I'll have a cup of tea while you're on your feet, love....

This is mainly about inequality in the family. You know, who does the housework, that sort of thing. Some sociologists look on the bright side and say that things are getting more equal. Others say they still aren't equal enough. Remember to look at the possible causes and social construction of inequality. And learn some of the statistics — it gets you more marks.

Roles and Relationships within the Family

This page is about sociological perspectives on the dark side of family life — domestic violence and child abuse.
Page 23 is about how our view of childhood has changed, and how social policy relating to childhood reflects this change.

Radical Feminists See *Domestic Violence* as a Form of *Patriarchal Control*

First of all, here's some **evidence** of domestic violence in Britain.

Dobash and Dobash (1992) found that **25%** of all serious assaults recorded in the UK were on women by their husbands.

The fourth **United Nations Women's Conference in 1995** reported that **25%** of women worldwide experience domestic violence.

Easy stats to remember, those. Quarter of assaults in the UK, quarter of women in the world.

Radical feminist theory says **violence against women** is treated **differently** to **other violent crime**.

1) Dobash and Dobash's first UK study (1979) found the **police usually didn't record** violent crime by husbands against their wives.
2) Since 1979 the police have set up **specialist domestic violence units**, but still the **conviction rate is low** compared to other forms of assault.
3) **Before 1991**, British law said a husband was **entitled** to have **sex** with his wife **against her will**. In 1991 **the rape law changed** to say that a husband could be charged with raping his wife.
4) Evidence like that above is used by **radical feminists** to support their argument that **laws** and **social policies** in society have traditionally worked to **control women** and keep men's power in society going.

Radical feminists believe that **violence against women** within the **family** is a form of **power and control**.

> "Violence was used by the men they lived with to silence them, to win arguments, to express dissatisfaction, to deter future behaviour and to express dominance." — Dobash and Dobash 1990

The **social climate** helps to **maintain this situation** by making women feel **ashamed** and **stigmatised** if they talk about the violence. The shame and stigma are part of the **ideology of patriarchy** — the school of thought that says women should know their place.

Shame also comes from the idea that women **should know better** — not get involved with violent men in the first place. There's a tendency to **blame the victim**.

Dobash and Dobash found that most women who left violent partners returned in the end. This was because of **fear of being stigmatised** — and because they were **financially dependent** on their partner.

Abusive partners often **condition** their victim into thinking that nobody cares and there's nowhere to go. The pressure not to leave an abusive partner comes from **the relationship** as well as from society.

Radical Feminism is *Criticised* for *Overemphasising* the *Power* of *Men*

There are **two main criticisms** of **radical feminist** theory of the family.

1) It **over-emphasises** the **place** of **domestic violence** in family life. **Functionalists** argue that most families operate **harmoniously** and **postmodern theory** argues that individuals have much more **choice** and **control** to avoid, leave or reshape their family relationships.
2) It presents men as **all-powerful** and women as **powerless** when in reality women often hold some power over men. The journalist **Melanie Phillips** (2003) highlights the fact that **women abuse men too** and **male victims** are often **ignored** by society and the police. The pressure group **Families Need Fathers** campaigns for men to have **equal rights** in **family** and child law.

Some Sociologists See *Child Abuse* In Terms Of *Power*

Sociologists study the issue of child abuse by parents and carers in terms of power relationships.
You need to be able to **explain abuse** as a **form of power** rather than explore **details** of abuse itself.

A parent or carer is able to abuse a child by **manipulating** the **responsibilities and trust** which go along with the role of parent or carer. Families are **private** and separate from the rest of society. This makes it less likely for children to report abuse.

Social policies have been **adapted** to give some **protection** to children. The **Children Act 1989** was set up so the state can **intervene** with families if social workers are **concerned** about children's safety.

Roles and Relationships within the Family

Childhood is Partly a **Social Construction**

Sociologists say **childhood** is not only a **biological stage of development** but a **social construct** (see p.24) as well. The idea that children are **different** from adults in their **values**, **behaviour** and **attitudes** isn't the same everywhere in the world, and it hasn't been the same for all time. In other words, it's **not universal** — different societies, with different cultures and values, can view childhood in different ways.

An example of this is how the school leaving age in Britain has moved from 12 to 16 in the last century. It would now be not only **socially unacceptable**, but also **illegal**, to leave school and work full-time at the age of 12. Effectively, the age at which childhood ends and adulthood begins has moved in line with social attitudes.

Aries says a **Cult of Childhood** Developed After Industrialisation

Sociologist Philippe Aries' work on the construction of childhood is a classic study.

Aries (1962) looked at paintings

Aries said that the concept of **childhood** in Western European society has only existed in the **last 300 years**. Before this, in medieval society a child took on the role of an adult as soon as it was physically able. Children in medieval paintings look like mini adults.

With **industrialisation** social attitudes began to value children as needing specialised care and nurturing. The importance of the child reinforced the importance of the role of the **housewife** — it was the housewife's job to look after children.

This **'cult of the child'** as Aries referred to it first developed in the middle classes and over time has become a part of working class values.

You need to be aware that although Aries' work is very important, he has been criticised. E.g. Pollack says that Aries' work looks weak because it uses paintings for its main evidence.

British Society in the 21st century is **More Child Focused** than Ever

There's now lots of **social policy** related to childhood. Children are recognised as having unique **human rights**. The **United Nations Convention on the Rights of the Child** was ratified (agreed to) in 1990 by all the UN members (except the USA and Somalia).

In Britain the Child Support Act 1991 established the **Child Support Agency**. This gave children the legal right to be **financially supported** by their parents, whether the parents are **living with the child or not**. This Act also made courts have to ask for the child's view in custody cases and take the child's view into consideration.

Children also hold more **power** in modern British society than at any other time in history. This has been identified by advertisers who recognise the **financial power** of children — this is often referred to as "**pester power**". Advertisers advertise a product to children because they know the children will **pester** their parents to buy the product.

Practice Questions

Q1 What sociological evidence is there of violence between husbands and wives?

Q2 Explain the feminist argument that domestic violence is treated differently to other violence in society.

Q3 Dobash and Dobash found most wives who were victims of domestic violence returned to their husbands. What was their explanation for this?

Q4 Describe how the notion of childhood has been socially constructed.

Q5 List two social policies which have affected children in 21st century Britain.

Exam Questions

Q1 "Domestic violence is part of the ideology and practice of patriarchy in modern society". Discuss. (15 marks)

Q2 Evaluate sociological study of the child in society. (20 marks)

Brrrr... not pleasant, is it...

You'd be forgiven for thinking that the stuff on page 22 is all a bit depressing. Unsurprisingly, the main idea on page 23 is that childhood is socially constructed. Remember that it's not enough to say that something is a "social construct" — you need to say how and why.

Definitions of Health

Most people believe they're unwell if they don't feel like they normally do. Sociologists see health as more than just not feeling poorly. ***The whole of section three is just for AQA. See you OCR folk on page 34.***

Sociologists see Health as More than Absence of Illness

"Health" is defined in everyday language as an absence of physical symptoms of illness. This view is based on the **biomedical** model of health which is current in modern, Western societies. Some sociologists favour the **social model** of health, which sees health and illness as "**social constructs**" serving the interests of a powerful **medical elite**.

A "**social construct**" is an **idea that's created by a society** — as opposed to an idea that's based on objective and testable **facts**. It's specific to the **values and behaviour** of that society — it's not universal. *But* people living in that society will usually accept it as **natural** and "**common sense**."
For **example**, in **modern**, **Western society** it is widely accepted that **democracy** is the **best form of government**. This idea is a **social construct** based on Western society's culture, values and experience.

The Biomedical Model says Health and Disease are Natural, Physical Things

The **biomedical model** is based around the idea that health and disease are **natural phenomena** which exist in an individual's body. **Disease** is something **physically wrong** with the body, and health is the **absence of disease**. The interaction of the individual and the social world is **not relevant** in the biomedical model.

Health professionals generally follow the **biomedical model of health**.

Key characteristics of the biomedical model

1) Health is seen as the **absence of biological abnormality**.
2) The human body is like a **machine** in that it needs to be **repaired** by treatment when it breaks down.
3) The health of society is dependent on the **state of medical knowledge**.

Nikki Hart (1985) identifies **five features** of the **biomedical model**:

1) Disease is **physical**	The **biomedical model** concentrates on **physical systems** of disease, not social and environmental factors. Disease happens in an **individual's body**, not as part of society.
2) **Doctors** are an **elite**	The **medical elite** (doctors) are the only people sufficiently **qualified** and **skilled** to **identify** and **treat** illness.
3) Medicine is **curative**	The body can be **repaired** with drugs and surgery.
4) Illness is **temporary**	Illness can be cured by the medical elite. **Wellness** is the **normal** state of affairs.
5) **Treatment** is **special**	Treatment of disease takes place in **recognised health care environments** (doctor's surgery, hospital), which are **distinct** from the environment where the patient got ill.

Example: A **biomedical view of disability**.

The biomedical model **looks in** at the patient and tries to **fix** the disability through medical practice.
Medical practice is **interventionist** — it's something that's **done to** the patient.

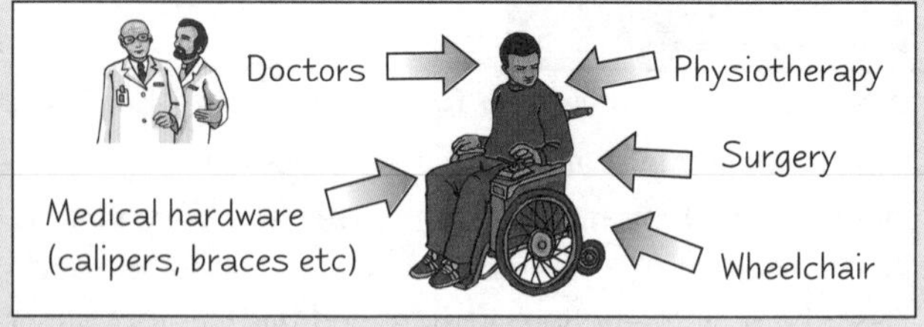

The Biomedical Model has been Criticised

1) Some sociologists, e.g. **McKeown (1976)**, say that **improved nutrition and hygiene** have been more important in improving health — starting with 19th and 20th century public health reform.
2) **Ivan Illich (1975)** and others have argued that modern medicine actually **creates disease**. Medical accidents, infections in hospitals and complications following surgery are examples of this sort of thing. There's a lot more about this on page 30.
3) **Marxist sociologists** in the 1970s accused biomedicine of distracting attention away from what they see as the real causes of illness — the **social causes**.

Definitions of Health

The Social Model says there's More to Disease than Physical Symptoms

1) **The medical elite** (doctors) **haven't always dominated** the definition and treatment of illness and disease — it's a modern phenomenon. For example, in the 1700s, mental illness was often thought to be caused by evil spirits — a religious thing, not a medical thing.
2) In modern society illness is only recognised as illness if it has been **diagnosed** by the medical elite. The social model says **definitions of health and illness** are "social constructs" — not actually always related to real physical symptoms.
3) The medical elite have been **influenced** by powerful groups to **control** people's behaviour. For example, **homosexuality** could be defined as a "mental illness" by the medical elite in America right up until the 1980s.

The Social Model of Health emphasises Social and Environmental Factors

McKeown (1976) thought that the biomedical model was wrong in several ways.

1) McKeown said that **medical science** is **barking up the wrong tree** because it **assumes** the **body is a machine**. He thought this was a **mistaken assumption**.
2) Medical science says that **intervention by doctors** is needed to **protect** the body from disease. According to McKeown, **this is wrong as well** — external factors are the main reasons why people are well or sick.
3) Also, McKeown thought that the biomedical model **neglects** those "machines" which **can't be easily repaired** e.g. the disabled or chronically ill. He reckoned that **most ill people** can't be easily put right again by doctors.
4) A social model of health would look to see which **environmental, social and behavioural factors** have contributed to make an individual person ill. There's more about McKeown's study on page 30.

Intervention means tinkering around with the body — by operating on it or giving it drugs, etc.

Example: A **social view of disability**.

The social model looks **outwards** from the individual to the **environmental** and **social** factors which disable an individual e.g. lack of access, rights, and opportunities.

A person using a **wheelchair** might feel more disabled by the **lack of a wheelchair ramp** than the fact they can't use their legs to walk.

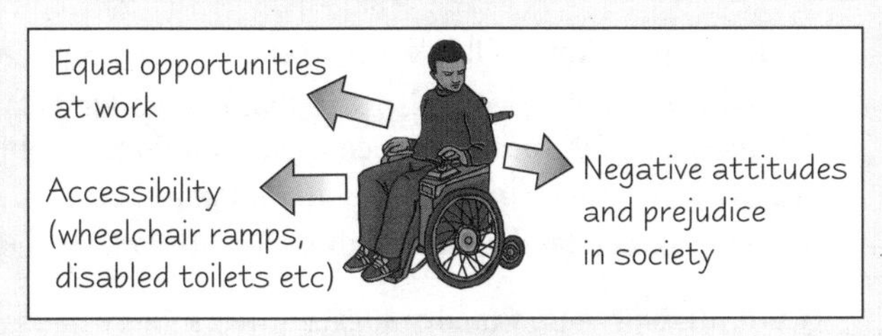

The social model of health **challenges** the idea that **wellness** is the normal state of affairs. Individuals with an illness are seen as **"living with"** their condition instead of having something **"wrong"** with them.

Practice Questions

Q1 Why are doctors seen as part of a "medical elite"?

Q2 List the five main features of the biomedical model of health and illness.

Q3 Give three criticisms of the biomedical model, and explain each one.

Exam Questions

Q1 Identify and briefly describe two differences between the biomedical and the social view of health. (8 marks)

Q2 Examine how social and environmental factors might contribute to disability and illness. (20 marks)

All I care about is why do I feel ill...

Hmm... the social model of illness seems a bit odd at first — how can it be society's fault that I've got a sore throat... But when you look into it, you have to admit that things like clean water, proper sewers and good diet are at least relevant to health. As always, you're expected to know the key points of each theory, as well as their faults and pitfalls.

Inequalities in Health

The working class tend to suffer worse health than higher social groups. Some sociologists blame the workers themselves for their lifestyle choices, others blame the effects of poverty.

Studies Show Working Class People have Relatively Poor Health

1) The **working class** have a **higher infant mortality rate** than the national average. The **wealthiest social groups** have **lower infant mortality rates** than the national average.
2) **Working class** people are statistically **more likely** to suffer from **serious medical conditions** such as heart disease, strokes and cancer.
3) **Working class** people are more likely to **die before retirement** age than the average.
4) According to government statistics, people born in **social class 1** (professional) can expect to live for **seven years longer** than people born in **social class 5** (manual workers).
5) People in the **south** of England are healthier and live longer than those in the **north**.
6) Some **ethnic minority groups** have a much higher infant mortality rate than the national average.
7) In general, **women live longer** than men.

These statistics are from the Social Trends report that the Office of National Statistics produces.

If getting ill was **pure chance**, you'd **expect** disease rates and life expectancy to be **the same across the board**. They **aren't**. So it **can't** be pure chance.

Cultural Deprivation Theory blames Bad Health on Working Class Values

Cultural deprivation theory says that the **working class** lead **relatively unhealthy lifestyles** with relatively poor diets, more smoking, less exercise and more drinking. Their poor health is therefore blamed on their **values** and their **choices**.

1) **Cultural deprivationists** think that working class people are **less likely** to do **exercise**.
2) Cultural deprivation theory also says that the working class are less likely to take advantage of NHS **public health measures** such as **vaccinations**, **health screening** and **ante-natal care**.
3) **Howlett and Ashley (1991)** found that **middle class** people are better **informed** about health, with more **understanding** of health issues. Therefore, they tend to follow **healthier lifestyles**.

Cultural deprivation theory suggests that society needs better **health education** to make people more **aware** of health issues. It's resulted in lots of **government initiatives** through the **Health Education Authority** — trying to get people to give up smoking, eat less fatty food, etc.

Cultural Deprivation Theory has been Criticised

Sociologists who **disagree** with **cultural deprivation theory** point out that **working class behaviour** is more **likely** to be caused by **real material deprivation**. They **don't think** it's an expression of different **cultural values**.

1) **Healthy diets** can be **expensive**, and **gyms** are often **very expensive**.
2) **Smoking and drinking** may be related to **stressful lives**, not **cultural values**.
3) Working class people are **less likely** to be able to afford **private health care**.
4) The fact that working class people often **don't take advantage** of **public health facilities** has also been blamed on feeling **intimidated** by health care and **health care professionals.** Health care professionals are **mostly middle class** and health care in general seems like it's set up to suit middle class people.

Work it, baybee, work it.

So it **might** not be the patient's own fault after all...
...and like so much in sociology, it might be **a little bit of both** — a bit of smoking because you feel like it, a bit of not going to the gym because it's so expensive...

Inequalities in Health

Social Administration Theory Blames *Unequal Distribution* of *NHS Resources*

1) The **quality** of health care **isn't the same** across all areas of the UK. This is often called the "**postcode lottery**" — the quality of hospital or clinic you get to go to depends on where you live (your postcode in other words).
2) **Julian Tudor Hart (1971)** wrote "The availability of good medical care tends to **vary inversely** with the **need** for it in the population served". In other words, those with the **most** need for health care get **least**, and those with the **least** need get **most**. This is called the **Inverse Care Law**.

Another important report, the "Inequalities in Health Working Group Report (1981)" (also known as the Black Report), confirmed the Inverse Care Law.

Tudor Hart's conclusion can be seen as **out of date** — a tremendous amount of reform to the structure of the NHS has gone on between 1979 and 2004.

Some sociologists have criticised his conclusions by saying he **didn't have hard evidence**.

On the **other hand**, politicians still talk about the "postcode lottery" of the healthcare system.

Marxists Blame the *Exploitative Nature* of the *Capitalist System*

now there's a surprise...

OK, remember that Marxists define **capitalism** as "**commodity production**" (a commodity is a product for sale in the marketplace, for profit). Marxists tend to see healthcare in capitalist societies as **just another commodity**.

According to **Doyal and Pennell (1979)**, the **pursuit of profit** has **negative health consequences** for the working class:

1) **Physical health consequences**
Industrial accidents and **industrial diseases** are far more common in the **working class**. **Keeping workers safe** from these risks would **cost money** and **eat into profits**.

2) **Economic consequences**
Capitalism **keeps wages low** to **keep profits high**. Marxists say this makes the working class **poor**, and poor people have higher health risks.

3) **Psychological health consequences**
Workers doing **repetitive tasks** on a production line are more likely to suffer from **stress related** health problems than workers with more varied roles.

Critics of the Marxist view point out that people in **communist countries often have poor health**, and that **Western capitalist society** has made a lot of **advances in health care**.

Marxists Disagree about whether the *NHS* has *Reduced Inequality*

Ian Gough (1979) saw the NHS as a **good achievement** that the **working class** gained through political action. He pointed out that health provision for workers was pretty lousy before **1947**.

Vicente Navarro (1976) wasn't keen on the NHS. He thought that the NHS and biomedical elite played an **ideological** role — drawing attention **away** from the **social** and **environmental** causes of disease and illness (see p.24-25 for more on the biomedical elite, and the social model of illness).

Navarro also suggests that the NHS helps give the **illusion** that capitalist society is a **caring** society.

Practice Questions

Q1 According to cultural deprivation theory, why do working class people have poorer health than middle class people?

Q2 What is meant by the Inverse Care Law?

Q3 Outline some criticisms of the Inverse Care Law.

Exam Question

Q1 Identify and explain inequalities in health and healthcare provision in relation to social class. (20 marks)

Everyone blames someone...

An awful lot of this sociology business is about blaming some system or another for the World's problems. Usual scapegoats are "working class values" and "the capitalist system". Marxists blame absolutely everything on the capitalist system. Make sure you know what the Inverse Care Law is — it's important for this whole module.

Access to Health Care

The National Health Service was set up to give free and equal health care for all. It was mostly a success. Mostly.

*There are **Inequalities** in the Health Care **Provided** by the **NHS***

The **NHS** was set up in 1947. It aimed to provide **free** and **equal** health care for **everyone** in the country.

Unfortunately, although the NHS was **generally a success**, it **doesn't give 100% equal health care** to all.

1) NHS **money** is **shared out unequally** between different areas of the country.
2) NHS money is **spent differently** in different areas of the country.
3) **Specialist** hospitals, e.g. heart hospitals, **aren't spread out equally** across the country.
4) There's a **north-south divide** in the **supply of health care**, as well as in people's health.

See p. 27 for more on the "postcode lottery"

Sociologists and politicians often claim that there's a **two-tier system** in the NHS — which means that it provides a **lower level of care** to some, and a **higher level of care** to others.

Politicians have introduced **lots of reforms** to try to **make the NHS work better** and **make it cost less money**.

*The **Internal Market** in the NHS had **Good** and **Bad Consequences***

In the **1980s**, Mrs Thatcher's Conservative government tried to **reform** the NHS to make it **more efficient** and **less expensive** (a lot of taxpayers' money is spent on the NHS). They introduced an **internal market**.

This meant that **health care providers** would **compete** with each other to provide services, and **GPs** would be **responsible for their own budgets**. The idea is that **competition drives prices down**. It's an **economics** thing. More **hospital management** was brought in to manage and supervise these changes.

The government **encouraged private hospitals** and **private health insurance schemes**. This was to take some of the **pressure** off the NHS by getting people who could afford private care to go private.

Like most things in Sociology, there are pros and cons, and lots of different opinions.

Positive Consequences

1) There's **more choice** for some "health care consumers" (patients).
2) **Competition** tends to **drive down costs**.
3) In some cases, health care became **more responsive to local needs**.

Negative consequences

1) **Inner city GPs** look after **more people** and **sicker people** than GPs in **middle class** areas. **Money has to go further**, so inner city GPs can't afford the same quality of treatment — it's a **two tier system**.
2) Increased numbers of **NHS managers** and **accountants** could be a big **waste** of money.
3) **Competition** between health care providers means that **two hospitals very close together** might offer almost exactly the **same services**. This can also be seen as a **waste** of money.

*Some People Worry that **Foundation Hospitals** will **Increase Inequality***

1) In 2003, the **Labour government** planned to set up **foundation hospitals**. These would be free to **opt out** of **government guidelines**, **raise their own money**, and **set their own priorities** for how to **treat patients**.
2) The plans for foundation hospitals were **criticised**. Critics pointed out that only the **top hospitals** would be able to become foundation hospitals — they'd get **better funding** so they'd be able to attract **better staff**. They claimed this was a kind of **two tier system** — the **best hospitals** would be given more money to **get even better**.

New Labour's **Private Finance Initiative** will let private investors pay for building new hospitals. Some sociologists think it's the first step towards a **privatised NHS**.

Most Health Care** in the UK is Provided by **Women

1) Around **75%** of all **NHS workers** are **women**.
2) However, only **25% of doctors** and **13% of consultants** are **women**.
3) **Over 90%** of **nurses** are **women**.
4) Studies have also discovered that the vast majority of **informal care** of **children** and **elderly relatives** is carried out by women.

Radical feminists think the NHS is a **patriarchal institution** — in other words, one where men dominate.

Access to Health Care

*The **Inverse Care Law** can be Applied **Today** to **Inequalities** in **Health***

Remember the Inverse Care Law from page 27.

The **Inverse Care Law (Tudor Hart 1971)** states that people whose **need** for health care is **greatest** are actually **least likely** to get it.

Working class areas tend to have the worst health facilities, the **fewest doctors** and the **fewest hospitals**. South Wales is an example.

Julian Le Grand's survey (2003)

Le Grand's conclusion was that the **middle class** get far **more benefit** from the **NHS** than the working class. The benefit the middle classes got wasn't in proportion to their actual health needs.

Le Grand found that the middle class were 40% more likely to get a **heart bypass** operation than the working class. Also, the working class were 20% less likely to get a hip replacement despite being 30% more likely to need one.

Even with something as simple as **consultation times** in GPs surgeries, Le Grand found that professionals were likely to get on average two minutes more of a doctor's time than working class patients.

This evidence supports the idea that the health care system is biased towards middle class people.

Research by **Cartwright and O'Brien (1976)** suggests that **middle class patients** tend to have a **better relationship** with their **doctor** than working class patients. Working class patients said they **felt** like the **doctor doesn't listen**.

*The **Inverse Care Law** Could Also Apply to **Ethnic Minority Groups***

Ethnic minority health needs were identified as **relatively high** in a report published by the **Department of Health in 1992**. Remember, "**relatively high**" doesn't mean "shockingly sky-high" or "loads higher than the white population". It means anything from a **tiny bit more** to a **lot more** than the **average population**.

1) **Heart disease** is significantly higher in men and women of **Indian** origin.
2) **Afro-Caribbean** people have higher incidence of **stroke**, **HIV/AIDS infection** and **schizophrenia**.
3) **Suicide** rates are **relatively high** amongst **Asian** women.

Some sociologists think that **ethnic minorities** have **relatively poor health** because they're **less likely** to get the **full benefit** from NHS services. **Various possible reasons** have been suggested for this:

1) The **cultural values** of the NHS might be **different** from those of some ethnic minority groups. Some advisers say the NHS **needs to adapt** to **fit** the **cultural values** of ethnic groups.
2) Some people from ethnic minorities, especially the elderly, **might not speak enough English** to communicate well with health care staff.
3) There's some evidence that **discrimination** and **racism** affect access to healthcare. E.g. Research in the 1980s found that **Asian women** in family planning clinics experienced racism.
4) **Some ethnic minority groups** tend to see illness and disease as a part of life you can't do much about — and **don't bother** to go to the doctor.

Practice Questions

Q1 List the advantages and disadvantages of an internal market in health care.

Q2 What are foundation hospitals?

Q3 Give three ways in which it can be said that the Inverse Care Law operates in today's NHS.

Exam Question

Q1 "The people who need health care the most are least likely to get it." Evaluate this view. (20 marks)

In the great drought of 1811 they introduced a two-tear system...

See, there's that Inverse Care Law again. There's still inequality in people's access to health care. Some think it's getting better, others think it's not. Sociologists are most concerned about a two-tier NHS, and about discrimination within the NHS. Governments keep trying to tweak NHS policy to make the NHS work better, or to make it cost less, or both.

The Role of Medicine and Health Care Professionals

There are sociologists who dispute the role of the medical elite in improving public health in modern times. Some even say doctors are the cause of much illness and disease. Blimey.

Medical Intervention** Hasn't Done a Lot of Good — According to **McKeown

1) **McKeown (1976)** claims that **medical intervention** by the biomedical elite **hasn't had much impact** on improvements in health over the last 200 years.
2) McKeown thinks that big health improvements have been mainly down to **social factors** — things like **sewage disposal**, supply of **clean water** and **improved diets.**
3) The **social changes** that McKeown says changed people's health all happened in the **19th century** — before the medical elite came to dominate health.
4) McKeown uses evidence like **life expectancy** and **infant mortality statistics**. He points out that life expectancy went up and infant mortality went down **before** biomedical techniques came in. For instance, mass immunisation for TB (a biomedical approach) only happened after the death rate for the disease had already gone down.

The bathroom — where social health really happens.

Illich** Says the **Medical Elite** Actually **Cause Bad Health

1) **Illich (1975)** defines **health** as the **capacity** to cope with the **human reality** of **death**, **pain**, and **sickness**. This is a very different definition to the mainstream biomedical definition.
2) Illich believes that medicine has **gone too far**, and started to "**play God**" — trying to **wipe out** death, pain, and sickness. OK so far... he then says that **trying to control death and illness** is a bad move which **turns people into consumers** or even objects. In his opinion, this messes up people's natural capacity for health and **makes people ill**.
3) Illich uses the word **iatrogenesis** to mean this kind of illness that's caused by modern medicine. He says there are **three types of iatrogenesis**:

> 1) **Clinical iatrogenesis** — the **harm** done to patients by **ineffective** treatments, **unsafe** treatments or getting the **wrong diagnosis**.
> 2) **Social iatrogenesis** — the idea that **doctors** have **taken over control** of people's lives, and individuals can't make decisions about their problems. More and more of people's problems are seen as **suitable** for **medical intervention**. This is called the **medicalisation of social life**.
> 3) **Cultural iatrogenesis** — the **destruction** of **traditional ways** of **dealing** with and making sense of **death**, **pain**, and **sickness**.

Illich thinks the **worst** is **cultural iatrogenesis**. He puts it like this:

> "A society's image of death reveals the level of independence of its people, their personal relatedness, self reliance, and aliveness."

According to Illich's view, dying has become the ultimate form of **consumer resistance** (when you're dead, you can't buy any more Nike trainers, I'd imagine). **Death** isn't seen as something normal. It's become a **taboo**.

***Functionalists** See Illness as **Deviant** — Doctors **Control** this Deviance*

1) According to **functionalists** like **Talcott Parsons (1951)**, doctors have an **important function in society** — they control the amount of time people take off **work** and **family duties**.
2) Illness is "**deviant behaviour**" which **disrupts** work and home life — you're not supposed to take time off sick.
3) Parsons said that sick people take on a "**sick role**". While a person is sick, they're allowed to stop functioning in their **normal role**. They don't have responsibility for making themselves better — but they are **expected** to **want to get better**, and to do whatever the doctor tells them.
4) Doctors are in charge of **confirming** that the patient is **actually ill**. Doctors **allow** the sick person to take limited time off, and **make them better** by using their **expert medical knowledge**. Parsons thought that doctors always put the patient's needs before their own needs.

Critics of Parsons say the medical profession don't always put patients first — they say private medicine is proof that doctors are self-interested. However, it **can't be denied** that doctors really do give people **sick notes** so they can take sick leave.

The Role of Medicine and Health Care Professionals

Marxists see *Medicine* as an *Institution* Which *Supports Capitalism*

Marxists believe that the medical profession only do good for the **capitalist** class — they **keep class inequalities going**. Marxists say that the medical profession have a **conservative** role in society.

1) Doctors keep the workforce **healthy** and **productive**. **Healthy** workers can **work harder** and won't have to take **time off sick**. This means **more profits** for the capitalist class.
2) Doctors **check** that **workers** aren't spending **too much time on sick leave**. They say **how long** a worker can **stay off work**.
3) Marxists believe that doctors **hide the real social causes of illness** (poverty, class inequality etc.) by focusing on the individual and their physical symptoms.

Some Marxists think that **doctors** are **agents** of **large drugs corporations** — they believe that health care exists mainly to produce **profits** for drugs companies.

Weberians see the *Medical Profession* as *Self-Serving*

Weberians think that doctors **arrange** things so that they **keep** their **high status** in society.

A Weberian is a follower of German sociologist, historian and economist Max Weber (1864-1920)

They suggest that the medical profession is **self-serving**.

They argue that the medical profession has managed to **shut out** other forms of healing such as homeopathy, aromatherapy, faith healing and other types of **alternative medicine**. This makes modern medicine a monopoly.

Feminists see the *Medical Profession* as serving *Patriarchal Interests*

1) Some feminists say that most **contraceptive methods** (e.g. the pill and IUDs) are designed for men rather than women. This doesn't mean men are supposed to use them — it means they have **significant health risks** for women that **men would never put up with**.
2) **Oakley (1984)** has said that the process of childbirth has been "**medicalised**". In other words, women giving birth are treated like there's **something wrong with them**. **Control** over giving birth is taken away from women and given to **men**. Male doctors are often in charge, not midwives or the women who are actually giving birth.
3) Women tend to have **subordinate** roles in medicine — **nurses** and **auxiliaries** tend to be **women**, **consultants** tend to be **men**. Some feminists think that the role of being a nurse has been made to look like being a "doctor's handmaid" — a female servant obeying the male doctor.
4) **Cosmetic surgery** is criticised by some feminists as the "medicalisation of beauty", and also as a **social control** over women.
5) Feminists see the diagnosis and treatment of **depression** in women as another kind of **social control**. There's more on mental health and feminism on the next page, by the way.

Of course, not everyone agrees that drugs for depression are prescribed to make women shut up and stop whingeing. It depends on your ideological viewpoint...

Practice Questions

Q1 What does McKeown claim is responsible for improvements in health in the last two hundred years?

Q2 What does iatrogenesis mean?

Q3 What three types of iatrogenesis does Illich identify?

Exam Questions

Q1 "Health and sickness are defined by the powerful". Discuss this view. (20 marks)

Q2 To what extent can the NHS be described as a patriarchical institution? (20 marks)

If doctors make you ill, do teachers make you thick...

Blimey, this iatrogenesis idea is a bit radical — it's actually the doctors' fault that we're ill... Still, you can kind of see some reasoning behind it. Oh, and as ever, you need to be able to compare and contrast functionalist (all for the best), Marxist (all set up for the benefit of the bosses), Weberian (all for the benefit of doctors) and feminist (all unfair to women) views. It's a right laugh.

Mental Health

These pages will help you revise different perspectives about mental health in the UK.

Mental Illness *in UK Society is* ***Unequally Distributed***

Sociologists and psychiatrists can't agree whether mental disorders have **physical causes** or **social causes**.

Sociologists have tended to favour the view that there is a **social basis** for mental illness. Given the **social inequality** in who has good or bad mental health, maybe the sociologists have a point. For example:

1) **Afro-Caribbean individuals** in the UK are **more likely** to be **admitted to a psychiatric hospital** than other ethnic groups. They're more likely to be "**sectioned**" under the Mental Health Act — **admitted against their will**. Afro-Caribbean men are more likely to be diagnosed with **schizophrenia**.
2) Women are statistically more likely to be diagnosed with **depression** or **acute stress** than men. They're also much more likely to be on **drug treatments** for **mental illness** — antidepressants etc.
3) **Working class** men and women are statistically **more likely** to be diagnosed with mental illness than **middle class** people.
4) **Single women** have **better mental health** than **married women**.

There are **different perspectives** on these trends including **medical**, **feminist** and **interactionist** approaches.

The ***Medical Approach*** *is to Treat Mental Health as a* ***Biomedical Condition***

1) The medical approach to mental illness focuses on the **abnormal individual** rather than the **environment** that the individual lives in. It concentrates on the **physical symptoms** of mental illness. For example, a **medical approach to schizophrenia** would say it's caused by a **chemical imbalance in the brain**.
2) The medical approach is **cure orientated**. It emphasises the importance of treatments such as **drug treatments** for depression.
3) The medical approach suggests that treatment is best carried out in the **medical environment** (e.g. a hospital rather than the community) and should always be carried out by the **qualified elite** (doctors).

Compare this with the key features of the biomedical model of illness on page 24.

1) In the 1930s, mental disturbance was sometimes treated **surgically**. Doctors actually **severed** neural connections between certain parts of the **brain**. This is called a **lobotomy**. It often had unwanted side effects, such as adverse effects on the patient's **intellect**. Lobotomies aren't done any more, although more refined brain surgery is sometimes used in extremely severe cases.
2) In the 1940s, **electroconvulsive therapy (ECT)** was used to treat depression. It's still sometimes used to treat very severe depression. In ECT, an **electric current** is passed through the patient's **brain**, to create a **seizure** a bit like an epileptic fit.
3) **Drugs** are used to treat all sorts of mental illness. Some drugs have **severe side-effects**.
4) Mental illness is also treated by **psychotherapy**, where the patient **talks** to a **therapist** who tries to get them thinking in a more healthy way.

Feminists *see* ***Women's Mental Illness*** *as a Result of* ***Patriarchy***

Joan Busfield (2001) thinks that women might be diagnosed with more than their fair share of mental health problems because of **sexism** in the **male dominated medical elite**. She thinks that doctors **label** and **interpret** behaviour differently depending on whether it's a man or a woman doing it. For instance, an **angry**, **stressed**, **upset woman** might be labelled **mentally ill** but an **angry**, **stressed**, **upset man** might just be "**overworked**".

Psychologist **Paula Nicolson (1998)** thinks that **post natal depression** is more a **social thing** than a **physical thing**. She disagrees with the standard medical view that post natal depression is a **mental disorder**, and that it's **normal** to be a **happy new mum**. Nicolson argues that it's **natural** for women to get **depressed** after having a baby.

Marxist feminists think that women's mental illness is caused by their "**dual oppression**" as **housewife** and **worker**.

Radical feminists suggest mental illness in women is a consequence of **patriarchal society** in which women have **low social status**, the **stress** of **housework** and **child care** and the stress of **social isolation**.

Mental Health

*The **Interactionist Approach** Sees Mental Health as a **Social Construct***

Thomas Szasz (1971) reckoned that **mental illness doesn't really exist.**

1) He thought that what we call "mental illness" is really just another "**social construct**" — a **label** society uses to **control non-conformist behaviours**. He said that people who behave in a way that the rest of society sees as **unacceptable** or **dangerous** are defined as "mentally ill".
2) People who are labelled as "mentally ill" can be admitted into psychiatric hospitals against their will. Szasz compared **forced treatment in mental hospitals** to the **persecution of witches** in the Middle Ages.
3) Szasz prefers a **system** where individuals are **free** to get psychotherapy **if they want to.** He says it's important that there's **no threat of force**, coercion or **loss of liberty**.

R.D. Laing was a psychiatrist who wrote in the late 1960s. He believed that "mental illness" is really a natural response to being in an unbearable situation. He also thought that mental illness needn't always be a negative thing. He had an idea that **mental breakdowns** could turn into **mental breakthroughs**.

1) **Erving Goffman (1961, 1970)** saw mental illness as a **stigma** caused by **negative labelling**.
2) Goffman was particularly **harsh** on the **role of mental institutions** in **reinforcing these labels**.
3) He thought that individuals in psychiatric institutions have to learn to **conform** to their label as "mentally ill". He said they **lose their old identities** in the process. Goffman calls this process a "**deviant career**".

Goffman (1961) studied patients and staff in psychiatric institutions

Goffman described how patients respond to being labelled "mentally ill".

Withdrawal Patient doesn't communicate with other patients — doesn't believe he / she belongs with them.

Rebellion Patient refuses to cooperate with staff.

Cooperation Patient plays along with the staff idea of how a mental patient behaves. Patient starts to act crazy.

The staff respond to the patient's "crazy" behaviour by **punishing** the patient — they take away the patient's liberty and privacy and they don't let the patient make choices. This is called "**mortification of the self**". It ends up with the patient losing their personality.

The patient becomes **institutionalised**, which means they can't manage on their own outside the institution. After this, the staff can start from scratch, building up a "sane" conformist personality.

If a patient said "I don't belong here, I'm not mad" the staff would think "that's just what a mad person would say, you must be mad".

This is what happens to Jack Nicholson's character in the film *One Flew Over The Cuckoo's Nest.*

1) Many sociologists have criticised the **institutionalisation** of mentally ill people. **Care in the Community** was introduced in the 1980s as an **alternative**. Mentally ill people are looked after in the community, instead of in institutions.
2) Care in the Community allows patients to **stay at home** and **make their own choices**.
3) It's also a **cheap** policy — which makes it popular with governments.
4) On the other hand, it doesn't usually monitor the patient 24 hours a day. **Seriously mentally ill** patients can stop taking their medication and become **disruptive** or **violent** in the community. Patients can end up being **neglected**.

Practice Questions

Q1 Which social groups are statistically most vulnerable to mental illness?

Q2 How would a "medical approach" define and treat disorders such as depression or schizophrenia?

Q3 According to Szasz, what is mental illness?

Exam Question

Q1 Assess sociological explanations for inequalities in the distribution of mental health problems between different social groups. (20 marks)

If you say you're sane, it's proof you're not...

Mental illness is particularly interesting for some sociologists because it can be as much about social deviance as it is about mental health. In Stalinist Russia, you could get locked up as insane just for saying something the authorities didn't like. It's scary to think of. Learn about the medical treatments for mental health, the gender inequalities, and the negative labelling bit.

Ownership and Control of Mass Media

The mass media is one of the most powerful influences in modern society because it's part of all our lives. The power and influence of the media is so wide-ranging that it's important to know just who owns and controls the media.
This section is for both AQA and OCR. Whee.

The Media is **Owned** by a **Few Powerful Companies** and **Individuals**

The **same companies** often own **different forms of media** — films, TV, radio and newspapers.
This is called **cross-media ownership**. It's often not publicised.

1) Media companies **diversify** — they buy other companies that make **different kinds of media**, and companies in **other business sectors**. For example, **Granada** was the first UK media company to buy a stake in a **football team** (Liverpool F.C.). **BSkyB** own 9.9% of Leeds United, Chelsea F.C. and Sunderland A.F.C. and **NTL** own 9.9% of Newcastle United and Aston Villa. BSkyB tried and failed to buy Manchester United PLC for over £600m in 1998.
2) In the US, in 2000 **Time Warner merged with AOL** to create a **huge company** with massive power and influence. Time Warner was already huge (it owns CNN, New Line Cinema, and lots of magazines and record labels) and AOL is the World's biggest ISP (Internet Service Provider).
3) Some media companies **own media** in **several different countries**. Rupert Murdoch's **News Corporation** owns **Fox TV** in the **US**, **Star TV** in **Asia**, **BSkyB** in the **UK**, **Fox Sports** in **Australia**, an **international** TV guide publisher, the **New York Post** newspaper in the US, several **Australian newspapers** and several **British newspapers**. Blimey.
4) **Bagdikian (1997)** found only **ten** major companies owned **25 000** media outlets in America. Wow.

Media group	% share of audience
BBC	19.7
News Corporation	10.6
ITV Network	9.4
Daily Mail Trust	7.8
Mirror Group Newspapers	7.6
United Newspapers	5.7
Carlton Communications	3.1
Channel 4	2.9
Other	33.2

This table shows "media concentration" measured by the time that British audiences spent using media owned by each media group. Source — Congdon et al (1995)

The individuals who own and control those companies have **huge power and influence** in society. They can **control** the information we receive **if they want to**. A **great example** is **Italy**, where the **Prime Minister** Silvio Berlusconi **owns most of the media outlets** and some people claim he is able to use them to **control the reporting** of his political party and the opposition.

Marxists say **Media Ownership Controls Media Content**

1) Traditional Marxism — media owners control what we see in the media

The idea is that the owners of the media **exploit their power position** to **manipulate** the content of the media. Capitalist media owners **tell news editors** what **stories** to cover and what **views** to put across There's a lot of **anecdotal** evidence about newspaper proprietors **personally telling** the **editors** of their newspapers **what view to take on important stories.** The media ends up putting across views that **serve the interests of capitalism.**

2) Neo-Marxism — what we see in the media reflects the ideas of the ruling class, including owners

Neo-Marxist theory is **more complicated**. It says that control over the media is **indirect**. It's a bit vague and hand-wavy, but bear with me for two ticks... Neo-Marxism says the **world view of the elite class** is **broadcast** and **reinforced** by the media. The **values** and **ideas** of the **ruling class** (including media owners) are presented as the **only views to have**, or the **natural**, **common-sense** views to have.

Pluralism says the **Media Reflects** the **Values** and **Beliefs** of Society

The pluralist view is that **society gets the media it wants** — media outlets have to **respond to market demand** or they'll go out of business. Pluralist theory says the media **reflects attitudes already present** in society, and **doesn't** try to **influence** society. In other words, it **doesn't really matter** who **owns** the media — it's the **market** that matters.

There's a definition of pluralism on page 123.

Ownership and Control of Mass Media

There Are **More Forms** of **Communication** and **Entertainment** These Days

Since the sociology of the mass media began there's been a wild and crazy explosion in new methods of mass communication. The two biggest developments have been with the **Internet** and **satellite broadcasting technology**.

1) The **Internet** has made a phenomenal, **humungous amount of information** available to a massive audience.
2) **Email** and **text messaging** are common today, but they didn't even exist ten years ago. Text messaging at 10p a pop is a **big income source** for mobile phone networks.
3) New, **"third-generation" mobile phones** can carry a large amount of information — pictures, Internet, streaming video of news and sport, advertising etc. There's been a lot of **investment** in these — the **government** made an absolute packet **selling the licences** to run the networks.
4) **Digital technology** means you can fit a **whole lot more TV channels** into the airwaves. There are more channels broadcasting to more "**niche**" special interest markets — e.g. DIY, motor sport, shopping.
5) The growth of **digital satellite** broadcasting has meant a big change in the way that **sport** is funded — particularly football. Satellite and digital broadcasters pay big money to buy the rights to **Premiership games**, and terrestrial TV is left with a highlights package.
6) **DVDs** can include documentaries, screen savers, interactive features etc. A DVD of a film has **added value** compared to a video cassette of a film.

There's more choice of media for the individual but not really much more choice in who **owns** and **controls** the media. The **large companies** have **expanded** into the new areas, e.g. Virgin have an Internet Service Provider.

> In the UK, television is **regulated by the state** to make sure it **acts in the public interest** (see p.48 for more on this). Some say that the huge growth in the **number of TV channels** means that the public will soon be able to get **whatever they want** from TV. This would mean there'd be **no need** for state regulation. Not everyone agrees though.
>
> The fact that there are lots of channels **broadcasting to the UK from abroad** means it's **impossible** for the state to regulate the content of those channels.

Merchandising is **Linked** to **Media Ownership**

A **film** or **book** release will be "**tied-in**" with other products, e.g. each **Disney** film release coincides with a new range of **toys** and **gifts** with children's meals at fast food chains, films with **cult appeal** often have tie-in posters and screenplays sold through high street music stores (e.g. 'Pulp Fiction'). This merchandising helps **advertise** the film or book and also makes **profits** for the companies making the tie-ins, which are sometimes owned by the same **parent company**.

The **media** have also used technological advances like text messaging and interactive TV to make more money. Reality TV is a great example of this — think Big Brother, Pop Idol and any kind of show where the audience has a **vote** on how the programme develops. The **production company** behind the show **makes money** on **every text vote**, interactive TV vote or phone vote received.

Practice Questions

Q1 What is cross-media ownership?

Q2 Explain how the ownership of the media in the UK is concentrated.

Q3 List three examples of mass media developed with modern technology.

Q4 Give an example of tie-in merchandising.

Exam Questions

Q1 Examine the view that the media is a tool of the capitalist class used to perpetuate the system. (20 marks)

Q2 "The content of the mass media reflects society". Discuss. (30 marks)

I own my own TV — I've got the receipt for it and everything...

The debate over ownership of the mass media boils down to whether media owners use the media to manipulate society or whether they use it to present all facts and opinions. I've got to say — if I owned a newspaper I'd be awfully tempted to use it to spread my own views. Just casually like, nothing blatant. You know, I really must stop modelling myself on Dr Evil.

Theories about Mass Media

*These two pages focus on ideology and theory and mention things like "neo-Marxism" and "pluralism" — which also appeared briefly on page 34. Page 34 concentrated on media ownership. These pages concentrate on the ways in which **ideology influences the media** and its content.*

Traditional Marxists Say** Media Serves the **Economic Power** of **Ruling Class

1) According to **traditional Marxism**, the media presents what's **important** and **relevant** to the **ruling class**. For example, stocks and share prices are featured on national news bulletins but only a small percentage of the population have a lot of shares. Marxists say that the poor are ignored by the media because they don't have money to buy the things that capitalism sells.
2) Marxist theory says that it's the "**logic of capitalism**" that the institutions in society will always be used as instruments of power by the capitalist class. It's all about serving the interests of capitalism.
3) For example, advertising is in magazines and on TV to **create the demand for goods** produced in the **capitalist economy**. Advertising also gives the idea that there's a wide range of choice for the consumer when, in reality, a few companies own the vast majority of products.
4) **Herbert Marcuse (1964)** was a Marxist who reckoned that the media promotes **consumerism** and gives people "false needs" — the belief that they "need" things that they don't really need.

There's more about Marcuse and his "false needs" on page 74.

Marxist sociologist **Miliband (1969)** thought that the media encourages the proletariat to be **subordinate** and happy to serve the bourgeoisie. Remember what Marx said about **religion** being the **opium of the people** — keeping the working class **subdued** and in support of a system which works against their interests. Well, Miliband reckons that the mass media is "**the new opium of the people**".

*Some **Neo-Marxists** Say the Ruling Class **Indirectly Control** Media Content*

In Marxist thought, one of the key powers of the ruling class is the power to **control ideas**, **values** and **attitudes**. The mass media is a useful tool for doing this. The values of the ruling class have dominance in society — this dominance is called **hegemony**.

This theory says that the **ideas** and **values** of the ruling class are **spread** by the mass media, and presented as if they're the most natural, obvious, common sense things to assume and believe.

"The ruling ideas are the ideas of the ruling class."
Marx, (1874) *The Communist Manifesto*.

1) Media content is controlled by an **approval process** — articles written by journalists are given the OK by editors. **Editors** are mostly from **white, middle class backgrounds** so they **select content** which **reflects** their own values. The idea is that they do this **unconsciously** — they **don't even realise that they're doing it**. Which is a bit odd and a bit scary. (Journalists also tend to come from middle class backgrounds — that's who newspapers and broadcasters tend to employ).
2) Some events are given **less media coverage**, and some are **left out completely**. Marxists believe that the media are **trained** to present a **certain view of the world**. This view becomes natural and "obvious" to them and the audience. Neither the media nor the audience are conscious that the media are pushing a certain view.
3) This neo-Marxist view doesn't say that **alternative** views are **suppressed** — it says they're **allowed**. This gives the impression that all views get a fair shout — which makes it seem OK and perfectly fair for the dominant view to stay on top. Alternative views are often made to look silly or immature.
4) Marxist sociologists say the control of ideas **doesn't just happen in news** or factual programmes. For example, family entertainment programmes are presented as light-hearted fun but they present a specific **idea of British family life**.

Gerald liked to get good press.

Critics of Marxism don't think all journalists think the same way, and they point out that not all media stories are covered from the same viewpoint.

They also say that the media doesn't always reflect the opinions of the dominant class. For example, the BBC reports of government evidence of weapons of mass destruction in the war with Iraq undermined those in power rather than supporting them.

Pluralists point out that media audiences aren't completely stupid, and don't all believe everything they see on TV and read in the papers.

Theories about Mass Media

Pluralism — Media Content Reflects Diversity of Society

The Pluralist view is that society is made up of lots of **different** and **interacting** parts and the state oversees them to keep them in check. Pluralists think that the **content of the media reflects the values of society**. The **free market economy** is the key to a pluralist media — any media which reflects the values in society will be **popular** and stay in business, any that doesn't will go ti... er, bosoms up. This is how pluralist theory says the media **regulates itself**.

Pluralists realise that the media will express **some opinions more than others**. Pluralists reckon this isn't because of bias from journalists, editors or owners — it's only a reflection of the **most common** views in society.

Nick Jones (1986) studied reporting of strikes

Jones studied the reporting on **industrial disputes** by the **UK media**. He concluded there was balanced and equal reporting. Individual reports may have been biased but the overall picture was **neutral**. He said apparent bias was down to the opposing sides managing to get good media coverage — the media were happy to publicise any relevant view.

Pluralism is criticised for **assuming** the diversity and neutrality of the mass media and **not showing evidence** for it.

Critics of pluralism point out that studies are often **carried out by people who work in the media**. Jones is a BBC Radio news journalist. This means that the research **might not be impartial**.

Katz and Lazarsfeld (1955) studied media before a US election

They wanted to find out how much the **media** influenced people's **political opinions** and votes. They concluded that the influence of the media is rather **unpredictable** and is often severely **limited**. They believed it was difficult to influence people through the media. People don't all get exposed to media messages, and don't always pay attention. People's attitudes can completely distort their understanding of a message. People also paid more attention to what their spouse, parents, co-workers and friends said than what the media said.

There's more on this on page 44.

Postmodernism — Media Content Gives Society a Consumerist Identity

1) Postmodernism says that **consumption** is **more important** than **class** identity. It sees Marxist views about economic power as irrelevant nowadays.
2) Postmodernism says that people's **identity** comes from **what they buy** and what kind of **culture and media** they **choose to consume**. Postmodernists think the media has a very important part to play in **showing people what they can buy** and what kind of **lifestyles** they can choose from.
3) French postmodernist **Baudrillard** says that society is **media-saturated** and full of lots of different images. He believes that audiences merge what they see on the media with their own experience to make their own individual sense of reality.
4) Postmodernists also say that there's no dominant set of ideas — **no dominant ideology**.

Many sociologists don't trust postmodernism because it's mainly theoretical — there's not much evidence to support it.

Practice Questions

Q1 What is hegemony?

Q2 What do traditional Marxists think advertising is for?

Q3 Why do Neo-Marxists think that alternative, anti-establishment views are allowed on TV and in the papers?

Q4 What do Pluralists think regulates the media?

Exam Question

Q1 Identify and explain two criticisms of the Marxist view of the relationship between media and audience. (20 marks)

CGP — subconsciously disseminating Cumbrian values since 1995...

Hmm. Subtle. Anyway, the big difference between Marxist and Pluralist views is whether the media controls the audience or whether the audience controls the media. You've got traditional Marxists, who think the media's all about making profits for capitalism, and you've got Neo-Marxists who say it passes on ruling class values without even meaning to.

Selecting and Presenting the News

Sociologists have studied the news as an example of how the media works because it reaches so many people. It's the main source of information on the World for most of the population. The news is a social product full of ideas and values — it's not an objective reality out there waiting to be discovered by journalists.

News is Influenced by ***Practical Constraints*** *— Time, Space and Money*

The news is **presented** to us as the most **factual**, **objective** form of media — the reporting of what's happened in the World that day. In reality, newspapers, radio and television run to very tight **deadlines** and **constraints** which **influence** what finally appears as the news.

1) **Time constraints** mean the most **easily available stories** make it onto the TV/radio news or newspaper. Editors and journalists have **contacts** they use **again and again** for convenience, meaning a **limited number of viewpoints** are used.
Also, all news organisations have a "news diary" of regular events.
This means they can plan coverage of regular events in advance.
2) **Technical constraints** influence the news. Some places are **easier** to get **cameras**, **microphones** and **journalists** into and these are the places **top stories** will tend to come from. A story will rise and fall in significance **partly** on **how easy it is to report**.
3) News organisations all run to a **budget**. Stories and reports from **places where they already have reporters** or **established contacts** are **cheaper to produce**. Many newspapers **can't afford** to have **many reporters** of their own so they **buy stories from news agencies**. These agencies then have a **huge influence** over what becomes news.

This can lead to, for example, disasters in far-flung places being ignored or under-reported.

It's common these days for celebrities, politicians and groups in society to issue a **press release**. Press releases give the story **straight to the newsroom**, which makes it much more likely to be used because it **saves time and money**.

Also remember stories have to shrink or expand to **fit the space available**.
The same story could be on page two one day and page seventeen the next, depending on **what else has happened** or what else is available to report.

Big hint — key studies to use in an exam answer are **Cohen and Young (1981)** *The Manufacture of News* and **Grossberg et al (1998)** *Media making*. Both refer to all of the above as common practices in the media.

News is Influenced by ***Values*** *and* ***Practices*** *of* ***Journalists***

Journalists who report the news learn to follow **certain rules** and ideas, which tend to be based on what they believe the general public want to hear about. Sociologists have referred to these as "**news values**". There are different types of news values which influence the type of news the media chooses to report.

Bureaucratic news values:

News should be **current**.
News should be **simple**.
News should be **brief**.
Big news is better than **small** news.

Cultural news values:

News should be **unexpected**.
News should focus on **important people**.
News should be **relevant to the audience**.
Bad news is preferred to **good news**.

The relative importance of the different news values to an individual journalist will depend partly on the type of publication or programme they work for.

Two key practices used by journalists which you must know are **Agenda-setting** and **Gate-keeping**.

Agenda-setting

Journalists and **editors** "control the news agenda". News **only becomes news** when **journalists** and **editors select it** as news. When a story is selected, journalists choose what **angle** to take when reporting it.
This has a **direct effect** on how the audience will **perceive** the story. Agenda-setting may not be **conscious**.
It comes from **learnt practices** of journalism — usually based on what **catches the audience's attention**.

Gate-keeping

This comes from work by **Gans (1974)** which describes how the editor decides **which stories are featured** and **how much space** is given to each story. Gans says it's like a gate — the editor opens it for some stories and closes it for others. **Dutton (1986)** concluded from his research: "editors fulfil a filtering role since there is usually an excess of material available to fill limited newspaper or broadcasting space".

Selecting and Presenting the News

Case Study of Selection and Presentation of News

The Glasgow University Media Group studied television news

The Glasgow University Media Group (GUMG) studied **television news** over a long time-span (1970s and 1980s) to look for evidence of bias. They focused in particular on coverage of workplace **strikes**. They used **detailed content analysis** of **television news bulletins**.

Finding		Examples
The **selection of news** was biased in favour of dominant class values.	→	**Picket line violence** was **reported more** than police violence.
The **voice-overs** were biased in favour of dominant class values.	→	Words such as "**trouble-makers**" and "**pointless strike**" were argued to be **neutral**.
Management were given **more access** to the media than striker leaders.	→	Television interviews with management were **more frequent** and longer than those with strike leaders.
The **filming** and **editing** was biased in favour of the police.	→	Cameras were often placed **behind police lines** showing the police viewpoint.

The work of the Glasgow University Media Group is used to demonstrate **bias in the news** and in the **values and assumptions** of the individuals who **produce** and **construct** the news. Their work is **highly respected** because they've studied **a lot of news** in **great detail**. Remember though, the work was done in the 1970s so think before you start blithely applying it to the news in 2004.

The **image** of the news as objective reporting of fact makes this bias more **important** and more **powerful**. Because people **think the news is unbiased**, they're **more likely to believe it**.

News is Influenced by Society — it's Socially Constructed

All media sociologists agree the **news is socially constructed** but they disagree over whose values are behind the social construction of news — those of the dominant class or those of the majority of society.

1) From a **pluralist** perspective, **practical constraints** are more significant in influencing the content of the news than ideological bias. The values of journalists are the **common values in society**.
2) From the **Marxist** perspective, the **ideological influences** are most important, and practical constraints can't be separated from ideology. Journalistic values are part of the **dominant ruling class ideology**.

Practice Questions

Q1 Describe what is meant by "news values".

Q2 Explain how the process of gate-keeping takes place in news production.

Q3 How does money influence the presentation of the news? Give two examples.

Q4 What is meant by the term 'socially constructed' in relation to the news?

Exam Question

Q1 Journalists create rather than discover the news. Discuss. (20 marks)

It's funny how the World's events always exactly fill the newspaper...

You think you know what news is, and then you read these pages. Suddenly, you know a lot more about news, but it isn't so clear cut any more. News is as much of a social construct as anything else. People choose what to put in the papers and on the telly, and people aren't unbiased and neutral — they're affected by all sorts of social factors, and all sorts of ideas.

Media Stereotypes

The role of the media in representing social groups is very influential. These pages look at the images of particular social groups, how they're formulated and what effect they might have.

Stereotypes are Inaccurate Generalisations

Stereotypes are **generalisations** about **social groups**. They are **inaccurate** and often **derogatory** — e.g. "Women can't read maps", "Gay men are camp", "Chinese women are submissive."

Media Messages Go Through Four Stages from Production to End Effect

In "sociology speak" this is called the **process of message trajectory**.

Stage 1 — Media Message is formulated by editors

Media messages are **formulated** (put together) by those in **powerful positions** in media institutions. These individuals aren't usually members of the social groups which the media stereotypes. For example, very few media editors are female, disabled, black, working class, openly gay, under 25 or over 65.

Stage 2 — Media Message content reflects groups in power

The content of the media **reflects the values** of the people who **formulate** it. Groups who aren't in power have **limited representation** in the media.

Stage 3 — Media Message is received by the audience

The messages are then **received** by the audience and **interpreted** in different ways — depending on **context** and **experience**.

Stage 4 — Media Message affects the role and treatment of social groups

Opinions and behaviour of **individuals** and **institutions** in society are **influenced** by **messages in the media**. The **impact of the media** depends on how you view the **interaction between media and audience**. It's all very theoretical.

There's plenty of detail about this on pages 44-47.

You need to **know these four stages** and to be able to give **examples** for the **social groups on the following three pages** (gender stereotypes, class stereotypes, disability stereotypes, ethnic stereotypes, age stereotypes and sexuality stereotypes). You can choose other groups but you'd need to **do your own research** to find your own examples.

Media Messages About Women Are Stereotyped

1) Most **editors** are **men**. Research by **Croteau and Hoynes (2000)** gives evidence for this. They found that in the mid 1990s in the US only 6% of top newspaper management were women and only 20% of top TV management. Women wrote 19% of front page stories and presented 20% of TV news reports.
2) Women **don't appear on the media as often as men**. A Broadcasting Standards Council survey by **Guy Cumberbatch (1990)** found 90% of all advertising voice-overs were male and 66% of all people in adverts were male. Also, women in ads were likely to be young, blonde and not to appear in a workplace setting.
3) Women in the media are often presented as **ideals** for other women to aspire to. **Naomi Woolf (1990)** and **Susan Orbach (1991)** both reckon that the rise in eating disorders in women is a direct result of distorted and idealised images of women's bodies in the media.
4) The media tends to portray women in a limited range of roles. **Tuchman (1978)** argued there were only two female roles portrayed in the media: **domestic** and **sexual**.
5) Women in the media are often presented in a way to **appeal to men** — as attractive, well-groomed and sexy.
6) Women are often represented as **victims** by the media — of sexual violence, domestic violence etc.

Ferguson (1983) looked at a wide range of **women's magazines**. She found the magazines gave **advice and training** on **being feminine**. She called this a "cult of femininity" which **reinforced stereotypes** of women as **sexual**, **domestic** and **romantic**. **McRobbie (1978)** studied **teenage girl's magazines**. She concluded that the **main theme** of the magazines was **how to get a boyfriend** — how to be attractive to men.

Postmodernist **Hermes (1995)** thinks people respond to images and stereotypical portrayal of women in a **variety** of ways. Individuals can **reject media messages** in the light of other knowledge and experience they have — people aren't all easily led.

Media Stereotypes

Some Sociologists Say There Are **Class Stereotypes** in the Media

1) **Editors** are almost all **middle class**. **Journalists** are often hired partly on the basis of whether their "face fits", so they're usually from the **same middle class background** as the editors.
2) **Middle class** people **appear on TV** more often than working class people, both on **dramas** and on **news** programmes.
3) **Drama roles** for working class characters are mostly limited to **soap operas**. **Upper class** characters are often seen in **historical costume dramas** — which tend to give a **romantic** picture of life and class.
4) In the **news**, **working class** people are often represented as a **source of trouble** — trade union unrest, strikes, crime, vandalism, "anti-social behaviour" etc.

Glennon and Butsch (1982) looked at TV in the USA

Glennon and Butsch carried out a massive research project into 40 years of family programmes on American TV.

They found that only **4% of sitcoms** featured a family where the head of household was a **manual worker**. In real life, **36%** of American families were like this.

Nearly **half** the **TV families** had a **professional** as head of household. In real life, only 25% were like this.

Most of the families were wealthy and glamorous.

Glennon and Butsch thought that most **working class dads** were portrayed as **stupid** and **comical**, for the audience to laugh at.

"Look," said Saskia. "Do you see what I see?" "Golly," said Rupert. "Working class people on the telly. Whatever will they think of next?"

This is their opinion though, not necessarily the opinion of the actual TV audience.

Stuart Hall (1982, 1992, 1996) thinks that the media has always portrayed the **middle classes** in a **positive** light and the **working class** in a **negative** light. He says that the media has reinforced people's class identities — which keeps the divide between the classes going strong.

Ann Gray (1992) looked at how women from different social classes used TV and video. She found that **working class women** watched a lot **more TV** and video. Women in **higher social classes** had a strong preference for "classic" and "quality" programmes.

Practice Questions

Q1 Write a summary of the four stages of a media message in no more than four sentences.

Q2 Give two examples of social groups which have been identified as being subject to stereotyped media portrayal.

Q3 List two pieces of research which illustrate the argument that the media is a patriarchal institution.

Q4 What contribution has postmodern theory made to the understanding of the portrayal of women in the media?

Exam Questions

Q1 With reference to sociological studies, assess the view that the mass media is biased in its portrayal of women. (20 marks)

Q2 How does social class play a role in the construction of stereotyped images in the mass media? (30 marks)

Learn the studies, you'll need them...

Remember, it's not just women who are stereotyped by the media. Men are also portrayed in a limited way, which tends to be as a strong, capable breadwinner. Most dramas which contain violence generally portray men as the aggressors, and they're more likely to be shown as criminals too. So, if a question asks about gender stereotypes, remember to talk about men as well as women.

Media Stereotypes

The media sends out stereotypes about disabled people, ethnic minorities, young people, old people and gay people. That's a lot of people.

Disabled People are Under-represented in the Media

1) Disabled people are **poorly represented** in **powerful positions** in the media. Those who do hold powerful positions tend to have specialised in disabled issues — e.g. Peter White, the radio journalist.
2) There's really **very little representation of disabled people** in the media at all. Government statistics show that about 20% of the adult population has some form of disability, yet the Broadcasting Standards Commission (1999) reported that people with disabilities only appeared in **7% of television programmes** and had only **0.75% of all speaking roles.**
3) **Roles** for disabled people are very **limited**. Research by **Cumberbatch and Negrine (1992)** looking at British television over six weeks found the roles for disabled people were based on **pity** or **comedy**. They found that **disabled actors** never appeared **just as actors** playing a person who **just happened to have a disability**, only in **roles particularly about disability**. However, there are **some positive portrayals** of disabled people in films and on TV — e.g. *Four Weddings and a Funeral.*
4) **Audience response** depends on people's **actual experience** of disability. Cumberbatch and Negrine researched audience responses as part of their study. They concluded that people with limited or **no real life experience** of disability **accepted** the media images with **little concern**. People **with experience** of disability were **critical** of the media and **rejected** stereotyped images.

Media Representations of Ethnicity are Stereotyped

1) New technology means there are more satellite and digital TV channels. Lots of small specialised channels have developed. Many of these **cater for specific ethnic minorities** and they're managed and controlled by people from those ethnic minorities (e.g. Zee TV, Bangla TV, Punjabi TV).
2) However, there aren't many people from ethnic minorities in positions of **power** in **mainstream media**. Have a good look at the difference between this and point 1. Ethnic minorities are **marginalised** in the media — shunted off into non-mainstream **specialist** media organisations.
3) There aren't very many **roles** played by members of **ethnic minorities** on TV. For example, a study of **American TV** by **Greenberg et al (1983)** found **97%** of characters on daytime soaps and dramas were white and **87%** of characters on primetime soaps and dramas were white. This is starting to change though.
4) Roles for ethnic minorities are often **stereotyped** and **limited**. **Stuart Hall (1982)** said that **in the past** there were three main stereotypes: **slave, "native" and entertainer**. Remember that Hall was talking about the past, not the present. Ethnic minority characters in soap operas are getting **less stereotyped** — e.g. characters on EastEnders.
5) There's evidence that ethnic minorities are presented **negatively** in the papers — as criminals, as illegal immigrants, as terrorists or as victims of famine. **Van Dijk (1991)** made a detailed analysis of **headlines** in five British national newspapers. He found **negative images** far outweighed positive images in all five papers. It's well worth your while learning a couple of statistics from this table of his results:

Newspaper	The Times	The Telegraph	The Guardian	The Mail	The Sun
Negative image of ethnic minority	19	32	14	16	25
Positive image of ethnic minority	4	4	5	4	1

6) **Audience response** to ethnic minority stereotypes varies depending on the **real life experience** of the audience. People don't swallow media stereotypes if they know better themselves.

Maria Gillespie looked at how **Punjabi teenagers** responded to **British TV** from 1988 to 1991. She concluded that the media gave teenagers the opportunity to **compare** Punjabi culture with **Western** culture.

Hartmann and Husband (1974) analysed children's response to media

They compared the responses of children in two parts of Britain and found that in the **area with low ethnic mix,** children **believed negative media content** and thought of "race relations" in terms of conflict. In the **area with a high ethnic mix**, children **rejected media stereotypes** in favour of their own experience.

Media Stereotypes

Images of Young and Old are Stereotyped in the Media

1) The **people with power** in media organisations tend to be **older**. It takes **time** to get **experience**, so this makes sense.
2) There's often a sexist **double standard** in the way older people are represented in the media. The **older** a **woman** gets, the **less likely** she is to get a leading film role or a TV presenting job. It's a different story for men. In films, older male actors like Sean Connery and Harrison Ford are "allowed" to be romantically paired with cute young women. There are lots more **older men presenting TV programmes** than there are older women.
3) **Biggs (1993)** focused on entertainment programmes and found lots of representation of older people. However, they were often in stereotyped roles of "forceful", "vague" and "difficult" — especially in sitcoms. In America, **Signorelli (1989)** studied television characters and found that both young and old were under-represented on prime-time television. TV was biased towards **middle-aged** people.
4) **Featherstone and Hepworth (1995)** found that magazines aimed at older people tended to push an image of "youthful" old people — enjoying holidays and sports, wearing fashionable, "young-looking" clothes, etc.
5) There are also **stereotypes** relating to **young people**. **Children** are represented as **innocent**. Slightly older "**youth**" are often seen as a **social problem** — prone to drug abuse, binge drinking, petty crime and unplanned pregnancy.

Stan Cohen (1973) first used the term "**moral panic**" to describe how **media reporting** of expected "trouble" could **create panic** in society.

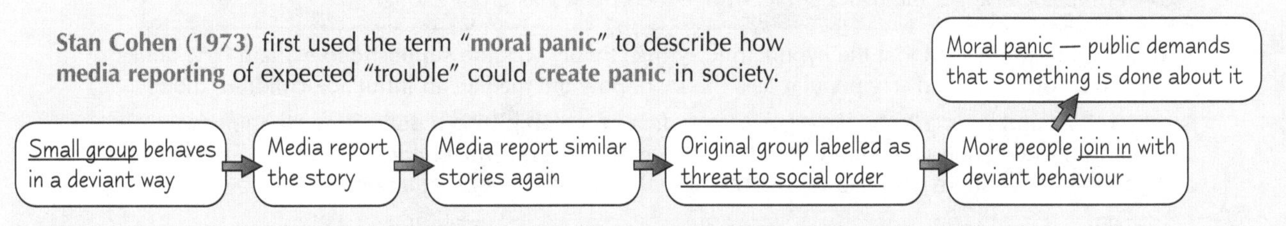

Cohen used the example of the **Mods and Rockers** in the 1960s. The media reported that there would be **fights** between two youth subcultures — the Mods and the Rockers. Lots of people turned up to fight or watch, partly because of the **media publicity**. The public then **panicked** over reports of how many people turned up to fight.

You can easily find **contemporary** examples of a moral panic — e.g. the concern over trouble at **So Solid Crew** gigs. The possibility of **gun violence** led to some shows being cancelled because **media reporting** of the concern led to **panic**.

Representations of Sexuality in the Media are Stereotyped

1) Gay men are often stereotyped as "**camp**". TV shows often use "camp" gay characters as **comic relief**.
2) Homosexual relationships and heterosexual relationships are shown differently in the media. For example, much more explicit heterosexual sex is shown on television than homosexual sex. **Coronation Street** and **EastEnders** have both had storylines involving a **gay kiss** which got widespread media attention. You don't get any outcry in the papers when a **man and a woman** kiss on a soap opera.
3) There was a **political** aspect to early **media reporting** of **HIV/AIDS**. It was initially openly characterised as a "gay disease". A *Daily Mail* headline in the 1980s referred to AIDS as a "gay plague".

Practice Questions

Q1 Briefly explain the findings of Cumberbatch and Negrine (1992).

Q2 Give an example of newspaper bias in relation to ethnic minorities in Britain.

Q3 How does real-life experience affect how people respond to stereotypes in the media?

Exam Questions

Q1 Examine the view that the media are biased in their representation of ethnic minorities. (20 marks)

Q2 With reference to sociological studies, evaluate the claim that the media are ideologically biased. (30 marks)

Learn these studies...in fact learn ALL the studies...in the world... EVER...

If you do a question on media audiences and ethnicity, disability, age or sexuality, you have to be prepared to mention some sociological studies to back up your points. It's the only way to get the marks. The stuff on these pages makes you think a bit. British society, and the media especially, has a way to go before it treats everyone equally.

Mass Media and its Audience

The media constructs and sends out messages to the public — but the impact of the messages depends on how the audience responds. People can accept media messages, or dismiss them as complete rubbish.

The **Hypodermic Syringe** Theory — Media **Directly Influences Audience**

Way back in the **1920s**, when **radio** and **newspapers** were just starting to get **important** in society, sociologists developed theories about how the media affected people.

1) The **hypodermic syringe theory** says the media **injects** its message into the mind of the audience in the same way as drugs are **directly injected** into the body. The idea is that the media is **so powerful**, its message **directly influences** the individual and they're **powerless** to **resist** the message or **reject** it.
2) This theory says that **all individuals** in the audience are **affected** in the **same way**.

> In **1938**, Orson Welles recorded a radio production of HG Wells' story *The War of the Worlds* in which Martians invade Earth. The broadcast included **fictional news bulletins** reporting the Martian invasion. Some radio listeners **believed** the fake bulletins were true, and **panicked**. This was used as **evidence** of the **dangerous** and **direct power of the media** and it created concern in society. For the hypodermic syringe theorists it was proof enough.

3) Some sociologists decided that the hypodermic syringe theory was **too simplistic** to explain how adults view media content. It did stay popular as a theory of how the **media** can **influence children**, though.
4) **Bandura, Ross and Ross (1963)**, played children a **film of a man hitting a doll**. They then left the children to play with the **same doll** which they'd seen on the film. The children who'd seen the violence on film hit the doll, those who hadn't seen the film played with the doll in a non-violent way.

Critics of the hypodermic syringe theory think it treats people as **passive** and very easily led. They also point out that **not all audience members react in the same way** to the same piece of media. Studies showed this as far back as the 1920s.

> Don't assume that this theory is dead in the water. Think about the **concern** that **fictional TV** and **film violence** can cause violent acts in society. In 1992, two 11 year old boys were convicted of **killing two year old Jamie Bulger** — when the judge was summing up he said that **watching a violent film** was "partly responsible".

The Media Message is **Interpreted** and **Passed On** by **Key Individuals**

The **two-step flow model** was developed in the 1950s. It says that the media does influence people, but **not everyone is influenced directly**.

> 1) The **first step** is the **media message** reaching an audience member. All simple so far.
> 2) The important **second step** is how their **understanding** of the message is **shaped** by **social interaction** with other audience members. For example, if workers in an office chat about a soap opera during their coffee break then these discussions affect individuals' opinions of the storyline and characters.
> 3) **Katz and Lazarsfeld (1955)** said that there were **key individuals** in each community whose reaction **directly influenced others**. These "**opinion leaders**" openly expressed their reaction and opinions, and others **followed** their lead. Katz and Lazarsfeld studied **media influence on American voters**. They concluded that most people followed the opinion leader's views on who they should vote for, but the opinion leaders themselves often got their **ideas straight from the mass media** messages.
> 4) It doesn't have to be just two steps — a message can go through several stages of interpretation. **Hobson (1990)** studied an office environment and found that a few **key individuals** influenced what the others watched on television and their **reactions** to the programmes. These opinions were **passed on** to another bunch of colleagues. A **social norm** of what to watch **spread** through the **whole office**. **New recruits** had to **conform** to fit in.

It's easy to imagine this happening in a school or a workplace. "Did you see Big Brother?" "Isn't she such a COW?" "He loves himself, doesn't he?". If you don't watch the programme, you're left out of the conversation. If you don't agree with the ~~bigmouth~~ opinion leader, you're made to feel a bit of an outsider.

Mass Media and its Audience

Social *and* ***Cultural Context*** *Affect how an* ***Audience Responds*** *to the* ***Media***

1) The **Cultural Effects theory** introduced the idea that **social context** is important when looking at the effects of the media. In short, they argued that **different people** interpret the media in **different ways**.
2) The idea is that an audience **interprets the media** in the **context** of the **culture** they already belong to. This means that the effect of the media is quite complex — it's not the same for everyone.
3) "**Culture**" refers to the **small, sub-cultural groups** an individual belongs to and also to the **wider, general culture of society**. For example, in England an individual's response to Arsenal winning the Premiership will **depend** on whether the **individual** supports Arsenal or not. But audience response to media reports of **England winning the World Cup** would be broadly **similar** because there's a **cultural norm** of supporting your country's sports teams.

Here's a **second look** at the audience response to the *War of the Worlds* broadcast — this time from a **Cultural Effects viewpoint (Cantril, 1940)**.

1) The response was **caused** by the **cultural context** in which it was heard. If it was on the radio **today** it wouldn't create the same response.
2) At the time of the broadcast there was **insecurity** in American society because of a **financial crisis** and the move towards **war in Europe**. Radio programmes were **frequently interrupted for news reports**, and there was a general expectation of bad news.
3) People **wouldn't have been surprised** to hear a **real report** of bad news interrupting a drama programme on the radio. This made it **more likely** that some members of the audience would **believe** the story.

The Effects of Media Messages ***Build Up Over Time***

1) The Cultural Effects theory made sociologists look at the **long term effects** of the media.
2) Media effects build up over time to **create** or **reinforce** cultural **norms**.
3) For example, **images of women** in the media create **stereotypical images** and place **expectations** on girls and women. There's been a long-running campaign by some feminists to remove pictures of **topless women** ("Page Three Girls") from national newspapers, because they argue that these images reinforce the dominant view that it's OK to objectify women as sex objects.

Practice Questions

Q1 Briefly explain the hypodermic syringe theory.

Q2 In which study did sociologists show children a film of a person hitting a doll?

Q3 Define the two steps in the two-step flow model.

Q4 Explain what's meant by the term "opinion leader".

Q5 Briefly explain Cultural Effects theory.

Q6 Name the sociologist who did a study of *The War of the Worlds* panic in 1940.

Exam Questions

Q1 Evaluate the claim that audiences are passive in their response to media messages, with reference to at least two sociological theories. (20 marks)

Q2 "The hypodermic syringe model is outdated." Discuss. (30 marks)

The Hypodermic Syringe theory — it gets right under your skin...

You read one theory and think "ah, that explains it", then you read the next theory and think "ah, that explains it" — and they're two totally contradictory theories, so they can't both be right. I suppose they can both be right some of the time, or they can give you a part of the picture. The most important thing is that you can write about them in the exam.

Mass Media and its Audience

Here's more about how people interpret what they see and hear from the mass media.
Some sociologists think people can be quite active in deciding what media messages they want to see and hear.

Audiences **Actively Use** and **Interpret** the Media to **Suit Their Own Needs**

There's a bunch of media theories which are grouped together as "**interpretive theories**".
They all argue that the audience responds **actively** to media content and messages.
There's a switch from "what the **media** does **to** people" to "what **people** do **with** the media".

Uses and Gratifications Theory

1) This theory was developed in the **1960s** by **Blumler and Katz** (they of "two-step flow" fame). It says that people **use** the media to **meet their needs**. The audience **actively chooses** what media to experience, using such cutting edge tools as free will and the remote control. Everyone chooses for themselves, so each person's media diet is **unique**.
2) A good example is the study of **soap opera audiences** by **McQuail (1972)**. He looked at how audiences used **Coronation Street** to fulfil a need for **social companionship**. Audiences felt part of the characters' lives and felt interest and concern for what would happen next in a storyline.
3) **Lull (1990)** listed the social uses of television in the UK — and found men, women, young and old all used the media to meet different needs.
4) Uses and Gratification Theory is **functionalist** — it says the media exists to serve the **needs** of the public.

In media language "to engage with" a piece of media means to find it interesting and pay attention to it — to be "into" it.

Selective Filter Model

1) This theory says the audience **choose** which media to **experience** and also **control** which parts of the media message to listen to and **engage with**. The audience pick out the parts of a message which **fit in with their view of the world** and **ignore the rest**.
2) **Fiske (1988)** says individuals become very **experienced readers of the media**. He says that individuals can understand one "**media text**" in several **different ways** on several **different levels** — and in relation to **other** "**media texts**" on the same subject.
3) Here's an example to make it clear: when watching a **TV drama series**, you can get **caught up in the fictional drama**, and at the same time **know a character is going to die** because you read it in a **newspaper article** about the series. Or you might like a character because he's played by an actor you liked in another TV series. This is called an "**intertextual response**" in the exciting language of media sociology.
4) This model emphasises the **power of the individual** to control his / her experience of the media and says that people use media in a **sophisticated** way. It's kinda postmodern in that way. However, it's been criticised for **overestimating** the control of the individual over very **powerful media messages**.

"Media text" means a piece of media — a TV programme, a newspaper article, a magazine article, an advert. Academics really like to call things "texts" for some reason. Oh well, if it makes them happy...

Structured Interpretation Model

1) This theory says there's a **dominant interpretation** of media messages which audiences go along with. Like the other two theories, individuals actively **pick** which media they **engage with**, but this theory says the process takes place in a **social context**. The social context creates a "**preferred reading**" of the media message (by "reading" they mean "interpretation"). For example a film is written, presented and promoted with a **preferred reading** in mind — the makers of a film like *Cold Mountain* want you to find the love story **moving** and **tragic**, not stilted and laughable.
2) **Different social groups** have **different dominant interpretations** of the same text. So, this theory isn't the same as earlier theories which saw the audience as a mass who all respond in the same way.
3) **Morley (1980)** studied how the television audience responded to one **news programme** — *Nationwide*. He showed the same programme to several **different social groups** and found that their responses to the programme **varied** hugely **but within each group** most **individuals responded in the same way**. Trade unionists saw it as biased towards management and management trainees saw it as pro-union.

Mass Media and its Audience

Postmodern Theory *Says the Audience Gets* ***Lots of Meanings***

1) **Postmodernists** say that there are **many**, **many meanings** to any social or cultural aspect of life. They say there **isn't any aspect of life** where there's one single, objective **truth** or **reality** that absolutely everyone experiences. That's a really important part of postmodernism.

2) Another important fact about postmodernism is that it can **make your head swim** if you try to think about it too hard. Just warning you because I care...

> **Baudrillard (1988)** says that the development of the media and technological advances have meant everyday life is **chock-full of images** and messages all competing and **conflicting** with each other. Audiences experience all these messages alongside each other — leading to a state he calls **hyperreality** where **no single word** or **image** has a **straightforward meaning**. *Whoah*. Like, *dude*. Seriously, whoah.

3) The media presents so many different **images** and **stories** which have been **woven into everyday life** that the **boundary** between **reality** and the **media** is **blurred**.

> **Turkle (1996)** reckons that individuals can relate to a **simulated world** as easily as **reality** — the characters in the pretend world become significant in their own right. The explosion of **reality TV** and the **obsessive interest** people have with **soap stars** are good examples of this. With **reality TV**, **real** people get put in an **unreal situation** which is presented as **real**, and the audience follows it like a **soap**. With a soap, **pretend** characters get treated by the press and by audiences **as if they're real**. So it's real, not real, real, not real and real again. At the same time. Again, *whoah*.

Conclusions of Postmodernism

1) The **conclusion** from postmodern theory is that the media is not only **complex** and **interactive** but it actually isn't **concrete** or **definite**.
2) There's no one **dominant message** or truth which is being conveyed — there's a range of **varying realities** for the **individual** to **interpret**.
3) This suits the idea of the **postmodern audience** who don't follow one clear path through life but **pick** and **choose** between a range of opportunities and alternatives.

Critics *say Postmodernism's too* ***Theoretical***

Postmodernism is criticised for being too theoretical. It's really **hard to find** (or even think of) any kind of **evidence** which would **prove** postmodernism **right** or **wrong**. I mean, if you're starting out from the premise that no idea has a straighforward meaning and individuals create their own reality so that there is no one definition of what is 'real' or 'true' — *where on earth do you go from there...*

Postmodernism doesn't acknowledge there's **inequality** in society and in the media. In real life, **not all messages**, views or "realities" **ever get presented** by the media.

Practice Questions

Q1 What do sociologists mean when they refer to an audience actively responding to the media content?

Q2 Give an example of a criticism of the uses and gratifications model of audience response.

Q3 Explain the term "preferred reading" in relation to the media.

Q4 Explain why *Big Brother* is a good example of postmodern TV.

Exam Questions

Q1 Compare and contrast the differing models of audience response known as interpretive theories. (20 marks)

Q2 "Media audiences actively select and filter the content and messages they receive". Discuss. (30 marks)

Whenever I fancy feeling like I've shoved my head in a blender...

... with an Amazon tree frog and a shot of ouzo, I read some postmodernism. There is kind of a point behind it, though. If you limit it to "people pick and choose what they believe" and "people think things are real when they're not really" it's not too bad. Having said that, I dare you to read Jacques Lacan or Jacques Derrida. I double dog dare you.

Censorship and Mass Communications

All governments control the media to a greater or lesser extent. The media reaches a large section of the population on a regular basis and it's influential in changing behaviour and attitudes — so it's not surprising there's some control and regulation over media content to protect the public from being misled or manipulated. ***These 2 pages are for OCR only.***

The **Media** can be **Self-Regulating**

Different branches of the media have different ways of **making sure content and practices** are kept to a **good standard**.

1) In Britain the press is "free". This means all **newspapers** and **magazines** are **commercial**, not funded by the state. There's **no obligation** for the press to be **impartial** or **unbiased** — in fact many daily newspapers **openly support** a particular **political viewpoint**.

2) The press set up their own organisation, the **Press Complaints Commission (PCC)** to monitor standards and to deal with complaints. The PCC can order newspapers to print apologies if a complaint's been upheld. A **frequent beef** people have with the PCC is that when apologies are printed they're often in tiny print at the bottom of an inside page — even when the initial story was on the front page with a **MASSIVE HEADLINE**.

3) **Broadcast media** (TV and radio) are **more regulated by the government**. They also often publicise **standards of their own** which **their journalists** have to stick to.

The **Media** Must **Obey The Law**

Both **public** (BBC) and **commercial** broadcasting are subject to **legal guidelines** and **restrictions**.

1) There are **laws** restricting **what can be shown on TV and when**. There is a "**watershed**" of **9pm**. Before 9pm you can't show **nudity**, **sex**, **violence** or **bad language**. After 9pm a **warning** must be given before programmes that have nudity, sex, violence or bad language.

2) UK television is required by law to be **impartial** — unlike the press. For example, in 2004, a public inquiry strongly criticised the **BBC** for it's **reporting** of issues relating to **Iraqi weapons of mass destruction** (WMDs). The reporter involved, as well as the Chairman and Director General of the BBC all resigned as a result.

3) There are various **laws** the government can use to **ban programmes**. Under the Official Secrets Act and the Prevention of Terrorism Act, the government can issue "**D notices**" which stop dangerous material being broadcast. For example, in **1989** the government banned a documentary ***Death on the Rock*** which questioned the official view of how three members of the IRA were killed in Gibraltar.

4) In **1989** TV and radio broadcasters were **banned** from using **words spoken by members** of **11 political and paramilitary groups** in **Northern Ireland**, including **Sinn Fein**. The ban was in place for **five years** — during that time the words of Sinn Fein politicians were spoken by **actors**.

5) The **law of libel** makes it **illegal** to make **defamatory** or **damaging** comments about **anyone**. Anyone and any organisation can be **sued** for **writing** (libel) or **saying** (slander) defamatory or damaging comments. This includes newspapers, magazines, Internet sites, TV, emails — even repeating comments initially made by someone else. Media providers often use **lawyers** to check **controversial material** before it is printed or broadcast.

Charters and **Legal Contracts** Restrain the Media

1) The **BBC** was established by a **Charter** which all its TV and radio content has to stick to. The BBC has to be "**independent**, **impartial** and **honest**" at all times.

2) The BBC has to **follow the rules** of its Charter to get **funding** from the government. It has 12 **governors** to make sure it does stick to the charter.

3) **Commercial TV and radio broadcasters** don't have to follow this Charter. Before they can broadcast they have to get **legal contracts** which tie them to certain standards. These contracts run for several years and are **issued by the government**.

4) In January 2004 **Ofcom** was established as the **new government regulator** to oversee the conduct of **all communications industries**. It deals with complaints and it can **fine** or **close down** broadcasters who break the rules.

Ever heard a presenter **panic** if a guest swears on TV or radio — this is because broadcasters are **heavily fined** for breaking regulations "regarding **standards of taste and decency**". There are two ways to avoid these fines: 1) broadcast on a **time delay** so you can bleep out the swearing and 2) **never** invite John Lydon onto your programme*.

The **Power of Advertising** is a **Restraint** on Commercial Media

Commercial media needs **funds from advertising** to **survive** — it'll always be careful not to have **bad publicity** or content which advertisers don't like. If content doesn't fit with the advertiser's image the media outlet is likely to **adapt the content** rather than **risk** losing an advertiser.

**Only kidding, Mr Lydon, sir. May I say what a truly great band Public Image Limited were, by the way.*

Censorship and Mass Communications

There are Several Arguments about Violence in the Media

Some sociologists argue that violence in the media has an effect on people

1) Early studies by Bandura, Ross and Ross (see p.44) show that children would **copy violent behaviours** they'd seen on film. This is often called "**copycat violence**".
2) Some sociologists say that violence on TV and film **desensitises** viewers to real violence. Seeing violence in the media makes people **less shocked** by violence in **real life**.

Other sociologists disagree with these ideas

1) **Catharsis theory** says that watching violence on screen **gets violent thoughts out of the viewer's system**. Watching a good gore-fest makes you **less likely** to grab a chainsaw and rampage through your own neighbourhood. So said **Feshbach and Singer (1971)** in their study of boys aged 8-18. Boys who watched aggressive and violent TV were less aggressive themselves.
2) **Buckingham (1993)** said that audience members actively interpret film and TV violence, and **make their own minds up** about the rights and wrongs of what they see on screen. Even young kids do this.
3) Some sociologists think that watching violence is a "**rite of passage**" for young people, especially boys. It's a phase they go through to prove they **aren't kids** any more.
4) **Morrison (1999)** makes a really important distinction between **serious, disturbing violence** and **lighthearted comedy violence**. For example, a photo of a prisoner of war getting shot in the back of the head is serious while the sitcom ***Bottom*** and the cartoon ***Ren and Stimpy*** are lighthearted violence. It's a darn obvious difference when you see it like that, but a lot of research has ignored it.

Censorship of Violence in the Media is a Tricky Area

1) There are clear regulations for public broadcasting which all programmes and films have to follow. Films can't be shown on TV or in cinemas in the UK until they've been **passed by the British Board of Film Classification (BBFC)** and given a **grading** which tells you **how old you have** to be to watch the film — U (Universal), PG (Parental Guidance), 12, 15 or 18.
2) Obviously, it's more difficult to censor and regulate media which is viewed privately in people's homes — e.g. **videos** and **DVDs**.
3) A real concern is that censorship doesn't prevent controversial material being produced — but drives it **underground** where it can't be monitored. The **Internet** has been used to sell and distribute **violent** and **pornographic** material which would be banned from other media outlets. However, high profile police campaigns using **sophisticated tracking technology** have meant individuals can be **traced** and are now being **prosecuted**.

Practice Questions

Q1 Explain the difference between public and commercial media.

Q2 Name two legal controls which both public and commercial media have to adhere to.

Q3 What differences are there in how print and broadcast media are regulated?

Q4 Give an example of how an advertiser could influence the content of a media publication.

Q5 Describe the regulatory arrangements for the BBC.

Exam Question

Q1 "The media is regulated to protect the public from biased and inappropriate media in Britain today". Evaluate this statement with reference to at least two forms of media. (20 marks)

TV makes me violent — I have to slap the telly to make it work...

Imagine — TV might be even worse if there weren't any controls or regulation... The question of whether violence on TV makes kids more violent and aggressive is an old one. There are those who say it does, and those who say it doesn't necessarily. Kids can be a lot more clever at telling the difference between real and pretend than you'd think.

The Role of the Education System

Section 5 is for AQA only. *Different theories try to explain the role or function of education in society. Some of them look at the positive functions. Some look at how education oppresses pupils and maintains inequality. Some look at pupil interaction in the classroom. Some say we should get rid of school altogether... Yay.*

Functionalism *Says Education Has* ***Three Functions*** *that Help Society*

1) Education teaches the **skills** needed in **work** and by the **economy**.
2) Education **sifts and sorts people** for the **appropriate jobs**. This is called the **allocation** function.
3) Education plays a part in **secondary socialisation**, passing on **core values**.

1) **Durkheim** said that education passes on **norms** and **values** in order to **integrate** individuals into society. Education helps to **create social order** based on cohesion and value **consensus**.
2) **Parsons** describes school as a bridge between the family and adult roles of society. Schools pass on a **universal value** of **achievement**. Parsons says that education **selects** children into **appropriate roles** because it's **meritocratic** (meaning that the best students rise to the top). He agrees with Durkheim that education helps to make people agree about norms and values.
3) **Davis and Moore (1945)** say that every society sorts its members into different positions. They think that there are **rules** for how education does this — called "**principles of stratification**". They believe that there has to be a system of **unequal rewards** (more money or status) to **motivate** people to train for the top positions.

The **functionalist** perspective says that education is **meritocratic**. A **meritocracy** is when social **rewards** are allocated by **talent** and **effort** rather than being **born** into a position.

Talent + motivation + equal opportunity = qualifications and a high position in society

Marxism *Says* ***Education Legitimises Inequality*** *through* ***Ideology***

1) Education **prepares children** for the **world of work** by giving them **skills** and **values** they'll need.
2) Education **justifies inequality**.
3) Education passes on **ruling class ideology** that **supports capitalism**.

1) The neo-Marxist **Althusser** sees education as part of the "ideological state apparatus". In other words, it's a tool of capitalism which is used to pass on the belief that society is fair. Althusser thinks education produces a **docile and obedient workforce**.
2) **Bowles and Gintis (1976)** say that there is a close link between school and work. They say that there's a **correspondence** between **pupil experiences of school** and **adult work**:
   - Pupils are taught to accept the **hierarchy** at school. Work also has a hierarchy.
   - Pupils are **motivated by grades** to do **boring work**. Workers are **rewarded with pay** to do **boring work**.
   - The **school day** is broken into **small units**. So is the **work day**.
   - At school and work **subservience** (following the rules) is **rewarded**.

   Bowles and Gintis say that the '**hidden curriculum**' (things like being on time for lessons, and doing your homework) **prepares people for work**. They also say that meritocracy is a **myth** which is used to **blame people** for not succeeding.
3) **Willis (1977)** says that education **doesn't turn out** an **obedient workforce**. Some kids form an **anti-school subculture** and cope with school and then adult work by mucking about.
4) **Bourdieu** used the concept of **cultural capital** (language, skills, knowledge and attitudes) to explain how the middle-class get into the top positions. There's **plenty** on this on pages 52-53.

Radicals like Illich Want to Get Rid Of School Completely

Illich (1971) believes that education has four functions:

1) Education **looks after kids** during the day.
2) Education **sorts pupils into job roles**.
3) Education **passes on dominant values**.
4) Education helps people learn **skills and knowledge**.

Illich agrees with functionalists about the functions of school — but he thinks the functions aren't good enough. So we should give up school as a bad idea.

The problem for Illich is that schools **don't create equality** or **develop creativity**. Illich wants to "**deschool society**". He wants everyone to have **access to education throughout their lives** according to what they need.

The Role of the Education System

*There are **Problems** with **Functionalist** and **Marxist Views***

Criticisms of Functionalism

1) Evidence of **differential achievement**, in terms of class, gender and ethnicity suggests that education is **not meritocratic**.
2) "**Who you know**" is still more important than "what you know" in some parts of society. So the allocation function isn't working properly.
3) It can be argued that the education system **doesn't prepare people** adequately for **work**. For example, the dearth of engineering graduates indicates education is failing to produce what **employers** and the **economy** needs.
4) Functionalism doesn't look at how education may serve the interests of particular groups in terms of **ideology** and **values**. It **doesn't explain conflict**.

Criticisms of Marxism

1) Marxism assumes people are **passive victims**. It **exaggerates** how much working class students are **socialised** into **obedience**. Willis showed how students actually resist authority.
2) Most people are **aware of the inequality** in education. Most people don't believe that society is fair.

The problem with both approaches is that they don't look at interaction and social processes within the school.

*There are **Similarities** and **Differences** Between **Functionalist** and **Marxist Views***

1) Both Functionalism and Marxism look at the **big picture** — institutions and the whole structure of society. They tend to **ignore social interaction** — with the exception of Willis. Both say education has a **huge impact** on the individual and that there's a **close link** with the **economy** and **work**.
2) The biggest **difference** is how they see **inequality**. Marxists say education helps to **maintain inequality** and **make people accept inequality**. Functionalists say education passes on the value of **meritocracy** and lets people **better themselves**.

Feminists** say that the Education System is **Patriarchal

1) Some feminists argue that the hidden curriculum unofficially **reinforces gender differences**.
2) There are still **gender differences** in **subject choice** in schools. Gender stereotyping may still exist.
3) Girls are now outperforming boys at school — but **boys** still **demand more attention** from the teacher.
4) **Men** seem to dominate the top positions in schools (**head teacher**, **deputy head**) and even more so in universities.

Liberal feminists want **equal access to education for both sexes**.
Radical feminists believe men are a bad influence, and want **female-centred education** for girls.
Marxist feminists want to consider gender inequalities **combined with inequalities** of **class** and **ethnicity**.

Practice Questions

Q1 Name three functions that the education system performs.

Q2 What is meant by meritocracy?

Q3 Name two functionalist studies of education.

Q4 What did Bowles and Gintis say education had a close correspondence with?

Q5 Give two problems with the Marxist theory of education.

Q6 What is the difference between Marxist and Functionalist approaches to education?

Exam Question

Q1 Assess the Marxist view that the function of the education system is to pass on ideology and reproduce the existing class structure. (20 marks)

Getting rid of school sounds good, but what'd you have instead?

*Mmm, there's lots of theory here. If you know what Marxism, Functionalism and Feminism are, then their views of school **shouldn't come as a big shock**. Functionalists think education brings social harmony. Marxists say school is there to produce an obedient workforce. Feminists think school reinforces gender inequality and difference. They're so predictable.*

Class and Differential Achievement in Education

Sociologists have investigated how social class affects how well people do at school. Financial and cultural factors are studied, as well as in-school factors like streaming.

Social Class** tends to Affect **Educational Achievement

1) Pupils from **professional** backgrounds are significantly **more likely** to enter **higher education** than those from unskilled backgrounds.
2) Pupils from **middle class** backgrounds are more likely to study **A-Levels**, whereas **working class** pupils are more likely to take **vocational** subjects.
3) Pupils from disadvantaged backgrounds are **more likely** to **leave school at 16** and **less likely** to start school being able to **read**.
4) Pupils from **unskilled backgrounds** on average achieve **lower scores** on SATs and in GCSEs and are more likely to be placed in **lower streams** or **bands**.

I wonder if class affects how well you do in a school of fish...

Some sociologists have suggested the relative intelligence levels of different socio-economic and ethnic groups accounts for discrepancies in educational attainment (**Eysenck (1971)** and others). But it is difficult to isolate whether IQ or social factors are the key to determining educational achievement.

***Processes Inside School** — Labelling, Streaming and Subcultures are Factors*

1) **Negative labelling** of students can lead to a **self-fulfilling prophecy of failure.** **Becker (1971)** and **Keddie (1971)** say that teachers tend to evaluate pupils in terms of an **ideal student**, by looking at appearance, personality, speech and social class.
2) Negative labelling can mean students get put into **lower streams or bands**. **Ball (1981)** found that the pupils in the top bands were from **higher social classes**. Teachers had **higher expectations** of them and they were **taught in different ways**. Keddie found that teachers allowed pupils in the top streams access to higher levels of knowledge. Working class students didn't get this knowledge.
3) As a response to negative labelling and frustration with low status, pupils may form **anti-school subcultures**. **Hargreaves (1975)** found that those in the **bottom streams** were more likely to be non-conformist. **Woods (1983)** responded by saying that there are lots of different reactions to school, but **non-conformist** reactions were more likely to come from **working-class** students.

These explanations are useful when looking at day to day experiences in schools. The problem is that they don't explain how **factors outside of school** (e.g. poverty, cultural deprivation) can influence achievement.

Labelling theory is also too **deterministic** — it says that once you're negatively labelled that's it, you'll fail. This isn't always the case.

***Material Deprivation Outside School** Can Affect Achievement*

The theory of **material deprivation** says that **economic poverty** is a big factor in low achievement at school.

1) In 1997, the **Joseph Rowntree Foundation** classified **one in ten** children as **poor** — which was defined as being in a family that couldn't afford at least three things other families took for granted.
2) **Halsey (1980)** found that the **most important factor** preventing working class students staying on at school was **lack of financial support**.
3) **Douglas (1964)** found that children in **unsatisfactory living conditions** (poor housing, lack of nutritious food, overcrowding) didn't do very well in ability tests compared to kids from comfortable backgrounds.
4) **Unemployment** or **low income** means less money for books, the Internet and school trips. Low income families can't afford **nurseries** and **private schools** and they can't afford to support their kids through **uni**.
5) Poverty and unsatisfactory living standards may cause **health problems** and **absence from school**.

***Cultural Deprivation Outside School** Can Affect Achievement*

The theory of **cultural deprivation** says that **working class culture** and **parenting** aren't aimed at educational success.

1) **Douglas (1964)** thought **level of parental interest** was the most important factor in affecting achievement. Middle class parents are more likely to visit schools for open evenings. Bear in mind that **working class parents** may not go to open evenings because they work **inconvenient shifts** — not because they aren't interested.
2) Some sociologists say that working class kids don't have the **knowledge** and **values** that help achievement. **Museum visits**, **books** and **parental knowledge of education** may help middle class pupils to succeed.
3) Some **styles of parenting** emphasise the importance of education more than others.

Class and Differential Achievement in Education

Some Sociologists say ***Class Affects Attitudes*** *to* ***Education***

1) **Sugarman (1970)** said that pupils from non-manual backgrounds and manual backgrounds have **different outlooks**. The pupils from **manual** backgrounds lived for **immediate gratification**. The pupils from **non-manual backgrounds** were **ambitious** and **deferred their gratification** — they invested time in studying and planned for the future.
2) **Hyman (1967)** said that the **values** of the working-class are a **self-imposed barrier** to improving their position. He said that the working-class tend to place a **low value** on education.

ethnocentric = believing your group/nation/culture is superior to others.

But...

Material and cultural deprivation theories **don't** explain how **factors inside school** affect achievement.

Cultural deprivation theory **generalises a lot** about differences between middle class and working class life. It **ignores** working class families who **do** place a high value on education, and tends to **assume** that working class families have **no culture** at all, or that working class culture can't be **relevant** to school. This is **ethnocentric**.

The **method** may be **unsound**, e.g. attending parents' evenings might not be a good measure of parental interest.

*The two Bs (***Bernstein*** and ***Bourdieu***) — Investigated* ***Differences*** *in* ***Achievement***

1) **Bernstein (1970)** found that working class pupils in the East End of London weren't comfortable with the style of language required by school. They used a **restricted code** — short forms of speech.
2) **Middle class students** knew how to use the same **elaborated code** as the **teachers** — a much more wordy style of speech with everything made very explicit.
3) In terms of **language**, the working class kids were at a disadvantage.

1) **Bourdieu (1971, 1974)** reckons middle class students are at an advantage because they have the right kind of "**cultural capital**" — the right **language**, **skills**, **knowledge** and **attitudes**.
2) He thought that the **more cultural capital** you have, the **more successful** you'll be in education — and he believed that working class pupils don't have **access** to cultural capital.
3) **Middle class** families **pass on cultural capital** and **expectations** from parents to children. This is called **cultural reproduction**.

Problems with Bernstein's theory	Problems with Bourdieu's theory
There are **variations within** the middle class and working class. Different sections of these groups **vary** in how they use the **elaborated code** — the "posh language" of teachers.	**Halsey (1980)** found that **material factors** are important. **Lack of money** may **stop kids staying on at school** or **getting to university**.
Some sociologists have developed his ideas to say working class speech patterns are inferior or somehow "wrong" — controversial... **Labov (1973)** thinks the elaborated speech code is just **different**.	**Not all working-class students fail**, even if they don't have cultural capital.

Practice Questions

Q1 Give two facts about social class and educational achievement.

Q2 Name two factors inside school that explain the links between social class and achievement.

Q3 For Halsey, what was the most important factor preventing working class students staying on at school?

Q4 Briefly outline the findings of Sugarman's 1970 research into class attitudes to education.

Q5 Who initially used the term "cultural capital"?

Exam Questions

Q1 (a) Identify and explain two factors within the school that influence working class pupils' levels of achievement. (8 marks)

(b) Assess the view that the home is the major factor in determining different levels of educational achievement between social classes. (20 marks)

Immediate gratification sounds good to me...

Just a quick word of warning. In the Exam you could get a question like "Assess how factors inside and outside school affect levels of achievement". This is a very broad question. You'd need to look at home and school factors for ethnicity, gender AND class. This means you'd need to have revised pages 54-57 as well as this page and the previous one.

Ethnicity and Differential Achievement in Education

Ethnicity is another factor that can influence how well people do at school.
Quick reminder — ethnicity means the shared cultural traditions and history which are distinct from other groups in society. Modern Britain is said to be a multi-cultural society made up of many different ethnic groups.

Some ***Ethnic Groups*** *Do* ***Better*** *Than* ***Others***

These figures are from **Modood et al (1997)** — the Policy Studies Institute's fourth survey of ethnic minorities in Britain.

All these statistics are averages. If you look at someone and say "she does well cos she's Chinese" you might be wrong.

Higher levels of achievement

1) The survey found that **Chinese**, **African Asians** and **Indian** groups were more qualified than whites. **Afro-Caribbean women** were more likely to have **A-levels** than white women.
2) Ethnic minorities were **more likely than white pupils** to continue into **further education** (from ages 16-19).
3) People from ethnic minorities who were **born** in **the UK** had much **higher qualifications** than people who moved to the UK from abroad.

Lower levels of achievement

1) **Bangladeshi** and **Pakistani women** were least well qualified. **Afro-Caribbean**, **Pakistani** and **Bangladeshi men** were least qualified.
2) **Pakistani** and **Afro-Caribbean** groups were **less likely** to get onto **university** courses, and **more likely** to get into **less prestigious universities**.
3) **Afro-Caribbean boys** are **more likely** to be **excluded from school**, more likely to be put in **lower streams** and more likely to do **vocational** courses.

African Asians means people of Indian origin who lived in Kenya and Uganda and then moved to Britain in the 1970s.

There are big **variations** between the **average achievement level** of different ethnic minority groups. There must be something behind it all — probably more than one factor, and probably some **social** and **economic** factors.

Some people say that **intelligence is inherited** — i.e. people underachieve because they've inherited low IQ.

HOWEVER... **IQ tests** can be **biased**. Sometimes they ask things that aren't really a test of brains, but really a test of **cultural knowledge**. The **Swann Report (1985)** found that if you took into account social and economic factors there were **no significant differences in IQ** whatsoever between different **ethnic groups**.

Processes Inside School — ***Labelling****,* ***Curriculum*** *and* ***Prejudice*** *are Factors*

Labelling theory says that teachers have **different expectations** of **different ethnic minority groups**. **Gillborn (1990)** found that teachers **negatively label black students**. Afro-Caribbean students were seen as a **challenge** to the school **authority** — and are more likely to be excluded from school. Gillborn calls this the "myth of the black challenge". Teachers had high expectations of Asian students. Negative labelling could result in a **self-fulfilling prophecy of failure**.

There's also an issue about whether the school curriculum is **ethnocentric** — i.e. that it might fit the mainstream, white, middle class culture better than other ethnicities. It could be **Europe-centred** too. Languages in the National Curriculum are mainly **European** — kids usually learn French and German, not Gujarati or Chinese. **Assemblies, school holidays** and even **history lessons** may not fit with the culture and history of particular groups.

Some sociologists see British education as "**institutionally racist**". This is where **policies** and **attitudes** unintentionally discriminate against ethnic minority groups. **Wright (1992)** found that even though members of staff said they were **committed to equal opportunities, Asian girls** got **less attention** from teachers and felt their cultural traditions were disapproved of (e.g. they might get told off for wearing a headscarf if it isn't part of the school uniform). **Afro-Caribbean boys** were more likely to be punished and **sent out of class**.

Some sociologists say that these factors may lead to a **low self esteem** for ethnic minorities.
Coard (1971) said that black students are made to feel inferior in British schools.

Low Self Esteem *Exists — But it* ***Isn't Really All That Widespread***

1) **Mirza (1992)** found that black girls had **positive self-esteem** and **high aspirations**. The girls experienced discrimination but had **strategies** to minimise the effects of racism. It **wasn't low self-esteem** that affected their achievement — it was being **unwilling to ask for help**, or unwilling to **choose certain subjects**.
2) **Fuller (1980)** found Afro-Caribbean girls in London **resisted negative labelling** and **worked hard** to gain **success**.
3) Negative labelling and racism can affect pupils' reactions to school. Pupils may use either a **pro-school subculture** or an **anti-school subculture** to maintain their self-esteem.

Ethnicity and Differential Achievement in Education

Factors Outside School — **Language Difference** Affects Achievement

1) **Language** was a barrier for kids from **Asian** and **Afro-Caribbean immigrant families** when they **first arrived** in the UK.
2) The **Swann Report** found that **language didn't affect progress** for **later generations**.
3) **Driver and Ballard (1981)** also found Asian children whose **first language** was **not English** were **as good at English** as their **class mates** by the age of 16.
4) **Labelling theorists** would say that language might not be a barrier, but **dialects** or having an **accent** might **influence teacher expectations** and lead to **negative labelling**. For example, a teacher might **assume** that a child isn't good at English because they have a foreign accent and put them in lower sets.

Factors Outside School — **Family Difference** Affects Achievement

1) Some studies say that **family life varies** for different groups and this can influence achievement.
2) **Driver and Ballard (1981)** say that the **close-knit extended families** and **high parental expectations** increase levels of achievement in **Asian communities**.
3) Some sociologists say the high levels of **divorce** and **single-parenthood** in Afro-Caribbean households could result in **material deprivation**. On the other hand, the **independence** of **Afro-Caribbean women** can mean that girls get **positive role models**.

A study at Essex University (2000) found that 39% of British born Afro-Caribbean adults under 60 are married compared to 60% of white adults. 50% of Afro-Caribbean families are single parent families.

Ethnicity Combines With Social Class To Affect Achievement

On their own, the inside school factors and outside of school factors may not seem all that convincing. If you bring **social class** and **material factors** into the equation you get a more complex explanation.

1) The **Swann Report** found that **socio-economic** factors affected the lower levels of achievement of **Afro-Caribbean** pupils.
2) **Pakistani**, **Bangladeshi** and **Afro-Caribbean** groups are more likely to be in **lower class positions** such as routine occupations (assembly line workers, factory workers) and elementary occupations (cleaners, labourers). This may result in poor housing, periods of unemployment, poverty and **material deprivation**.
3) **Chinese**, **African Asian** and **Indian** groups are more likely to be in **higher class** positions and **less likely** to experience material deprivation.

If you were answering an exam question on this, you'd need to bring in stuff from p52-53 about class and achievement.

Practice Questions

Q1 Give two facts about ethnicity and educational achievement.

Q2 Why do sociologists dislike genetic explanations about intelligence and educational success?

Q3 Name one inside of school factor that explains the underachievement of some ethnic minority groups.

Q4 How does language affect educational achievement?

Q5 Give an example of how social class combines with ethnicity to affect achievement.

Exam Question

Q1 Assess the significance of inside of school factors in explaining the educational achievement of different ethnic minority groups. (20 marks)

It's more complicated than you might have thought...

Remember that not all ethnic minorities underachieve — so don't go storming into your exam answer with a pre-prepared rant that it's all about white / black racism. There are always several different factors that affect each ethnic group. Also, remember that class, ethnicity and gender (see page 56) all mix together to influence how someone does at school.

Gender and Differential Achievement in Education

Gender is another factor that can influence how well people do at school.
Since the 1980s, things have changed. Sociologists used to talk about female underachievement.
Now there are worries that boys are falling behind. Geez Louise, make your minds up...

Here are **Six Facts** about **Gender** and **Differential Educational Achievement**

1) Girls get **better results** at all levels in National Curriculum tests.
2) Girls get **better results** in **most subjects** at **GCSE**.
3) Girls are **more likely** to **pass** their **A-levels**.
4) Women are more likely to go on to **university**.
5) **Men** seem to have most success at the **highest levels** of University.
A higher proportion of male students get **first class degrees** and **PhDs**.
6) **Girls** tend to go for **communication based subjects** like English and sociology and **boys** tend to go for **technical** ones like maths and physics.

Don't be tricked by these facts into thinking that boys are doomed.
You could say that there's been a bit of a '**moral panic**' about males underperforming (see page 43).

Understand the **Old Explanations** of **Girls' Underachievement**

There were three explanations for why **girls didn't do as well as boys** before the 1980s:

1) **Biological explanations** said that **girls matured at an earlier age** so they did better at younger ages. Boys would then **catch up** and overtake girls by age 16.
2) Sociologists used **early socialisation** to explain girls' underachievement. They said that **gender stereotyping** started before kids got to school. **Toys** and **media representations** of women helped to socialise girls into the stereotypical roles of **caring** and **mothering**.
3) **Behaviour in the classroom** was also used to explain why boys did better. **Stanworth (1983)** said that classroom interaction **disadvantaged girls**. Girls got **less attention** from teachers and were often **negatively labelled**. **Spender (1983)** argued that education was **controlled** and **dominated** by **men**. The curriculum was **male-centred**, boys got more attention and boys got away with being disruptive in class.

Factors Inside School Explain Why **Females Now Do Better**

1) **Mitsos and Browne (1998)** say teaching has been **feminised**. Women are **more likely to be classroom teachers**, especially in primary schools. This gives girls **positive role models**.
2) **Textbooks** and **teaching resources** have changed and are less likely to **stereotype girls** into passive roles.
3) The National Curriculum **forced** girls to do **traditionally "male"** subjects. For example, more girls started to do **science**. Other Local Education Authority and government initiatives tried to encourage girls to do these subjects, e.g WISE (Women In Science and Engineering) and GIST (Girls into Science and Technology).
4) **GCSEs** include more **coursework** than earlier qualifications. Some people argue that coursework suit girls better because they put in **more effort**, are **better organised** and can **concentrate** for longer than boys (that's quite a sweeping generalisation though...)

Factors Outside School Explain Why **Females Now Do Better**

1) Policies such as the **Equal Pay Act** and **Sex Discrimination Act** have helped to create **more equal opportunities** in wider society. This has **changed values** of society and attitudes in school.

> The Equal Pay Act (1971) makes it illegal to pay men and women different money for the same work. The Sex Discrimination Act 1975 means employers can't discriminate on the basis of gender.

2) **Sue Sharpe (1994)** found that girls' priorities have changed. They now want **careers** — and qualifications. More women go out to work, so girls see lots of **positive role models** in work. Girls nowadays often want to be **financially independent** — they don't just want to marry a rich man any more.
3) **Boys** tend to spend their leisure time being **physically active**. **Girls** are more likely to spend their leisure time **reading** and **communicating**. This means girls develop **language skills** that are useful for most subjects.
4) The **feminist** movement caused a **change in female expectations**, and made more people **aware of inequality**. People are now more careful about negative stereotyping, sex discrimination and patriarchy.

Gender and Differential Achievement in Education

Here are Some **Reasons** Why **Boys Underachieve**

Burly men in Santa hats can read books, too.

1) Boys may be having an **identity crisis**. The rise of **female independence**, the decline of the **breadwinner** role for men and the rise in **male unemployment** might mean that boys don't see the point of education. This may lead to anti-school subcultures.
2) **Interactionists** say that teachers have **lower expectations of boys**. Teacher expectations may lead to a **self-fulfilling prophecy** of poor behaviour. **Negative labelling** may explain why they're more disruptive. Boys are more likely to be **excluded** from school.
3) The **feminisation** of **teaching** means that boys don't have as many **role models** in school.
4) **Reading** is often seen as "uncool" or "girly". Boys who **avoid books** like the plague won't develop important **communication skills**.

Subcultures help to Explain **Gender** and **Achievement**

Negative labelling and putting students into different **streams** or bands can cause some pupils to rebel against school's values. They form **subcultures**. These can be either **pro** or **anti-school** subcultures.

1) In the 1970s **Willis** looked at why working class kids get working class jobs. He studied a group of boys called "Willis's lads". The lads **rejected school** and formed an **anti-school subculture**. They **coped** with their own underachievement by having a **subculture where it didn't matter**, and where having a laugh was more important.
2) **Mac an Ghaill (1994)** says that **subcultures are complicated**. There are **lots of different types**. Boys may join a **macho lad subculture** because of a crisis of masculinity. But boys could also join **pro-school subcultures** and be proud of academic achievement.
3) **Fuller (1980)** found that **Afro-Caribbean girls** in **London** formed a **subculture** that worked hard to prove negative labelling wrong.

There are Different Ways to Explain Gender and **Subject Choice**

Girls tend to go for **arts and humanities**. Boys tend to go for **science and technology**.

1) **Subject choice** may still be influenced by **gender socialisation**. The ideas of **femininity** and **masculinity** create different **expectations** and **stereotypes** of what to study. Kids often see Biology as "the science that it's OK for girls to do" and girls who do Physics as "super hardcore science chicks" (or "geeky girls who do Physics").
2) **Kelly (1987)** found that **science** is seen as a **masculine subject**. Boys dominate the science classroom.
3) **Parental expectations** and **teacher expectations** may encourage girls to follow what they see as the traditional "**normal**" choice for their gender. There's a pressure to **conform** to a social norm.

Practice Questions

Q1 Give two facts about gender and educational achievement.

Q2 Which sociologists studied how classroom interaction disadvantaged girls?

Q3 Name one inside of school factor that explains why girls now do better than boys.

Q4 Who found that girls' priorities have changed?

Q5 Why do subcultures form?

Q6 Give one reason why boys and girls choose different subjects.

Exam Questions

Q1 (a) What does the 'feminisation of teaching' mean? (2 marks)

(b) Identify and briefly explain two educational policies that led to improvements in girls' performance. (8 marks)

(c) Assess the significance of school factors on the differential progress of boys and girls. (20 marks)

Girls are DOOMED... no wait, boys are DOOMED... no wait... ah, forget it...

Once again, you can't look at gender without looking at class and ethnicity. Working class girls don't do as well as middle class girls. Also remember that there's a ***lot of generalisation*** *with these sociological theories. Of course not all girls prefer coursework to exams. I bet they prefer lounging around on the beach to doing exams though. Pity they don't test that.*

State Policy and Education

All Governments are interested in education. The 1870 Forster Education Act introduced elementary schooling for 5-10 year olds. A few years later all students up to the age of 10 had to do reading, writing and arithmetic. Since then there have been some major changes. Place your votes, please.

The **1944 Education Act** Introduced the **Tripartite System** and the **11+**

By the time of the Second World War, the main problem was that there was a **huge divide** between the type of secondary education available for the rich and poor. The **1944** Act (often called the **Butler Act** after the man who introduced it) tried to create education for all — secondary schools were made free for all and the school leaving age was raised to 15. You took the **11+ exam** (like an IQ test) and went to one of three schools:

1) **Grammar schools** were for the able kids who passed the 11+. Pupils were taught traditional subjects ready for **university**. **20% of kids** got in to grammar school.
2) **Secondary modern schools** were for the **75-80%** of pupils **who failed** the 11+. Secondary Moderns offered **basic education.**
3) **Technical schools** provided **vocational** education — hands on **job training** for 5% of the school population.

This **tripartite system** aimed to improve the education of all children, but there remained several problems.

1) The **11+ didn't necessarily measure your intelligence**. It was **culturally biased**, and suited the middle class more than the working class.
2) **Few technical schools were built** so the vocational part of the plan didn't work especially well.
3) The three types of school in the system were meant to have "**parity of esteem**" — **equal value** in other words. The problem was the **grammar schools** were seen as the **best**. Not a surprise, since you had to **fail something** to get into the other two...
4) Kids who failed the 11+ were **labelled as failures** which sometimes turned them off education.
5) If well-off middle class pupils failed, their parents could still afford to send them to **private schools**.

In **1965** the Labour Government made Schools **Comprehensive**

The Labour Government insisted that Local Education Authorities (LEAs) **reorganised most schools** so that everyone had equality of opportunity. "**Comprehensive school**" means it's universal — everyone's meant to get the same deal.

Positive aspects of the comprehensive system	**Criticisms** of the comprehensive education system
There's no 11+, so 75% of the school population don't get labelled as **failures.**	Comprehensive schools still **stream** pupils into sets depending on test scores. (So it's still possible to feel like a failure without the 11+.)
High-ability pupils generally still do well with this system. Lower ability pupils do better in comprehensive schools than in the old secondary moderns.	Schools in **working class** areas have **lower pass rates** than those in middle class areas.

The comprehensive system has not achieved equality of opportunity. Schools tend to be 'single-class' depending on the local area. Where people can afford to live (and whether there are good schools nearby) is important in educational attainment.

In **1976** the Push for **Vocational Education** Started

Labour Prime Minister James Callaghan thought British education and industry was in decline because schools didn't teach people the **skills they needed in work**. All governments since then have had policies to create a closer link between school and work. This is called **vocationalism**.

YTS were job training schemes for 16-17 year old kids leaving school.

1) **Youth Training Schemes (YTS)** started in 1983.
2) In 1993, **GNVQs** and **NVQs** were introduced — **practical qualifications.**
3) The introduction of the **New Deal** in 1997 means people on benefits must attend courses if they don't accept work.
4) Recently, **key skills** qualifications have started. These are supposed to be useful for all jobs.

There are some **problems** with vocational education:

1) Some sociologists argue that vocational education aims to teach **good work discipline**, not skills.
2) Some Marxist sociologists say that vocational training provides **cheap labour** and that governments encourage people into training schemes to **lower unemployment statistics**.
3) Lots of **young people** have **part time jobs** so they **already have work skills**.

State Policy and Education

*The **1988 Education Reform Act** — Choice, Inspections and More Tests*

In the late 1980s, the **Conservative** Government introduced some **major reforms** in education.

Education should link to the economy

The Government introduced **more vocational courses** and more **work placement schemes**.

There should be better standards in education

1) The Government introduced a **National Curriculum** of **compulsory subjects** for all **5 to 16 year olds**.
2) **OFSTED** (Office for Standards in Education) was set up to **inspect** schools and make sure they were doing a **decent job**. You might have seen **teachers** getting somewhat **frantic** before an inspection.
3) Schools could **opt out** of their local education authority and become **grant maintained schools**. This means that they got money **straight from the government** and could **spend it how they liked**. The government believed this would **improve standards**.

There should be a system of choice and competition

1) Parents could **choose** which school to send their child to — if the school had **space**.
2) Parents could use **league tables** to help them choose. **League tables** show **how many** kids at the school **pass their exams**, and how many get **good grades**.
3) Schools worked like **businesses** and **advertised** for students.

There should be more testing and more exams

Pupils had to sit **SATs** at **7, 11 and 14** and **GCSEs** at **16**.

New Labour** Try To **Mix** Some Of The **Old Ideas Together

In 1997, New Labour took over. They wanted to do something about **inequality**, but they also said there should be **choice** and **diversity** in education. It's a bit like the old Labour policies and a bit like the Conservative policies, **mixed up together** — it's called "**third way politics**".

The Government has made some changes since 1997:

1) They've **reduced infant class sizes** to a maximum of **30**.
2) They've introduced **numeracy hour** and **literacy hour** in **primary schools**.
3) New Labour have allowed **faith schools** and **specialist status schools**.
4) They've set up **Education Action Zones** to help in areas of deprivation.
5) They've tried to **increase** the **number of people going to university**.

A big change in 16-18 year olds' education came in 2000. Policy changed to make A-level education broader. Students now have to do **AS/A2s** and **key skills** and there are more **vocational courses**.

The Government are also keen on **citizenship education** to get pupils to be more **aware of politics**.

Practice Questions

Q1 What was the aim of the 1944 Education Act?

Q2 Name the three types of school in the tripartite system.

Q3 Briefly explain two problems with comprehensive schools.

Q4 Briefly describe two changes brought about by the 1988 Education Reform Act.

Q5 Name two changes in schools brought about by New Labour.

Exam Question

Q1 Assess the ways in which state policies have influenced educational attainment. (20 marks)

Can you ever really solve all the problems in every single school?

Governments have been trying to "Sort Out Education Once And For All" and "Shake Up Britain's Failing Schools" for ages. Some education policies have been more successful than others. Whatever happens, kids go to school, teachers teach 'em things, and there's exams at the end of it all — AS-levels, NVQs, vocational A-levels, key skills, GCSEs, International Bac...

Poverty and Welfare

The sociological questions here are: "Which groups have the most / least?", "Is inequality increasing or decreasing?", "How much should the State help the poor?" and "Why does poverty exist at all?" So, that's all pretty straightforward then. ***This is for AQA.***

Wealth is the Value of a Person's Possessions

Wealth is defined in official statistics as the **value of all the possessions** of an individual **minus** any **debt**. It includes houses, land, money in the bank, shares and personal goods.

Wealth can be divided into **marketable wealth** and **non-marketable wealth**. **Marketable wealth** means **things you can sell**. **Non-marketable wealth** means things like your **salary** or a **pension fund**.

Percentage of marketable wealth owned by:	
The richest **1%** of society	**22%**
The richest **5%** of society	**42%**
The richest **10%** of society	**54%**
The richest **25%** of society	**75%**
The richest **50%** of society	**94%**

These figures come from the 2003 edition of Social Trends. The pattern's pretty consistent over the last 25 years, by the way.

1) Every year **government statistics** on **wealth** in the UK are published in the **Social Trends** report.
2) The table shows that **over half** of the country's **wealth** is owned by a **small percentage** of the population. The **less well off 50%** of the population share only **6%** of the country's wealth. These dramatic patterns show a society where **a few people** are **extremely wealthy**.
3) **Wealth** largely results from ownership of **business** and **property**. Most of this gets **passed down** to the **next generation**, so wealth **stays in the same families** for years. However, lots of the richest people in Britain have generated their own wealth (see below).

The *Sunday Times* publishes a list of the **1000 richest individuals** in the UK every year.

1) The 2003 list revealed that the super-rich are **mostly men**. Only 77 out of 1000 were women.
2) 753 of them were **self-made millionaires**, 247 **inherited** their wealth. The ten richest individuals had money from **business** and **land**. The wealthiest individual in Britain in 2003 was the **Duke of Westminster**, but in 2004 it was Roman Abramovich, of oil and football fame.

Income is the Money a Person Receives on a Monthly / Yearly Basis

1) The vast **majority** of the British population **doesn't have significant wealth**. For most individuals their money comes from an **income**. Income is defined as the **personal funds an individual receives** on a **monthly / yearly basis**. This is usually from a **job** but can be from **benefits**, or **interest** on a savings account.
2) Household **disposable income per head** has **grown steadily** in the UK since the early 1980s. This reflects **overall growth in the economy**, and could be said to show that **everyone is getting richer** to some extent.
3) On the other hand, the **gap** between **rich and poor** has **widened** in recent years (according to Social Trends 2004). This means that the rich are getting richer whilst the poor are getting **relatively** poorer. Ahhh... the stuff sociology is made of...

There are Patterns of Which Social Groups are likely to Earn the Least

The **Social Trends** report shows how many people have an income of **less than 60% of the median income** (the government measure of poverty). The **median** income is the **middle** income. **Half** the population **earn more** than the median, **half** of them **earn less**.

1) Households where adults are **unemployed** are **most likely** to have an **income below 60%** of the median. Which makes sense — you don't earn a lot of money when you're unemployed.
2) In 2001, **22%** of pensioners lived in households with **incomes of less than 60%** of the median. Which makes sense — you don't earn a lot of money when you're **retired**, either.

The **Social Trends** report also includes statistics about how **ethnicity and income** are related.

1) Overall, people in **ethnic minority households** were **more likely** than people in **white** households to be in the **lowest earning category**.
2) **White**, **Afro-Caribbean** and **Indian** households were pretty much equally likely to be the **highest earners**.
3) **64% of Pakistani and Bangladeshi households** were in the **lowest earning category**.
4) **White** and **Afro-Caribbean** households were **fairly well spread** across **all income groups**.

Poverty and Welfare

Absolute Poverty is a Lack of the **Minimum Requirements** for **Survival**

1) An individual is in absolute **poverty** if they don't have the income to afford the basic necessities — **food**, **warmth** and **shelter**. By this definition there are **very few individuals in the UK in poverty**.
2) **Rowntree (1871-1956)** set up the first major studies of poverty in the UK in **1899** and measured it in absolute terms. He made a **list of essentials** needed for life and recorded how many families could **afford** them. Those whose income was **too low** were classed as **in poverty**. He found **33%** of the population in York were in poverty.
3) There are criticisms of Rowntree's study. His definition of poverty didn't allow for any wasted food and it assumed the **cheapest** options were **always available**. The lists of essentials were compiled by **experts** and **didn't match the lifestyle** of the folk he surveyed. He did listen to his critics though, and for two further studies (1941, 1951) he **added more items** to the list of essentials. By this time, **more people** could afford the basics on the list. His conclusion was that **poverty was disappearing fast** in 20th century Britain.
4) Probably the **most recent study of poverty in absolute terms** is **Drewnowski and Scott (1966)**. They devised a "**level of living index**" which worked out the income needed for **basic needs**, adding **cultural needs** to the list. It's debatable whether cultural needs like TV should be included in a study of **absolute** poverty.

Relative Poverty is a **Comparison** with the **Average Standard of Living**

Many sociologists (especially left-leaning ones) favour the **relative** definition of poverty. **Relative poverty** shows whether an individual is rich or poor **in relation to the other people** they **share** their **society** with, rather than whether people have the basics like food and shelter.

Townsend (1970) studied relative poverty in the UK

Method Townsend devised a "**deprivation index**" of 60 items central to social life in the UK. He selected 12 as essential to the whole population — the **level of poverty** was **the percentage** of the population **without** these. Importantly, Townsend didn't just focus on income and material basics but also the ability to have a **normal social life**.

Conclusion Townsend's study concluded that in 1969, **22.9%** of the population were living in poverty.

1) Townsend's work has been **criticised** too. **Piachaud (1981, 1987)** said that the deprivation index was inadequate and reflected Townsend's **cultural bias**. **Wedderburn (1974)** thought that the items on the deprivation index were **arbitrary**.
2) **Mack and Lansley (1985, 1992)** did their own research using a deprivation index compiled by **actually surveying the general public** for a list of items essential to social life in Britain. Their conclusion was similar to Townsend — **relative poverty is still a significant problem** in the U.K.
3) A **big problem** in measuring poverty like this is that **not everyone agrees** on what the **essential items** are. Sometimes people don't buy something because they **can't afford** it, sometimes they don't buy it because they don't want it.
4) A second problem is that **relative poverty levels** are **constantly changing**, because the economy grows over time. This makes measuring and tackling relative poverty much harder than absolute poverty. **Some sociologists** would argue that this makes it a **less useful concept**.

How much poverty there is out there really depends on how it's **measured**.
With an **absolute** definition of poverty, Rowntree concluded **poverty** was soon to be a **thing of the past**.
With a **relative** definition of poverty, Townsend and others conclude poverty **persists** in the UK.

But then again, it always will because it's relative.

Practice Questions

Q1 Give a one sentence definition of each of the following: wealth, income, relative poverty and absolute poverty.

Q2 How much of marketable wealth is owned by the richest 1% in British society, according to Social Trends, 2003? And how much is owned by the poorest 50 %?

Q3 What was Townsend's "deprivation index"?

Exam Questions

Q1 Identify and explain two sociologists' definitions of poverty. (8 marks)

Q2 Outline the problems faced by sociologists in defining and measuring poverty. (20 marks)

We can all dream of being rich...

Most rows between married couples are about money. It's troublesome stuff, but you can't live without it. Learn the basic pattern of distribution of wealth — if you can learn a couple of figures as well, that'll be useful. Get the difference between relative poverty and absolute poverty squared away — it's crucial for understanding the methodology as well as the theory.

Explanations of Wealth Distribution

Evidence shows that wealth is distributed unequally, and that incomes vary from small to huge. To sociologists, a pattern like this needs explanation — and of course there are lots of different explanations for the way that wealth is shared out.

Early Theories **Blamed the Poor** For Being Poor

1) The first theories of poverty **blamed the individual** for the poverty they're in.
2) **19th century** sociologist **Herbert Spencer** said the **poor** were those in society who had **failed** to do the best for themselves. He suggested that they were immoral, lazy and more interested in booze than an honest day's work.
3) Spencer said the **state shouldn't intervene** to help the poor because the poor are a useful **example to others** not to follow that way of life.
4) This attitude isn't necessarily Victorian, you know. The **European Commission Attitudinal Survey 1989** found **18%** of the **British public** thought **laziness** was a cause of poverty.

Functionalists Say **Unequal Distribution** of **Wealth** is **Good** for Society

Functionalism says some people are richer / poorer than others because **society functions that way.** **Functionalist theory** argues that as societies develop, they have to find a way of allocating people to suitable roles and jobs. The most **important jobs** need to be **rewarded more highly than others** to motivate **intelligent people** to **train** and qualify for them. The key study to know here is **Davis and Moore *Some Principles of Stratification*, (1949)**. Don't worry that it's old – it's classical functionalism.

Functionalist arguments have been **criticised** — they assume the best jobs are allocated on the basis of **talent** when in reality **discrimination** by social class, age, ethnicity and gender often influences who gets top jobs. **Tumin (1967)** reckons that Davis and Moore **ignore all the talent and ability in the working class** which society doesn't use.

Weberians Say Distribution of Wealth is Based on **Market Situation**

1) Weberian sociologists (followers of **Max Weber**) say that the distribution of wealth and income is based on what they call **market situation.**
2) An individual's market situation is how **valuable** their **skills** are for society and how **scarce** their skills are. It's about **supply and demand** of skills. High demand for your skills makes them worth more.
3) For example, currently **plumbers** can earn **higher wages** than other skilled manual workers, because there's a **shortage** of plumbers and people **need their skills**. So plumbers have a good market situation at the moment.
4) Weberians say **poor people** have a **poor market situation.**
5) There **isn't always the same demand** for the **same skills** — the same people don't always have the best market situation. This means there's always some **movement of wealth in society.**
6) Individuals **compete** to improve their market situation. **Powerful people** like judges, politicians and the directors of big companies can do most to keep themselves in a good market situation.

Car mechanics are always in demand in the tiger economies.

Marxists Blame Capitalism for Inequalities in Wealth and Income

1) Marxists say that the social groups which have **low levels of wealth** and **income** are the ones which are **powerless** in society.
2) According to Marx and his followers, **capitalism thrives** on **inequality of income** — if there were equal distribution of wealth there wouldn't be any profit for the capitalists. The capitalist class **needs profit** to keep up its **power in society.**
3) Marxism says **exploitation** is an **essential part of capitalism** — and inequalities in wealth and income are a central part of that exploitation.
4) Marx predicted that as capitalism develops, **more oppression** of the proletariat (working class) is needed. Marxists say the current **widening gap between rich and poor** is evidence of this.

As you may have noticed, the Marxist explanations for most things are quite similar. Capitalism, exploitation, etc, etc...

Explanations of Wealth Distribution

Recent **Changes in Society** Have **Increased** the **Gap** between **Rich** and **Poor**

1) The gap between the income of the rich and the income of the poor **went down** in the **1970s**. Under the **Labour government (1974-1979)**, **benefits** given to the poor **went up** and taxes paid by the rich were **very high**.
2) In the **1980s**, under the Conservative government, the **gap widened**. The top rate of tax went down so the **rich kept more of their earnings**. Taxes that everyone pays like **VAT** and **fuel tax** went up. The economy did well so rich people earned more money on their **investments**. **Benefits** went **down**.
3) There has been an **increase** in the number of **single parent households.** Single parent households tend to have less money (see below) and this means the statistics show **more poorer households**.
4) There are also more **two earner households** — e.g. families where both parents work. Income's measured by household, so a **household with two people** in **good jobs** is relatively rich. This contributes to the statistics showing an **increase in rich households**.

Some Social Groups are **More Likely to be Poor** Than Others

For these statistics, poverty is defined as having an income that's less than 60% of the average income.
Remember that the average income gets pushed up by a few people at the top getting paid huge salaries.

Women — in 1992, there were **5.2 million women** living in **poverty** in the UK, compared to **4.2 million men.**
Older people — in 1992, **32%** of households where the **main adult was over 60** were poor.
Single parents — in 1992, **58%** of **single parents** had an income of less than half the average.
Disabled people — in 1996, **47%** of **disabled** people had an income of less than half the average.
Ethnic minorities — in 1997, the Policy Studies Institute said that overall UK ethnic minorities are **more likely** to be poor. **Pakistani** and **Bangladeshi** households are the most likely to have **low income.**

1) Women tend to be poorer than men **partly** because they're **more likely** to be **single parents** than men. **Working mums** are more likely to be in **part time jobs** that fit in with childcare — but that pay less.
2) Older people tend to be poorer because they're **retired** — some retired people only get a **basic state pension**.
3) **Single parent** families tend to be poor because it's hard to get **good work** and **look after kids** at the same time.
4) **Disabled** people face **discrimination** in the job market. Disabled people, and people with long-term illnesses who can't work, live on **incapacity benefit** and **disability benefit**, which means they have a fixed, relatively low income.
5) **Some ethnic minorities** tend to be **richer / poorer** than others — and there's **variation** in the level of income within ethnic minority groups. It's not as clear-cut as the statistics suggests.

Practice Questions

Q1 Why did Spencer argue inequality of income is good for society?
Q2 How does an individual's market situation affect their wealth?
Q3 Did the gap between rich and poor decrease or increase in the 1980s?
Q4 Write down five groups in British society who are more likely to be poor than others.

Exam Questions

Q1 "Inequality in wealth serves society well". Briefly examine this view from two different sociological perspectives. (8 marks)

Q2 Examine the social composition of the poor in British society. (20 marks)

Ever seen how much plumbers charge...

Remember that the gap between rich and poor went down, then up again. It's mainly related to tax and benefits. Learn those Functionalist, Weberian and Marxist explanations for distribution of wealth. You can probably guess the Functionalist one "it's all for the best" and the Marxist "it's cos of evil capitalism, grr". Watch out for those Weberians and their plumber.

Why Does Poverty Exist?

Unsurprisingly, different schools of sociological thought have different explanations of why poverty exists.

Oscar Lewis said Culture was the Cause of Poverty

Lewis (1959, 1961, 1966) studied the poor in Mexico and Puerto Rico

Lewis thought that the **values**, **norms** and **behaviour** of the **poor** were **different** to the rest of society and these values were passed on to the next generation.

He said individuals learn how to be poor and learn to expect to be poor through the sub-culture of poverty they're socialised into.

He reckoned that this culture of resignation, apathy and lack of participation in wider society initially starts as a response to poverty but then becomes a culture which keeps people in poverty. He called it a '**design for life**'.

1) Lewis reckoned that the poor are **culturally different** from the rest of society.
2) Lewis's work was **controversial** and **criticised** from the start. Other research done at the same time in similar poor areas found **highly organised community facilities** and **political involvement**.
3) **Schwartz (1975)** concluded that the poor **weren't culturally different** from the well-off.

Situational Constraints theory says... guess what it says... it says that the poor are constrained by their situation. I tell you, it's a thrill a minute, this sociology lark.

1) Situational Constraints theory says that the poor have the **same values and norms** as the **rest of society** and any difference in the **behaviour** of the poor is because they're **limited** by their **poverty**. For example, unemployment restricts lifestyle options.
2) **Coates and Silburn (1970)** studied poor areas of Nottingham. They found that **some people** in poor areas **did feel resigned to being poor**, and that it wasn't worth trying to get out of poverty. But... they said this was actually a **realistic assessment** of an individual's situation. It **wasn't proof** of some kind of **alternative value system**.
3) Coates and Silburn's research supported the idea that **poverty leads to other forms of deprivation** which can trap people into a sort of **cycle of deprivation**.
   This means poverty is **practically hard to get out of**, not culturally hard to get out of.

New Right Theorists Blame Dependency on Welfare for Poverty

1) **Charles Murray (1993)** described a sector of society which he thought had a **culture of dependency on the state** and an **unwillingness to work**. He called this group the **underclass**.
2) Murray identified three factors — a **rising number** of **single parent families**, **rising crime** and **attitudes** of **resistance to work**. Murray accepts that not all poor people are workshy but he thinks that a significant group of the poor just don't want to work.
3) In Murray's opinion, **Welfare State benefits** are **too high**. He says this means there's not much encouragement to get off welfare and get a job.
4) Another right-wing sociologist, **Marsland (1989)** thinks that the **level of poverty** is **exaggerated** by other writers on poverty. He says society should **keep a small level of poverty** to **motivate** others to work. Marsland agrees with Murray that the **Welfare State is too generous** and encourages a **culture of non-work** amongst some groups.

Sociological **criticism** of Murray says his **evidence** for the existence of an underclass is **too weak**. **Walker (1990)** found **very little evidence** of **different values** and **behaviour** among the poor. His opinion was that **blaming** the poor **distracts** from the **real causes** of poverty such as the **failure of social policy**.

Weberian Sociologists Blame Inequalities in the Labour Market

1) **Max Weber** thought that an individual's **position in the labour market** was the key to their life-chances, wealth and status. The people whose skills were most **valued** and **needed** would always be the **wealthiest**.
2) **Dean and Taylor-Gooby (1992)** think that **changes in the UK labour market** have led to increased poverty. There are more casual and temporary jobs, less job security and there are far fewer "jobs for life". Dean and Taylor-Gooby say this means more people are likely to experience poverty at some point.
3) **Townsend (1970, 1979)** has the view that the key **explanation for poverty** is the **low status** of some workers, which doesn't give them much power to improve their labour market situation.

Why Does Poverty Exist?

Marxists Blame *The Capitalist System* for Poverty

Marxists think that the working class tends to be poor as a result of capitalist exploitation. They say it's a mistake to focus on the poor as a **separate group**, and that poverty comes from **class structure**, so sociologists should focus on the **working class** instead.

Marxists think that **poverty exists** because it **serves the needs of the capitalist class** in society.

You might wonder how poverty can be useful to anyone. Marxist sociologist **Kincaid (1973)** explains it like this:

1) The low-paid provide a **cheap labour supply** for the **capitalist class** which keeps **profits high**.
2) The varying pay levels within the working class keep individuals **competing** against each other to get the best jobs. This **divides the working class**. Remember, the working class is the **majority** in a capitalist society. Marxism says that if the working class all **united together** they'd be a **threat** to capitalism. That's why they say it's in the **interests of capitalism** to keep the **working class divided**.

Kincaid believes poverty is **not an accident** — he thinks it's an **inbuilt part** of the capitalist system. He said "It is not simply that there are rich and poor. It is rather that some are rich because some are poor."

Marxists say welfare benefits don't much good

1) Marxist sociologists **Westergaard and Resler (1976)** argue that state benefits only **blunt the extremes** of poverty.
2) They say that **welfare benefits stay low** to **make sure** that people **still need to sell their labour** even if their wages are low.
3) They also point out that most of the **money paid out in welfare benefits** has been **paid in by the working class in tax** or **subsidised by their low wages**. That means the working class are getting their own money back, not money from the rich. Westergaard and Resler say that the Welfare State "**redistributes within classes** rather than **between them**".

Marxist Explanations of Poverty Have Been *Criticised*

1) Marxist explanations of poverty **don't explain** why some groups in society are much more likely to experience poverty than others. Marxists treat poverty (and just about everything else) as a **characteristic of capitalism**, and as something that the **working class as a whole** suffer. They don't look for much **detail** about the experience of poverty for **individuals** or **groups**.
2) Marxism **ignores** the effects of **gender** and **ethnicity** on poverty. It doesn't explain why women are more likely to be poor than men, or why Bangladeshi households are more likely to be poor than Afro-Caribbean households.
3) **Townsend (1970, 1979) rejects** the argument that the Welfare State doesn't do much good. He believes that **social policy can and should improve standards of living** even within a capitalist system.
4) **Capitalism** creates **wealth** in the economy. This increase in wealth contributes to the **reduction of absolute poverty**.

Practice Questions

Q1 Give an example of an attitude and a behaviour which Lewis (1959, 1961, 1966) argues causes poverty.

Q2 What does Murray (1993) identify as the key processes which create an underclass?

Q3 Give an example of how poverty is helpful to the capitalist class, from a Marxist perspective.

Exam Questions

Q1 The claim that the poor are to blame for their poverty features in some sociological explanations of poverty. Critically examine the arguments for and against this view. (20 marks)

Q2 Evaluate the claim that the cause of poverty lies within the structure of society. (20 marks)

Blame the victim or blame the system...

It's not as easy as you might think to explain why people get stuck in poverty. Each of these theories makes some sense, but they don't all look at the big picture. When you're answering an exam question that asks you to "critically examine the arguments" bear that in mind — remember the downsides of each theory. Use one theory to criticise another.

Social Policy and Poverty

You need to know what kind of things governments do to sort out poverty.

*The **New Right** believes in the Reduction of the **Welfare State***

1) The **New Right** think that a **generous welfare state** actually **makes people poorer**.
2) British New Right thinker **Marsland (1989)** thinks all **universal benefits** (paid to everyone regardless of wealth) should be abolished because they **encourage dependency**. He says that benefits should only exist to support those in the most desperate need for the shortest possible time. He argues that this will encourage people to "stand on their own two feet".
3) **Right wing policy** encourages **business** so that **wealth will be created**. Right wing politicians would prefer everyone to make their own money and decide how to spend it, instead of paying lots of tax or getting benefits from the State.
4) American sociologist **Murray (1993)** recommended a "**moral**" benefits system to discourage people from forming **single parent families**. He thought that unmarried mums should get no benefit at all.

In the UK, the Conservative governments (1979-1997) were influenced by New Right theory. They **reduced spending** on welfare by removing some universal benefits and having benefits **only for the poorest**. They made it very clear that they wanted to **get rid of the dependency culture** by **reducing benefits** and **allowances**.

The idea was that people would be **better off working**.

The idea was also that resources freed up by these welfare cuts would **boost the economy** which would benefit society as a whole. Conservatives said the money at the top would "**trickle down**" to make **everyone** in society wealthier.

Examples of Conservative welfare reforms

1) **Stopped paying benefits** to **16-18** year olds.
2) **Replaced grants** for basic necessities with **loans**.
3) **Abolished** entitlement of **students to benefits** in the **academic holiday**.
4) Introduced the **Child Support Agency** — forcing **absent parents** to pay for the support of children, rather than the state.

People on low incomes used to be able to get a "social fund" grant to buy things like a new cooker. Nowadays they can get a loan, which they have to pay back.

So, some of the **New Right solutions to poverty** have **been tried** in the UK. They've been criticised by some sociologists for **increasing** relative poverty.

***Social Democrats** Believe **Social Policy Reforms** Could Solve Poverty*

Social Democrats see **institutions** in society as the cause of poverty. They believe **inequality** in **wealth and income** is the root cause of poverty, so they want government policy to **re-distribute wealth** and resources from **rich** to **poor**.

The big idea is that the state **should** work to stamp out poverty — and that the state **can** work to stamp out poverty.

1) Social democratic theory says **increasing welfare provision** will help to **solve poverty**.
2) **Mack and Lansley (1985)** suggest a big increase in benefits. They conducted a public opinion poll in which British people said they were **prepared to pay higher taxes** to get rid of poverty.
3) **Townsend** sees the solution to poverty in the **labour market**. He says **social policy** must have the job of **reducing inequalities** in the labour market.
4) The poor are most often unemployed or low-paid. This means **policies** are needed to **improve wages** and conditions and to **protect workers' rights**. The **National Minimum Wage** and **Working Families' Tax Credit** brought in under the New Labour government are examples of this kind of intervention.
5) British sociologists **Walker and Walker (1994)** argue for an "active employment strategy" where the government would actually **create work** for the unemployed.

Social democratic theory has been **criticised** by people on the **right wing** and on the **left wing**.

1) **New Right** theorists say the social democratic policy of **strengthening the Welfare State** and increasing the power of social policy would be an **absolute disaster** in terms of solving poverty. The New Right say these things led to the increase in poverty in the first place.
2) Left wing **Marxists** say the **state** will always **serve the interests** of those in **power**, which means that nothing the government does can make a big difference to poverty in capitalist society.

Social Policy and Poverty

*Since 1997, the **New Labour** Government has had a "**Third Way**" Approach*

When New Labour took power in Britain in 1997, it claimed its social policies would reduce poverty significantly. Their philosophy **combines** both the **New Right** and the **social democratic** theories — so it was called "**the third way**".

The theme was that the poor need "**a hand up not a handout**". The "hand up" part means the State should have **social policies** which **help the poor** — rather like the social democratic theory. The "not a handout" part means people **shouldn't depend** on benefits — rather like **New Right theory**.

They say the state has a responsibility to **help people in real need**, and individuals have a **responsibility to help themselves**. The "**New Welfare Contract**" of 1998 says that the **government** has to **help people find work**, make **work pay**, help with **childcare**, help the **poorest** old people and help those who really **can't work**. It says that **individuals** have to look for work, be as **independent as possible**, support their own family, save for retirement and not defraud the taxpayer by claiming benefit when they shouldn't.

Don't worry — you don't need to know all the New Labour social reforms in detail. Here are some examples which help show the ideology behind them.

Reforms to remove dependency on benefits — so working pays more than benefits...

1) **Working Families' Tax Credit** — tax reductions for the **low-paid but working**.
2) **National Minimum Wage** — to ensure every employer **pays more than benefit levels**.
3) **New Deal** — a **training** and **support** package for people **returning to work** from benefits.
4) **Welfare to Work** — a series of opportunities for **young, unemployed people** paid for by tax on profits of privatised gas and electricity companies.

Reforms to make the poor less socially excluded and isolated

1) **Social Exclusion Unit** — launched to provide support to **re-integrate excluded people** back into society.
2) The concept of **Stake Holders** — individuals could own a stake in organisations which affect them, either in financial terms or voting power.
3) **Child-care costs** paid for or subsidised by the government.

There is conflicting evidence as to whether the government has achieved a reduction in poverty since 1997. The 2003 Social Trends report shows that the distribution of wealth has changed little over the past 28 years. The number of people classed as unemployed has fallen though (see p. 78).

Marxists** say **Nothing** Will Work Except the **Overthrow of Capitalism

1) Marxists believe that the root cause of poverty is the **inequality** central to the **capitalist system**. Therefore, the Marxist solution to poverty is the **removal** of the **capitalist system**.
2) Marxists say that while the capitalist system keeps on going, poverty will still be around — **no matter** what **social policy** you throw at it. **Westergaard and Resler (1976)** think no big **redistribution of wealth** can happen until capitalism is overthrown and replaced by a **socialist** society where **wealth is communally owned**.
3) Marxist theory says that **capitalism** will eventually be **overthrown** — when the working class are sufficiently **united** to have a **revolution**. I wouldn't wait up for it if I were you.
4) The most **common criticism** of the Marxist approach is the **evidence** that **socialist** and **communist societies haven't eradicated poverty**. People were poor in Soviet Russia and there is poverty in Cuba.

Practice Questions

Q1 Why do the New Right think that the Welfare State can be too generous?

Q2 Give an example of a social policy which could be used to lessen poverty.

Q3 Explain how Marxist theory argues poverty could be eradicated in Britain.

Exam Questions

Q1 "The New Labour government of 1997 combined opposing policies of previous solutions to poverty in Britain." Explain and evaluate this statement. (20 marks)

Q2 "Ideology lies behind all solutions to poverty." Discuss. (20 marks)

Sounds great on paper — but will it work in real life?

Although the four theories here are different, they all make some kind of sense on paper. It'd probably be great if everyone earned enough money to buy the best kind of private welfare. It'd probably be great if the State provided really good public welfare for everybody. In real life it's hard to make things work. At the moment, the jury's still out on the Third Way idea.

Welfare Provision

Welfare means all the institutions that look after people — whether they're state-provided or not.

Four Sectors *provide Welfare —* ***Public****,* ***Private****,* ***Voluntary*** *and* ***Informal***

Public Sector

These are **state services** which are **funded**, **regulated** and **run by the state**. Examples — the **NHS**, the free **education system** and the **benefits system**. Most services are **free at the point of delivery** and are **funded by taxes** and **national insurance**.

Private Sector

These services are **run by companies for profit**. They often offer **alternatives** to state services — e.g. **private hospitals**, **schools** and **nurseries**. There's no state funding but they have to **meet state regulations**. The individual **pays for these services directly**.

Voluntary Sector

These services are provided by **charity**. They often provide **extra** facilities and services beyond what the state provides. E.g. the **hospice** movement and **Help the Aged**. They have to **conform to state regulations**. Voluntary services **may get some state funding**. The individual receives these services **free** or at a **subsidised low cost**.

Informal Sector

This means services and help provided by **friends and family** as and when needed. The informal sector often provides services **in addition to state services** or when there **isn't enough state provision**. Examples — **family carers**, **family childminders**. There's **little** or **no state funding** or **regulation**. It's usually **free** to the individual but **costs the provider money**.

In the British system **all four sectors are mixed together**. The **Conservative** governments of 1979-1997 encouraged more **private** and **voluntary** sector welfare provision and less **public welfare provision**. The New Labour governments since 1997 have not attempted to change this substantially.

The Welfare State — Health, Housing, Education, Social Work *and* ***Benefits***

1) The British **Welfare State** was set up in the **1940s** after the **Beveridge Report** was published. The Welfare State was designed to wipe out the social problems of society. Beveridge defined these as the "**five evils**".

Ignorance (poor education)	⟹ **1944 Education Act**
Disease (poor health)	⟹ **NHS set up in 1946**
Want (poverty)	⟹ **National Insurance Act**
Idleness (unemployment)	⟹ **National Assistance Act**
Squalor (poor housing)	⟹ **Council Housing Programme**

2) People in work would pay into a **national insurance scheme** which would **pay for the Welfare State**. The Welfare State was designed to be free at the point where you actually needed it. For example, going to the doctor = free.

3) The British Welfare State is **universal**. This means all benefits and services are given to **everyone** rather than **selectively** to the poorest. **Checking** that people are **poor enough** to get a selective benefit is called **means testing**.

4) The **cost of the Welfare State** has **risen a lot**. The Office of National Statistics said 61% of the total government budget was spent on welfare in 1993.

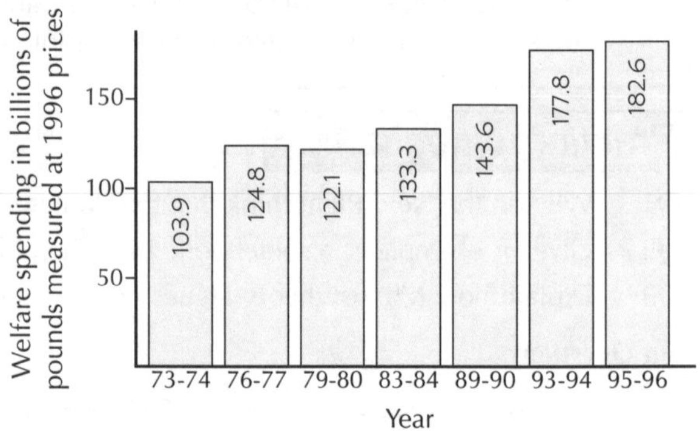

There have been a lot of **Conservative reforms** to **reduce the size** of the Welfare State and **cut costs**.

1) **Increase** in **selective benefits** — e.g. 1980 Housing Act, 1988 Social Security Act.
2) **Reduction** in **universal benefits** — e.g. general entitlement to free eye tests abolished.
3) **Privatisation** of welfare provision — e.g. local authority care homes closed, replaced by private care homes.
4) **Increase** in **voluntary** and **charitable** welfare provision — e.g. housing associations taking over council houses.

Under **New Labour** there's been an emphasis on trying to make the NHS and social security more **efficient** to **save money**. Most benefits and services cut by the Conservative governments **haven't been re-introduced**.

Welfare Provision

Social Democrats *believe the* ***Welfare State*** *can* ***Reduce Inequality***

The founders of the Welfare State thought it'd **reduce inequality** because the rich and poor would all get the **same benefits** and **services**. Resources would be shared out more **equally**. Part of the vision of the Welfare State was that these policies would help create a society where all people had **equal opportunities**. But...

...There's research demonstrating **persistent hard-to-shift inequality** in all five areas of welfare — **health**, **education**, **housing**, **unemployment** and **poverty**. A good overall study by **Le Grand (1982)** found not much evidence of redistribution of resources. Le Grand found that **middle class** families were more likely to use the free services of the welfare state — not the working class, or the poor.

Marxist sociologists **Westergaard and Resler (1976)** argue that the welfare state has failed to reduce inequality between social classes in Britain. Their research focused on **tax** and **benefits**, and concluded that the **working class contributed most** as a **proportion** of their **income** and that the **middle class benefited the most**. However, the middle classes as a group pay most in terms of the total tax received by the government. Some sociologists have argued that by focusing on the contribution as a proportion of total income, **Westergaard and Resler** emphasised the inequality aspect.

The New Right *Prefer* ***Selective Benefits*** *and* ***Means-Testing***

1) Remember, the New Right theory blames poverty on an **over-generous welfare state.**
2) So, from the New Right point of view, the ideal welfare state has a **small range** of **minimal benefits** which are only selectively available to the very **poorest**.
3) Selective benefits would be **means-tested** — the government would only provide them to people whose incomes were below a certain level.
4) The New Right say that governments must focus on creating a **strong economy**. In a strong economy **private welfare providers** can compete giving individuals **choice** and **value**. New Right thinkers reckon the **free market economy** is the **best way** to ensure services are provided at the **lowest prices** and the **best quality**.
5) The New Right think that a **strong market** will encourage individual endeavour, leading to an increase in standards of living for everybody. The Welfare State would only be needed as an **emergency back-up**.

For ***Marxists*** *the* ***Welfare State Reproduces*** *and* ***Legitimises Capitalism***

1) According to Marxists, the Welfare State makes sure the capitalist class always has a **healthy workforce** through the NHS. For Marxists, they don't do this to be **nice** to the individual worker but to **keep them working**, which is essential to keep **making profits**.
2) The Welfare State helps to portray the image of a **caring society** where the state **cares** for the individual. Marxists say this is **useful** to the capitalist class because it **hides** the real **oppressive** nature of capitalism and **keeps the working class quiet** — which prevents a revolution.
3) Not all Marxists agree, mind you. An **alternative Marxist view** is that the **Welfare State exists** because it was **fought for** by **workers' struggle** and the capitalist class wouldn't have provided it otherwise.

Practice Questions

Q1 Name four sectors which provide welfare.

Q2 What were the key social problems the Welfare State was founded to address?

Q3 List four Conservative reforms of welfare provision.

Q4 Outline the findings of Le Grand (1982).

Exam Questions

Q1 "The Welfare State has successfully reduced inequality in British society". Evaluate this statement. (20 marks)

Q2 Compare and contrast Marxist and New Right theories of the Welfare state. (20 marks)

Shall we give the poor some money, or shall we not bother...

You might think that the New Right theorists are all mean old grumpyboots with no heart, or that Marxists are just dreamers with no grip on reality. The thing is, they both genuinely believe they're doing the best for everyone. With these social policies, it's hard to tell who's wrong and who's right. You can look at real-life examples — most of these ideas have been tried somewhere.

Management and Organisation of Work

This section is for AQA. Ignore it if you're studying OCR. *What's work for one person might be leisure for another. If I play golf it's leisure (and better golfers might say it's also comedy). When Tiger Woods plays golf it's work. Luckily, sociologists agree on some characteristics of what constitutes work.*

*Ideas about **Work** and **Leisure** Are Fairly Modern*

The **distinction between work and leisure** is a **modern** idea. Before the Industrial Revolution, things were **less clear cut**. **Capitalism** and **industrialism** are the two big forces influencing work and leisure in the modern age.

Capitalism** and **Industrialism** are Defined in Terms of **Work

Capitalism is commodity production

Marx defined capitalism as "**commodity production**". A **commodity** is a **product** made **for sale**, **to make profit**. **Modern capitalism** involves these three features.

1) There's **private ownership** of the **means of production** (means of producing wealth).
2) **Labour power** (work) is **purchased** by employers for **wages** — work therefore becomes a "**commodity**".
3) The **overriding driving force** in capitalism is to make lots of lovely, lovely **PROFITS**.

Industrialism is mechanised commodity production in factories

Industrialism is the **mechanised production** of commodities by workers in **industrial plants** and **factories**. The production process is **managed** and **coordinated** by **specialist managers**.

***Mechanised Assembly Line Production** was Introduced in the 20th Century*

In 1911 **Frederick Taylor** devised a system of management called "**scientific management**". He used **time and motion studies** to see what workers spent their time on. He developed the idea of a **division of labour** — recommending that work should be broken down into smaller and smaller **specialised tasks** to increase control and profitability. Henry Ford put the idea into practice with his assembly line for making cars.

Henry Ford had the very first **moving assembly line** in the **Ford car factory** in 1914.

1) **Fordism** is a term for **industrial assembly line production**.
2) Assembly lines produce a **standardised product** that the **mass market** can afford.
3) Work is divided up into lots of **little repetitive tasks** which are done by a **line of workers** along a **moving conveyor belt or track**. The conveyor belt **carries the product** from one worker to the next, and **each worker does their bit**. Each worker does the **same thing** over and over again **all day**.
4) Workers **don't need to be skilled** to work on an assembly line. Most are unskilled or semiskilled.

***Braverman** Claims Labour is Progressively **Deskilled** under Capitalism*

1) **Harry Braverman (1974)** said that under industrial capitalism work is **degraded**. Workers become **deskilled** — their jobs used to need skill, but don't any more. **Fordism** leaves workers with boring, repetitive jobs, and almost no say in how they do their jobs. Braverman said this would get **worse and worse** as technology and mechanisation progressed.
2) Braverman bases a lot of his ideas on Marx's concept of "**alienated labour**". Marx believed that under capitalism work is **alienated** from the worker by capitalism's **obsession with profits**. There's **loads** more on this on page 73.
3) Braverman has been criticised for **exaggeration**. Some sociologists claim that workers are often **compensated** for their lack of control over the labour process through **good wages**.

Management and Organisation of Work

Post-Fordism is *Flexible* and Involves *Multi-Skilled Labour*

Remember — **Fordism** means **repetitive, deskilled assembly line work** that keeps **costs low**.

Braverman suggested that **Fordism** will **intensify** as **technology advances**. Several sociologists **disagree** and say there is a new "**post-Fordist era**" in the management and organisation of work.

Main Features of Post-Fordism

1) **Computer technology** — technological development means that **many of the boring repetitive** tasks of the factory can be done by **computer controlled machines**.
2) **Skilled labour** — modern firms require more **flexible** and **versatile, multi-skilled** workers rather than **unskilled** production line workers.
3) **Flatter Management** — there's less strict hierarchy. Modern firms involve workers in decision-making. This means the workers are more committed to the firm.
4) **New Organisation of Workers** — British economist **John Atkinson (1986)** reckons that the new industry organises its labour force in terms of **core workers** and **peripheral workers**. Core workers are **multi-skilled and motivated**. They're **full time employees** of large companies and tend to be disproportionately **white** and **male**. Peripheral workers are **low paid, temporary contract workers**. Peripheral workers are disproportionately **female** and **black**.
5) **Products Made for Quality not Quantity** — Products are aimed at a **discerning niche market**. It isn't mass production for a mass market any more.

Neo-Fordism is a *New Kind of Capitalism*

Some sociologists say that **post-Fordism** isn't really a good thing. They say it's more like **neo-Fordism** — a new kind of Fordism in slightly different clothes.

1) **Paul Thompson (1989)** thinks that rather than requiring **skilled flexible workers** modern firms simply train workers to **multi-task**, so that they can perform **any simple repetitive** task on a production line.
2) **Marxist sociologists** also say that **mass production isn't on the decline** — it's simply upped and moved to countries where the labour is cheaper. This is called the **globalisation of mass production**.
3) **Anna Pollert (1988)** thinks that the **peripheral** work force **isn't a new development** for capitalism at all. She says it matches with the desire to **maximise profits** by **reducing costs**. The use of a peripheral work force has made it simple to **weaken** the **trade unions** and **reduce industrial conflict**. Pollert calls this "**coercive pacification**" — making it so workers can't make a fuss.

Quick and Easy Profits No. 5.
Switch your factory to gold production.

Practice Questions

Q1 Give five features of work (as opposed to leisure).

Q2 What is meant by industrial capitalism?

Q3 What is meant by scientific management and Fordism?

Q4 What is deskilling?

Exam Question

Q1 Assess the validity of the post-Fordist views on the organisation and management of work. (20 marks)

Everything we do — is driven by a need to increase the profit margin...

You need to know the definitions of capitalism and industrialism before you start. A lot of the theory of management stuff is about factory work where workers make things on an assembly line. Make sure you learn the list of features of post-Fordism. Of course, you wouldn't expect all sociologists to agree on anything, so there's points to learn against post-Fordism as well.

Work: Satisfaction, Alienation and Conflict

The next four pages are about explanations and theories relating to attitudes to work.
I suppose you've probably got a fairly decent attitude to work if you're reading this book. Go you.

Many People think that **Today's Society** has a **Positive Attitude** to Work

According to sociologist **Keith Grint (1991)** this wasn't always the case in past societies.

1) In **prehistoric, hunter gatherer societies** it's unlikely there was any work ethic at all. Once enough food had been found then work stopped completely.
2) In **classical societies** like Ancient Greece and Rome, work was often rather **looked down on** and usually associated with slaves.
3) **Before** the **Industrial Revolution**, most people **worked at home** and were paid for each bit of work they completed. Workers had a degree of **control** over the work process. Evidence suggests that domestic workers saw work as a **necessary evil** and **resisted all attempts** to make them **work harder**.

Grint's work suggests that work has only become important to people in the modern industrial era. Wonder why that is...

Max Weber Suggests the **Protestants** Gave Society its **Work Ethic**

Calvinism is a **strict** kind of **Protestant Christianity**. It emphasises work and says **work** is a **calling from God**.

Max Weber (1958) identified **Calvinism** as an **important influence** on the **work ethic** of society today. **Victorian** attitudes to work were quite Calvinist. Victorians saw work as a **moral duty**, and they were very **harsh on laziness**.

Others, for instance social historian **E.P Thompson (1967)**, have suggested that the **Industrial Revolution** was behind the development of the modern work ethic. The Industrial Revolution introduced **working in factories** which demanded a change in attitudes towards work.

There was a big change from **task orientation**, where you work until a task is finished, to **time orientation**, where you keep working for a set time. If you worked at **home**, you could **stop for a break** any time you liked, but **machinery in factories** had to **keep going** through the **whole day**. At the start of the Industrial Revolution, workers had to be **taught** by employers to **work hard all day long** and not **waste time**.

Functionalists, **Marxists** and **Feminists** have **Different Ideas** About Work

Functionalists

Functionalists like **Emile Durkheim** take a **positive** attitude to work in industrial society. Durkheim compared the **different work tasks** carried out in a **modern economy** to the **different functions** carried out by the **different parts of the body**. Each function is needed for society or the body to **function harmoniously**. Durkheim referred to this as **organic solidarity**.

Marxists

Marxists see work in capitalist economies as characterised by **exploitation**. The big idea of Marxism is that a **small minority own the means of production** — the raw materials and machinery used to make things. Workers **create wealth** by working, but they only get a **tiny bit of it back** as wages. Marx also believed that under capitalism labour is **alienated**. There's a lot more about the alienation of labour on the next two pages.

Feminists

Feminists argue that there's a **sexual division of labour** which **excludes women** from **important** areas of work and restricts them to **low status areas.** Traditionally, there were "men's jobs" and "women's jobs", but this is changing. Up until the late 20th century, women (especially middle class women) were **discouraged** from **working outside the home** at all. Feminists point out that **most domestic labour** is done by women, and that nobody gets paid a penny for doing **housework**.

Work: Satisfaction, Alienation and Conflict

Marx Believed a **Person's Ability to Work** was Really Important

Marx said the **ability to work** was a person's **most important attribute**.
It's **through work** that people can **change** and **improve** their world.

He thought that under **capitalism** labour gets **alienated** from this positive role and instead turns into a series of **boring**, **repetitive**, **uncreative** tasks.

Alienated Labour is More than Just Boredom at Work

According to Marx, labour is **alienated** in the following ways:

1) Labour becomes just another **commodity** that can be bought and sold. Labour is alienated from its true role — it **doesn't belong to the workers** any more and they can't do what they want with it.
2) Workers' **tasks** under industrial capitalism are **boring**, **repetitive**, **uncreative** and **highly controlled**.
3) The **worker** becomes **powerless** because the capitalists own both the **labour process** and the **products** of labour. In Marx's language, the capitalists own the **means of production** and the **products of labour**.
4) The profits from a worker's labour are made to **work against the worker** by being **invested** back into the **capitalist system**.
5) Workers are also **alienated from each other** under capitalism because it's a **competitive** system.

Marxists say Workers' Labour is **Alienated** — Even if They **Don't Realise It**

For a Marxist, alienation is "an objective state due to the social relations of production". This means it's something that **definitely** happens to **all workers** because of the way **capitalism** is organised. Process workers and assembly line workers are **exploited** and their **labour is alienated** — **whether they feel it and believe it or not**. Marxism says that workers will only be free from alienation under **communism**.

Wright Mills (1951) found that it isn't only **manual workers** who suffer alienation. **Office workers** and **sales people** are alienated because they have to put on a **mask** of being "**nice**" or "**sincere**" and **can't express** their **real attitudes**.

Functionalists Are **Optimistic** About Industrialisation

1) **Durkheim** (writing in the 1890s) disagreed with Marx, and was fairly optimistic about industrialised labour. Durkheim suggested that **specialisation** could eventually **increase social cohesion** as people became **more dependent** on each other and therefore more likely to work together.
2) Durkheim was **concerned** that the **rapid speed of industrialisation** would lead to a state of "**anomie**". Anomie literally means **normlessness** — it means a state of confusion where **nobody knows how to behave**. The **upheaval** of industrialisation would be so huge that people **wouldn't share the same norms** and **values**.
3) Durkheim said **rising divorce rates** and **industrial unrest** were **evidence of anomie**. In some ways it was a similar idea to Marx's idea of alienation.
4) **Marx** thought that the only solution was to **overthrow the system**. **Durkheim** thought the solution was **codes of practice** between workers, owners and professionals to make the **existing system nice and workable**.

Practice Questions

Q1 Who said the work ethic in modern society come from the early Protestants?

Q2 Give three examples of ways that Marx said work could be alienated from the worker.

Q3 What is meant by organic solidarity?

Exam Questions

Q1 a) To what extent is the work ethic a modern phenomenon? (8 marks)

b) Discuss Marx's theory of alienated labour under capitalism. (20 marks)

Well, paint me green and put me on Mars...

Marx said that your labour is alienated even if you say it isn't. So, even if you like your job, Marx would say your boss is exploiting you by making you do boring work and keeping the profits from what you do. Thompson makes pre-industrial life sound nice — stopping for breaks any time you liked, being as lazy as a very lazy person from Lazyville. Was it really like that, though..?

Work: Satisfaction, Alienation and Conflict

Here's more on alienation from work and worker's attitudes to work...

Blauner Says Alienation of Labour Has Four Sources

1) **Powerlessness** — When workers **aren't in control** of their work process or activity.
2) **Meaninglessness** — When workers **don't see** the **function** or **meaning** of their activity in the context of the whole organization. Labour is alienated if you **don't know why** you're doing what you're doing.
3) **Isolation** — When workers **don't** see themselves as part of a **social group** or **community** in the workplace.
4) **Self-estrangement** — When workers **don't get involved** in their work and don't use it to express themselves.

Blauner (1964) Studied Workers' Attitudes

Method: Blauner gave **questionnaires** to workers in different industries — a traditional print shop, a textile mill, a car factory with a production line and an automated chemical plant.

Findings: From his results, Blauner figured that **different industries** have **different levels of alienation**. He found little alienation in craft technology (traditional printing) and a lot of alienation in assembly line production (the car factory). Blauner found very little **alienation** in **fully automated production**, because the boring manual work is done by industrial robots. Blauner thought that workers in automated production have plenty of responsibility and control — they operate a control panel to make sure the machines are doing the right thing.

Conclusion: Blauner thought that **production technology** was a big influence on alienation. He saw **automated production** with computerised industrial robots as the way forward.

Automated factories have computer-controlled machines. The machines do the production line work instead of human workers.

Marxists criticise Blauner, saying he **ignores the real causes** of alienation. Others criticise Blauner because they think he **interpreted** what workers said in the questionnaires in a **biased** and **unscientific** way.

Some Workers Don't Mind Alienation — They're Happy with the Money

Goldthorpe et al. (1969) studied process workers

Method: They surveyed a sample of 229 manual workers and 54 white-collar workers to find out about their **attitudes to work**.

Findings: They found that many manual workers **didn't** actually **expect job satisfaction**. They were prepared to put up with being bored and frustrated in return for **relatively high wages**. Goldthorpe et al. called this an **instrumental attitude** towards work — work as a means to an end. Good pay allowed workers to have a nice lifestyle and give their families a good standard of living.

Conclusion: Goldthorpe et al. concluded that many workers actually choose "alienating work" because it paid better. These "**affluent workers**" didn't look for satisfaction in their work. They looked for satisfaction and enjoyment in their **family life**.

You can say there's two types of job satisfaction. Intrinsic job satisfaction is pleasure workers get from work itself. Extrinsic job satisfaction is when workers enjoy good wages — and get satisfaction from what they can buy with them.

Some sociologists have **criticised** Goldthorpe et al. for **two main reasons**:

1) The men they studied weren't representative. They were all **married with kids** and perhaps more likely to be "instrumentally orientated" — concentrating on supporting their family. The men surveyed were **earning significantly more than the national average** — not all assembly line-type jobs do pay well. Also, they didn't study any women.
2) **Neo-Marxists** have suggested that the **preoccupation with lifestyle** and **what you can buy** is the result of exposure to a **capitalist mass media** (see just below for more on this).

Neo-Marxists Say False Needs Hide Alienation

The neo-Marxist **Herbert Marcuse (1964)** said that **work is horrible**, and **leisure time isn't much better**.

He said that **leisure** activities are mainly based around what he calls **false needs** — things people **don't really need**, and which **don't really satisfy** them. False needs are fed to workers through the **mass media**. Marcuse gives cars, expensive hi-fi equipment, fancy homes and expensive kitchen equipment as examples of false needs.

Marcuse calls workers who go after these false needs "**happy robots**". He says that **fulfilling a false need** results in a "**euphoria in unhappiness**" — a temporary high which hides the misery of alienation.

Marcuse suggests the term "**happy consciousness**" as a new version of traditional Marxist "false class consciousness". This "happy consciousness" gives people the **false impression** that **leisure makes them happy**.

Work: Satisfaction, Alienation and Conflict

Industrial Action Means *Conflict* Between Workers and their *Bosses*

There are **different types of industrial action**:

1) **Strike** — This is when workers **collectively withdraw their labour** — in other words, **stop working**. Strikes are often organised by trade unions.
2) **Sabotage or theft** — When workers **deliberately damage or steal equipment** belonging to the company they work for.
3) **Work to rule** — When workers only work to the **letter** of their contracts and won't do any tasks that aren't on the contract.
4) **Absenteeism** — When workers **deliberately go absent from work** without good reason.

A trade union is an organisation of workers usually centred round a particular trade that collectively negotiates on behalf of all its members — e.g. National Union of Mineworkers, National Union of Teachers.

There are *Many Different Reasons* and *Theories* as to *Why Strikes Start*

1) **Boredom** and **resentment** makes strikes more likely. In a study of strikes in the textile industries, **Edwards and Scullion (1982)** concluded that most strikes were caused by boredom and resentment of bad management.
2) **Communications failure** makes strikes more likely. Workers who find it hard to express grievances are more likely to go on strike.
3) **Wage disputes** account for over 40% of strikes in Britain. However in a study of the Pilkington glass workers, **Lane and Roberts (1971)** concluded that strikes that were **supposedly about wages** were often **really about worker resentment of management**.
4) **Certain groups of workers** seem to be **more likely** to go on **strike**. **Kerr and Siegel (1954)** concluded that **dockers** and **miners** were more likely to strike because they were **geographically and socially isolated**. This meant they tended to have a strong sense of solidarity with each other. This is called **isolated mass theory**.
5) **Marxists** see strikes as **inevitable byproducts** of an **exploitative capitalist system**. Marxists are often lukewarm about trade unions — they think collective bargaining legitimises the capitalist system.
6) **Agitators** sometimes cause strikes. An agitator is someone who gets **other workers** all worked up and **angry** about a situation and makes them **more likely to strike**.

Industrial Action is On The *Decline*

If you read the papers you might think people are **on strike all the time**. In fact, the number of strikes has been **going down** significantly since the **1980s**. Sociologists suggest the following reasons:

1) **Trade union laws** made it more **difficult** to call strikes. Some forms of industrial action have been made **illegal**.
2) **Trade union membership** has **fallen** a lot since the 1970s and 1980s.
3) **High unemployment** in the 1980s meant that workers became **less willing to risk their jobs** by striking.
4) **New Right** sociologists argue that increasing affluence means fewer people feel the need to strike.

Practice Questions

Q1 What are Blauner's 4 elements of alienation at work?

Q2 Give two criticisms of the work of Goldthorpe et al. (1969).

Q3 Give three reasons why workers might go on strike.

Exam Questions

Q1 Explain the difference between intrinsic and extrinsic job satisfaction. (4 marks)

Q2 Suggest three factors which may affect the degree of job satisfaction experienced by workers.
Explain your choices. (6 marks)

Show me the money...

It's hard to answer a question like "Are workers satisfied at work?" because it really depends on the particular worker, their boss and the company they work for. Sometimes people don't mind doing a tedious job if it pays well. Sometimes people fall out with their bosses and go on strike. Back in the 1970s, people were striking all the time, but it isn't so common now.

Impact of Technology

These pages will help you revise the impact of computer technology on the experience of work.

Sociologists Disagree about Technology

Technological Determinists See Technology as a Force Which Affects People

Technological determinists think technology is an **independent force** which forces work to be organised in a particular way. A good example of a **technological determinist** is **Blauner** (see page 74), who identified a link between technology and job satisfaction / alienation.

Social Determinists Think People are in Control of Technology

Social determinists think people control technological change. **Social forces** determine how technology develops and people **make choices** about how they're going to **react** to it. **Goldthorpe et al.** are good examples of **social determinists** — they claimed that workers' **attitudes to work** affected how they reacted to technology.

Here Are Views From Three Contemporary Sociologists

1) Shoshana Zuboff is in between Social and Technological Determinism

Shoshana Zuboff (1988) claims that "**smart machines**" are having a **really important impact** on the workplace — but **human choices** will decide whether it's a **positive** or **negative** impact. Zuboff says that with ICT, managers can choose to **automate** the workforce — cutting jobs, controlling work and deskilling. Or they can "**informate**" the workforce — adding value to jobs, giving workers more control, reskilling.

Hmmm, "informate"... sociologists do tend to make up odd words like this.

2) Jon Clark adopted a position closer to a technological determinist one

Clark, McLoughin, Rose and King (1988) studied the adoption of new computer technology in **British telephone exchanges**. They concluded that once a new technology is set up and running, it gets very difficult for workers to change their relationship to the new technology. Clark identified **critical junctures (moments)** during the introduction of technology when people can **influence** the way technology is used. However **once these moments had passed**, workers were **stuck** with the way they were using the technology. In Clark's words, "**social chances** became **frozen** within a given technology".

3) Rob Kling believes that the impact of computer technology depends on how it's used

Rob Kling (1991) rejected both Zuboff and Clark's conclusions about the impact of computer technology on work and **rejects any deterministic theory** that claims computers will **definitely** have a particular effect on work. According to Kling computers can **deskill** but they can also **reskill**. Sometimes computers have a really big impact and sometimes they have virtually **no impact** at all. It all depends on how they're used or **consumed**.

Technology can be **consumed in different ways** leading to very **different results**. For instance — if A-level students are given **fixed times** to use **computer suites** their lives become **regimented** by when they can use them. However, if they had **open access** to the technology to use it in their **own time**, the **effect of the technology** on **how they work** would be quite **different** — although the **technology itself is identical**.

Here's a Summary Of Their Positions

Zuboff	There's been a **computer revolution** — this can have either a **positive** or a **negative** impact on the experience of work. **Managers** can **choose** what the impact will be.
Clark et al.	Once computer technology has been put into place, it can **limit** and **freeze** someone's work **opportunities** and **experiences.**
Kling	The effect of computer technology on the experience of work mainly depends on how it's **used** or **consumed.**

Impact of Technology

The **Way People Talk About Technology** May **Influence** How it's Used

1) **Keith Grint and Steve Woolgar (1992)** studied how people **talk** about technology.
2) Grint and Woolgar **attack** the idea that **technology determines the effect it has** on the workplace **by itself**. They say it's **impossible** to **separate** a technology from the **interpretation** that people put on it — what people think about it in other words.
3) They argue that the **way people talk about technology** is the **crucial factor** in how technology will be applied in society. The people who succeed in **spreading their view about technology** are in a **powerful position** to use technology in their own interests. They point out that power isn't equally shared in the discussion about technology — recognised **experts** have a **disproportionate** amount of power.

Ethel and Rita's discourse on technology was going swimmingly.

Grint and Woolgar's work is interesting because it shows there are always **choices** about how a technology is used. But they can be **criticised** for **exaggerating** the influence that individuals have over how technology is used.

The talk about technology is called "the discourse surrounding it" in sociologists's language. Grint and Woolgar also refer to people as "social actors". Again, it's just the way sociologists are.

New Technology and **Manufacturing Techniques** Can Lead to **Exploitation**

1) **Harry Braverman (1974)** did a **Marxist** critique of mass production. The "**Braverman Thesis**" (also known as the "**deskilling thesis**") says that mechanisation leaves workers with low pay and unfulfilling work, because work gets **deskilled**. **Relations** between **bosses** and **workers** get **worse**. Braverman thought that this process would get faster as technology developed.

2) **Andrew Zimbalist (1979)** did a case study of the American **printing** industry which described the **deskilling** of labour by technology. Years ago, printing was a very **skilled** job. Every single letter on the page was put into place by a **skilled worker**. Zimbalist says that the **deskilling** of the printing industry led to the **print unions losing their power**.

3) **Andy Friedmann (1977)** is more **critical** of the Braverman thesis, suggesting that other factors may well be important. He is also more hopeful about the potential for **workers to influence** the **application of technology** — some workers would get more control over their own work.

4) **Shoshana Zuboff (1988)** found that some **office workers** felt that their jobs were becoming **deskilled**. She said that **automation** meant that jobs which used to have **face-to-face skills** were now done in front of a **machine**. Workers felt that they were forced to sit in front of their computer with their **heads down**, and **weren't allowed to talk** to each other. However, she also found that computer technology could also be used to **help communication** between workers, e.g. email.

Practice Questions

Q1 Who claimed that attitude and orientation affected how people reacted to technology?

Q2 Who claimed that managers can choose to either "automate or informate" the workforce? What does this mean?

Q3 Give an example where the way that a particular technology is consumed can have different effects on the workforce.

Exam Questions

Q1 Sociologists disagree about the impact of technology. Explain the two main sociological theories about this issue, with reference to the individual sociologists that support them. (8 marks)

Q2 Critically assess the Braverman Thesis, with reference to ideas from other sociologists. (20 marks)

Let's talk about fax, baybee...

Does technology rule people or do people rule technology...? Unsurprisingly, sociologists tend to think it's somewhere in between. Technology does change things, but people have the chance to influence how they use technology. At the end of the day though, if your boss comes in and says, "Here's a new computer system, use it!" then you're gonna be using it.

The Social Effects of Unemployment

Sociologists argue about the causes and consequences of unemployment.
In fact, they can't even bring themselves to agree about how it should be measured...

Unemployment in the UK Goes Up and Down

1) **Structural unemployment** is where a whole **big bunch of workers** lose their jobs because their **skills aren't needed** any more e.g. when coal mines close.
2) **Cyclical unemployment** is where people lose their jobs because the **economy** is on a **downer**. When the **economy perks up** again, more **jobs are created** and unemployment goes down.
3) **Frictional unemployment** is where people lose a job and quickly get another one.

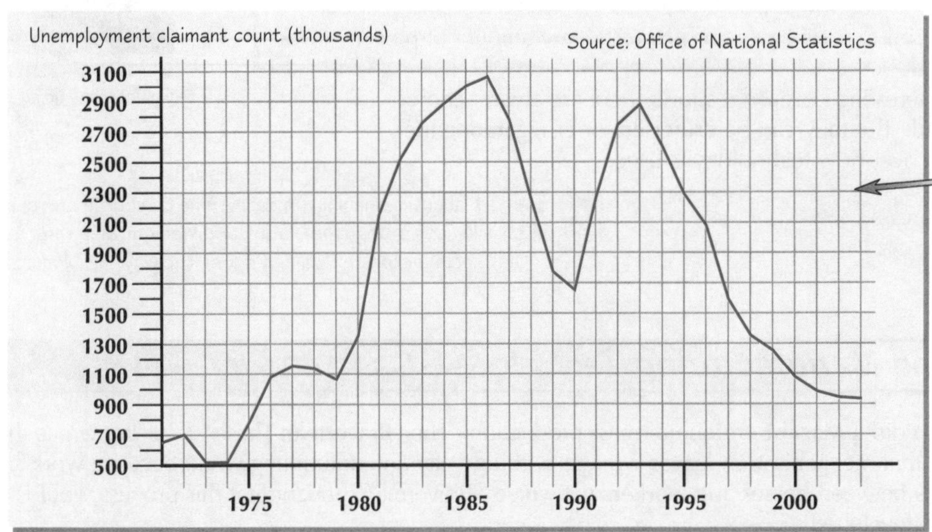

You can also look at the number of people claiming unemployment benefit as a percentage of the population. This went from 1.9% in 1973 to 10.5% in 1986, then down to 5.5% in 1990, back up to 9.7% in 1993 and down to 3.1% in 2003. You can also make an estimate of how many people are unemployed but not claiming benefit.

It's Hard To Measure — Some say the Figures are Fiddled

Measuring unemployment isn't as easy as you might think:

1) **Not everyone** who's out of work **registers** for **Jobseekers' Allowance**.
2) People who **have to leave work** because they're **ill** or **injured** **sometimes count** as unemployed and sometimes not.
3) **Housewives don't count** as unemployed — or employed either.
4) People who take **early retirement** sometimes count and sometimes they don't.

The problem of benefit fraud could be said to be a moral panic (see p. 43).

Politicians tend to suggest that **official unemployment figures** are **overestimated** because they include people who actually work but still claim Jobseekers' Allowance — "**benefit fraudsters**". There's not much hard research evidence to back up this position. **Pahl (1984)** found that the unemployed were no more likely to do informal cash-in-hand work than the employed.

The **Trade Union Congress** (TUC) suggest that unemployment is actually **underestimated** by around 1.5 million. Governments keep **changing the method** of calculating unemployment. The TUC think that governments change it to **get a lower figure each time**, so it'll **look like** unemployment is **going down** faster than it really is.

Not All Social Groups face the Same Risk of Unemployment

1) **Older workers** are more likely to get made **redundant**. **Young people** don't have the **experience** needed for many jobs. You could say both groups are victims of **ageism** in society.
2) **70% of the unemployed** are **unskilled manual workers**. The lower a person's skill level, the more likely they are to be unemployed.
3) **Ethnic minority groups** generally have **more unemployment** than the white population. This is partly down to **discrimination** and partly down to **differential levels of achievement in education** (see section 5).
4) There are big **regional** differences in unemployment in the UK. Unemployment hot spots include the **North**, **North West**, **Northern Ireland** and **Wales**, where there's been a **decline of traditional heavy industry** like steel works and mining. Unemployment is a lot **lower** in the **South East**, where there's been a big increase in the number of **service sector jobs**.

The Social Effects of Unemployment

Sociologists give Conflicting Causes for Unemployment

1) **Keynesian views — it's demand**
Followers of economist **J.M. Keynes** think unemployment is caused by **low demand** in the economy. Keynesians believe **state policy** and **investment** can **raise demand.**

2) **Marxist views — it's capitalism**
Capitalism benefits from **some unemployment** because a **"reserve army of labour"** keeps wages down. Even if **you** don't want to work for **low wages**, some **unemployed** guy probably will.

UNEMPLOYMENT

3) **New Right views — it's tax and welfare**
The New Right viewpoint is that **high business tax rates** hurt business and cause unemployment. They also think **welfare benefits** mean some people **don't bother to get a job.**

4) **The global economy — jobs are going abroad**
Some sociologists argue that unemployment is due to the **manufacturing** industry **moving** to countries like China, the Philippines and Vietnam. Such moves benefit businesses because **labour costs less** and there are **fewer regulations.**

*There's **Less Disagreement** on the **Negative Effects** of **Unemployment***

No one in Sociology says, "Well, unemployment's not that bad really, you get to watch daytime TV".

1) **Poverty** — **Income** from benefits is **low**. When there's not much money coming in, **standard of living** is **low**. **Housing problems** start because it's hard to pay the **rent** or **mortgage** (although people on low incomes can get housing benefit). It's often difficult to get new rented accommodation if you don't have a job.
2) **Social effects** — **Stress** and **no money** often cause **family arguments** — and more **stress**. Unemployed people often feel **isolated** from the world of work and they're **socially isolated** from other people.
3) **Physical health effects** — Unemployed people tend to have **worse health** than working people. There's more **long term illness** and disease among people who have been unemployed for a while.
4) **Mental health effects** — Unemployed people are more likely to be **clinically depressed** — it's not surprising that being unemployed is **depressing**. A person's sense of **identity** is often closely linked to their job. So if they **lose** that job, they lose that part of their identity, and as a result can feel **insecure** or **purposeless**. Unemployed people have **higher rates of suicide**.

Long term unemployment can lead to a **dangerous spiral downwards** — the unemployed person becomes **less and less able** to **rejoin the world of work** as their self-esteem, mental health and physical health all go into decline. This can affect **whole communities** — e.g. some mining communities were badly affected after the pits closed.

Practice Questions

Q1 What is cyclical unemployment?
Q2 Why is it difficult to trust official statistics on unemployment?
Q3 Give four causes of unemployment.
Q4 Give four consequences of unemployment for individuals.

Exam Questions

Q1 Name the three social groups which are at most risk of unemployment and explain why. (6 marks)

Gizza job, go on, give us one, I know you got one...

Unemployment is a total bummer. That much is agreed. Different sociological theories have different ideas about why unemployment happens, though. An interesting thing about unemployment is how hard it is to measure — two sets of figures might have been measured in completely different ways, which means you can't really compare them.

Leisure

Some people think it's quite easy to distinguish leisure from work — leisure's the time "left over" after work. It's not so clear cut for everyone, though. So, what do those sociologists make of it all...

Parker Defined **Categories** of **"Life Space"**

Stanley Parker (1976) came up with these definitions of different ways people spend their time:

Work	Time spent in paid employment
Work obligations	Time spent as a result of paid employment e.g. commuting to work
Non work obligations	Time spent on activities such as child care or housework
Physiological obligations	Time spent eating, sleeping, washing, and on the loo
Leisure	The time left over is "leisure"

Parker Says The **Type of Work** you Do **Shapes** your **Attitude** to **Leisure**

1) **Professionals** who have plenty of **independence** and **job satisfaction** show an **Extension Pattern** of work and leisure. The boundary line between work and leisure isn't always clear because **work is a central part** of that person's **life**. Leisure activities are often linked to work activities, for example a businessman might meet clients on a golf course.
2) **Clerical** and **semi-skilled workers** with less independence and job satisfaction show a **Neutrality Pattern** of work and leisure. There's a clear divide between leisure and work. Work isn't so important to the person. **Family life** and **leisure** are the central interests in life.
3) **Unskilled manual workers** working **tough** and **dangerous** jobs have an **Oppositional Pattern** of work and leisure. There is a **very clear distinction** between work and leisure. Leisure is of **central** importance and is used to "**compensate**" for hard work. Leisure activities are **fun**, not serious.

Stanley Parker has been **criticised** for **ignoring other sociological factors** which may influence attitudes to work and leisure, such as gender, culture and class.

Marxists say **Leisure** is Shaped by the Nature of **Capitalism**

Marxists claim that **before the industrial revolution** and the rise of capitalism there was **no clear dividing line** between work and leisure. The introduction of the **factory** system meant workers had to **work longer hours** in more **structured** surroundings. "Leisure time" as such only began to **emerge** in the **late 19th century**. The **freedom** and **flexibility** that people had before industrialisation **never** returned.

1) Under **capitalism**, leisure has been **commodified** and **commercialised**. It now involves the passive consumption of "leisure commodities" by consumers — things like films, going to the pub, going to bingo, going out to a restaurant. According to neo-Marxists **John Clarke and Chas Critcher (1985)**, the two most important factors are the **State** and the **Leisure industry**.
2) The **State regulates leisure activities** through licensing of pubs, bars, clubs and gambling. It regulates films and TV by censorship. This means that leisure opportunities are limited.
3) Marxists say that "bourgeois" middle class pursuits like playing golf and going to restaurants are seen as more **worthwhile** than working class ones like going to the pub.
4) The **leisure industry** is big business making huge profits. **Commercialised leisure** is **dominated** by **large companies** who, Marxists say, **manipulate choices** and **tastes** and **exploit** consumers.

Pluralists see the **Leisure Industry** as a **Democratic Market Place**

Ken Roberts (1978) sees leisure as a **freedom of choice** thing. He **rejects** the Marxist idea that leisure is defined and imposed on consumers by big business and government. Roberts takes a **democratic pluralist** view of the leisure market place, where State and commercial providers have to **respond to public tastes**. If the leisure industry didn't give people what they wanted, they'd **lose money**. Roberts says that leisure must involve **freedom of choice** — if you had to do it, it wouldn't be leisure.

Leisure

Feminists Say Men's Experience of Leisure is Different to Women's

1) Feminists point out that men and women do **different leisure activities**.
2) Women have **less access to leisure** because of relatively **low incomes**, **discrimination** in society and **stereotypical views** on women's domestic responsibilities.
3) Women who go out to work often have to do the **housework** as well. They have **less time available for leisure** than men.
4) **Looking after children** is **stereotypically women's work**, and women do most childcare in the UK. Childcare responsibilities don't leave much time for leisure. Also, looking after children is sometimes characterised as "spending all day playing with them".

Liberal feminists seek a **reformist** solution to these problems. They want to highlight discriminatory practices and get them reformed. Liberal feminism would like **equal pay**, access to free or **subsidised childcare**, and an **end to discrimination**.

Radical and socialist feminists suggest that gender inequality is created by the **patriarchical structure** of society and that only wholesale change in that structure will change women's experience of work and leisure.

Postmodernists Claim that Individuals Choose their Leisure

Traditional sociology says that class, gender, age and ethnicity have **some bearing** on **everything** we do. **Postmodernists** say that the effects of class, gender, age and ethnicity are on the **decline**.

1) Postmodernists such as **Lash and Urry (1993)** have claimed that advances in satellite, cable and Internet technology and the globalisation of culture has made leisure more **individualised** or "**privatised**".
2) **Consumers** have an absolutely **huge** number of **leisure choices** in postmodern society. Leisure activities are used by consumers to construct "**unique social identities**" for themselves. These unique identities aren't tied to gender, ethnicity or class.
3) Lash and Urry also suggest that people are **less likely** to take part in **group** leisure activities than they were in the past.

Critics of the postmodernists point out the lasting influence of **class**, **gender** and **ethnicity**.

For instance **ethnic minority consumers**, living in inner cities with low level incomes and suffering the negative effects of **racism** are unlikely to have access to 'postmodern' leisure activities. But on the other hand, it's different for well-off ethnic minority consumers living in the suburbs.

Feminists such as **Scraton (1994)** point out that women's **leisure opportunities** are **still** largely shaped by a relative lack of **disposable income**, societal expectations of **gender roles** and "open ended domestic responsibilities".

Practice Questions

Q1 How does Stanley Parker (1976) distinguish between work and leisure?

Q2 What is meant by?

a) An Extension Pattern of work and leisure

b) A Neutrality Pattern of work and leisure

c) An Oppositional Pattern of work and leisure

Q3 In what ways do men and women experience leisure differently?

Exam Question

Q1 Suggest three reasons why the leisure patterns of the unemployed might differ from the leisure patterns of the employed. (6 marks)

A bit of time off — now there's a good idea...

Leisure is a big part of modern life — and it's big business. Because it's big business, you can be sure that Marxists will have something snarky to say about it. You can argue that media and big business manipulate people's leisure interests and push people into liking films and football and pubs and bingo. On the other hand, you could say people just enjoy those things.

Religious Institutions

Religious groups organise themselves into different forms. They differ in leadership, relationship to the State and politics, how they worship and who they appeal to. Sociologists have put forward different classifications of religious organisations. ***This section is for OCR only.***

A Church is a Well Established Religious Organisation

Social historian **Ernst Troeltsch (1912)** distinguished between different kinds of religious organisation, and used the word **church** to mean a **large religious organisation**. He said churches usually have four main features:

1) A church claims **monopoly over the truth** — it says its claims are **absolutely true** and others are **false**.
2) Churches have a **complex rigid hierarchy** and a **bureaucratic structure** with lots of **rules and regulations**.
3) Churches often have a **close relationship** to the **State**. Some nations have an official national religion — Weber used the term "**ecclesia**" for this.
4) They are closely integrated into **mainstream society**. Churches act as a **conservative** force, resisting change. This is why the **upper classes** are more likely to join — even though churches are **universal** and **inclusive in principle**.

Examples of churches include the **Roman Catholic Church**, the **Church of England** or the **Episcopalian Church**.

Troeltsch studied churches in **16th century** Europe. **Steve Bruce (1995)** says that Troeltsch's points don't always apply to churches any more because there's **religious pluralism** these days. The Church of England doesn't claim a monopoly over the truth and it isn't always conservative.

Religious pluralism = lots of different types of religious groups.

Sects are Small, Radical Religious Movements

Troeltsch defined sects as being almost the **opposite of churches**. Few religious groups fall into the category of sect.

People who are **dissatisfied** with mainstream religion can be attracted to a sect. Sects are often formed by people **splitting off from a church** because they **disagree** with the church's **practices** or **theology**.

1) Sects claim a **monopoly over the truth** and are intolerant towards other religious organisations.
2) Sects have **no complex hierarchy**. They often have a **charismatic leader** who **persuades** members to **follow his / her teaching**.
3) Sects are **small**. Their members follow with **total commitment**, and they can be **manipulated** by the sect's leader.
4) Sects are separate from the state — they're in **opposition** to mainstream society. Sects can sometimes offer an alternative way of life for **deprived** and **marginal** groups

Examples of sects include **early Methodists** and **Calvinists** (although over time these have become more mainstream). This category also includes **extremist** groups like the **People's Temple** in America who were led to mass suicide by Jim Jones, or the **Branch Davidians** led by David Koresh.

These extremist groups are generally called cults in everyday language.
Watch out though — in sociology, cult means something else...

Denominations are Subsets of Churches

Troeltsch **originally classified** religious organisations into **churches** and **sects**.
The term "**denomination**" was added later.

1) Denominations don't usually claim **a monopoly over the truth**. They see themselves as a **possible route to the truth**. They are **tolerant** towards other religious organisations.
2) Like a church, they have a **hierarchy** and **bureaucratic structure** but it isn't as complex.
3) They have a reasonably **large membership**, but not as large as an established church.
4) Members of denominations are usually **not as loyal** as members of churches.
5) Denominations **aren't closely connected to the State**. They get involved in society and **comment** on **current events**.

Examples of denominations are **modern Methodists** and **Baptists**.

Cults are Mystic Movements — Often Wrongly Defined

Bruce (1995) defined cults as movements without a fixed set of beliefs. They emphasise the **inner power** of the **individual** and **mysticism.** Cults are usually loosely knit and don't have a hierarchy.

Religious Institutions

New Religious Movements can be Affirming, Rejecting or Accommodating

The term **new religious movement** (or NRM for short) includes a **huge range of movements** from diverse sources. They've increased significantly since the 1960s. They don't always fit the old church-sect-denomination-cult divisions. Sociologist **Roy Wallis (1984)** identified three types of new religious movement:

World-rejecting movements cut themselves off from society — similar to sects

1) World-rejecting movements are very **critical** of wider society and are often in conflict with the State.
2) **The Unification Church**, better known as the '**Moonies**', is one example of a world-rejecting movement.
3) World-rejecting movements require **total commitment**. They demand **significant lifestyle changes.** Members often turn away from family and friends — world-rejecting movements have developed a reputation for "**brainwashing**" members. It's often hard to leave a world-rejecting movement.

World-affirming movements are tolerant of other beliefs — similar to cults

1) They're similar to **self-help** and therapy groups — they try to "**unlock spiritual power**". **Transcendental Meditation** is an example of a world-affirming movement.
2) World affirming movements seek **wide membership**.
3) World-affirming movements **don't require** especially high levels of **commitment**.

World-accommodating movements are traditionally religious — similar to denominations

1) World-accommodating movements often come from **traditional** religions.
2) They try to rediscover **spiritual purity** lost in traditional religions. **Pentecostalism** is a movement within Christianity that aims to bring the Holy Spirit back into worship.
3) World-accommodating movements allow people to carry on with their **existing lifestyle**.

New Religious Movements Include New Age and Millenarian Movements

1) **New Age Movements** are close to cults and world affirming movements. New Age ideas often aren't linked to an organisation, but spread through a culture. Examples include **dowsing**, **feng shui**, **crystals, neo-paganism** and **Reiki**.
2) **Heelas (1996)** claims that New Age beliefs are dedicated to "**self-spirituality**" and the development of the self.
3) **Bruce (1995)** highlights **three themes** to New Age Movements: **New Science** rejects many claims of traditional science, **New Ecology** is concerned for the environment and **New Psychology** sees the self as sacred.
4) New Age appeals to **women** more than men and **middle class** more than working class.

Millenarian movements claim that members will achieve **salvation** through a **cataclysmic** event — a major disaster. Millenarianism is connected to **apocalypticism** which believes that **divine forces** will **overthrow** the existing social order.

The **Ghost Dance** of the indigenous **Plains Tribes** in **North America** is an example of a **Millenarian** movement. The tribes believed storms and earthquakes would return the buffalo to the prairies and end ethnic divisions.

Millenarian movements are associated with **deprived groups** or areas where there has been **radical social change**.

Practice Questions

Q1 Give two characteristics of a church.

Q2 Give two characteristics of a cult.

Q3 What are the key characteristics of a denomination?

Q4 Name the three types of new religious movement identified by Wallis.

Q5 What is a millenarian movement?

Exam Questions

Q1 (a) Identify and explain two differences between churches and sects. (15 marks)

(b) Identify and explain two differences between world-rejecting and world-affirming New Religious Movements. (15 marks)

It's a broad church...

Don't assume you already know what a church is, what a sect is, etc. The Sociological definitions are probably a fair bit different from the everyday definitions. So ***learn them****. Obviously, not all religious groups will fit neatly into one of these categories — but most will. And finally, make sure you can spell all those fiddly names like Millenarianism, Pentecostalism and Branch Davidians...*

Religious Organisations: Issues

Religions get bigger and smaller as they gain and lose members. Different religious groups attract different people. Easy (ish).

*The **Growth** of **New Religious Movements** isn't Easy to Explain*

The **interactionist** (also known as **interpretivist**) idea is that **new religious movements (NRMs)** provide **certainty** in times of **uncertainty**. When there's uncertainty, new religious movements have **greater appeal** and **grow** in numbers. Here are some of the **uncertainties** that people face:

1) **Marginality** — inequality, immigration and racism may **marginalise** some groups. So, some new religious movements may help marginalised people **make sense** of their situation, and may promise a better life after death as **compensation**. Theologians call this the "**theodicy of disprivilege**".
2) **Relative deprivation** — the concept of marginality doesn't explain why **white, middle class groups** join new religious movements. Although they aren't absolutely poor or deprived, some middle class people may see themselves as **deprived in comparison to their peers**.
3) **Social change** — transformation of society can result in **anomie** (see p.73) and **uncertainty**. The breakdown of **community**, the process of **secularisation** (see p.86), **cultural diversity** and bad news such as **terrorist attacks** may generate uncertainty.
4) **Modernity and post-modernity** — the **alienation** of capitalism, the increasing amount of **red tape**, bureaucracy and disillusionment with work may create **uncertainty**. The choice people have in constructing their identity may create **uncertainty** and a **crisis of identity**.

Melton (1993) didn't agree that NRMs emerged in periods of uncertainty. He looked at the founding dates of non-conventional religious organisations in the US. **Rapid growth** took place in the **1950s** — in a period of **stability** and **certainty**. Why do these sociologists never agree...

Wallis (1984) explains the appeal of the three different kinds of new religious movement

1) **World-rejecting movements** grew in numbers in the 1960s. There was a lot of **freedom** for people, but also **uncertainty**. It was a period of **radicalism** with lots of alternative world views — often called the "sixties counter-culture". Some people got **disillusioned** with this counter-culture and wanted more **concrete** beliefs.
2) **World-affirming movements** develop as a means of coping with a **crisis of identity** in more successful groups (e.g. the middle class). They try to unlock **human potential** and help people solve their problems. **Bruce (1995)** claims that they're a response to the **rationalisation** of the modern world where it's hard to find satisfaction from work.
3) **World-accommodating movements** appeal to those who are dissatisfied with existing religion.

New Age Movements** Appeal to People Already **Examining** their ~~**Navels**~~ **Identity

1) New Age beliefs appeal to people who have **turned away from traditional religion**. New Age beliefs say that people can find salvation, peace or perfection **inside themselves**. Modern society is more **individualistic** than before — **individual beliefs** are **trusted more**, and **authority** is **trusted less**.
2) New Age Movements help some people cope with the **uncertainties** of modernity. In the modern world, people have a lot of **different roles**. New Age beliefs can help people find a sense of **identity**.
3) New Age beliefs often appeal to **middle class** people working in "**expressive professions**" — actors, writers, social workers, counsellors, therapists etc.
4) New Age movements may also reflect a **cultural change** in mainstream society. People are surrounded by non-conventional religious ideas like horoscopes, feng shui and self-help books. **Mass communication** gives us an awareness of different movements.
5) New Age is quite a **postmodern** thing. In a **postmodern** society of **choice** and **diversity** people can **pick and mix** from all kinds of New Age philosophies to help them construct their own identity.

There are more and more belief systems in society. "**Spiritual shoppers**" are people who **sample** different systems of belief to find the **best fit**. This is an **individualistic** and **consumerist** attitude.

*A **Sect's** Popularity Can Be **Unstable***

1) Sects rely on a **charismatic leader**. If the leader **dies**, the group can often no longer hold itself together.
2) A problem arises when the **second generation** are born into a new sect. They didn't decide to join the sect so they sometimes don't follow with the same religious fervour.
3) If a sect **argues for change** in society and the change actually comes about, the sect **isn't needed any more**.
4) It's difficult to **maintain extreme teachings** and **totally reject society**. A sect can survive if its ideologies become **less rejecting** and **more accommodating**. Sects can eventually become **denominations** (e.g. Methodists).

Religious Organisations: Issues

Religious Participation Varies by Age, Class, Ethnicity and Gender

Age

Age affects how religious people are. The **old** and **young** tend to be **more religious**. The **elderly** are **more likely** to see themselves as **belonging to a religion**.

But some recent studies claim that the **elderly** are **increasingly losing faith** in God.

Middle aged groups are more likely to get involved in **world-affirming movements**.

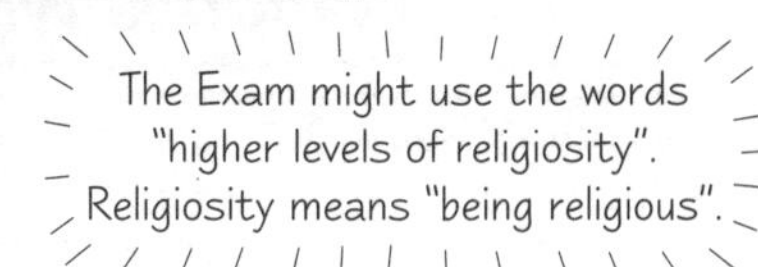

Class

Churches are **inclusive** so they recruit from a broad range of **classes**. However, the **Church of England** has a large **middle class** membership and its leaders tend to be from **privileged** backgrounds. Other **Protestant** denominations tend to have more **working class** membership.

Cults often recruit from **marginal** and **deprived** groups in society.

New Age movements and **world-affirming** movements generally appeal to the **middle class**.

Ethnicity

Ethnic minority groups are **more religious** and participate more in religion because they're more likely to come from **cultures** where **religion is significant**.

Religion can help maintain a sense of **community** and **cultural identity** within ethnic minority groups.

Gender

Women are **more likely to attend church**, and more likely to say they belong to a religion. Women are also more likely to be involved in **new religious movements** and **New Age movements**.

This has traditionally been explained by **differential socialisation**. The argument goes that girls are socialised to be **passive** and to **conform** — which fits in with the behaviour of more traditional and conservative religious groups. Another argument is that **differential roles** are a factor — women are less likely to be in **full-time work**, which means they have **more time for worship**.

Religious Organisations May Bring About Social Change

Whether or not an organisation brings about **social change** depends on these things:

1) **What they believe** — Some religious organisations put a lot of importance on **doing good here on Earth**. Others put more importance on worshipping God and having faith in God. Organisations that focus on **actions** in the here and now are more likely to bring about change. For example, **Liberation Theology** is a Christian movement which pushes for social salvation from repression as well as religious salvation from sin and death. Liberation theology has brought about change in Latin America (see p.90).

2) **Their relationship to the establishment** — **Radical** religious movements **want change** and fight for change. Most churches are fairly conservative, but their leaders do sometimes have the ear of politicians and leaders of society.

3) **Their structure** — A clearly **organised hierarchy** or strong sense of authority can get a group all pulling in the same direction. A well organised group wanting social change are more likely to get it than a loosely organised group.

4) **The background of their members** — Organisations that recruit from **persecuted groups** are more likely to want social change than organisations that recruit from privileged and well-off groups.

Practice Questions

Q1 Name two uncertainties that explain the appeal of New Religious Movements.

Q2 Who do New Age Movements appeal to?

Q3 Are women more or less likely than men to say they belong to a religion?

Q4 Name two factors that influence whether a religious organisation can bring about change.

Exam Questions

Q1 (a) Identify and explain two reasons why women are more likely to express higher levels of religiosity and religious participation than men. (15 marks)

(b) Outline and examine the reasons for the growth of New Religious Movements. (30 marks)

If you're spiritual shopping, can you pick up a cheap soul for me, ta...

Different religious movements are always going to appeal to different people. I mean, if you're a middle aged Protestant looking for a more exciting church you're probably going to go for something different than if you're a tofu-eating reflexologist looking for something to bring out your inner goddess. Class, gender, age and ethnicity affect how religious people tend to be.

The Influence of Religion: Secularisation

That's me in the corner...

Secularisation is When **Religion Loses Its Influence** Over Society

Bryan Wilson (1966) defined secularisation as a "**process whereby religion loses its influence over the various spheres of social life**". Secularisation is said to be a result of the social changes brought about by **modern, urban, industrial society**.

The "founding fathers" of sociology **predicted secularisation**.

1) **August Comte** claimed that **science** was the **final stage** in the **development of human thought**. He said modern society would be dominated by **science** and not religion.
2) **Max Weber** believed that **modern society** would be the age of **technology**, **rationality** and **bureaucracy**. He said rationality and efficiency **sweeps away magic**, **myth** and **tradition**.

Church Attendance and **Membership** is in Decline

Source: UK Christian Handbook: Religious Trends 1988/99

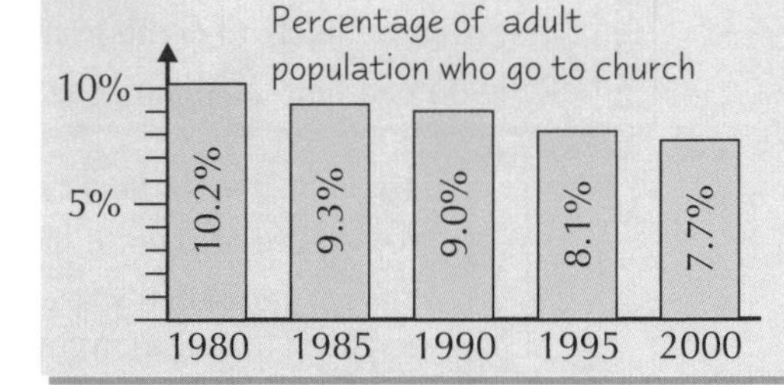

Counting bums on pews gives **supporting evidence for secularisation**:

1) **UK church membership** and **attendance** has gone down — **attendance** has fallen by almost 1 million in the last 20 years.
2) Attendance at ceremonies such as **baptisms** and **marriages** has also dropped. **27%** of babies were baptised in 1993 compared to **65%** in 1900.

Measuring secularisation by counting **bums on pews** has **limitations**:

1) People may **attend church** but **not believe in God**. They might attend a service, baptism or wedding out of friendship for the people involved, for respectability or because of family duty. Or even to get their kids into a certain school.
2) People may **not attend church** because of their **lifestyle** but they do still believe in God. **Not being in church** doesn't tell you about **belief**. The last Census found that 72% of the population identified themselves as Christians.
3) To make comparisons with the past you have to use **old statistics**, which may not be reliable.

Pluralism Gives People **Choice**

Religious pluralism is about **diversity** in types of religious organisations and beliefs in society.
As a result the **established, national church loses its influence** in integrating people into **shared values**.
Multi-cultural societies are more likely to have religious pluralism.

Some sociologists use pluralism as evidence against secularisation

1) The increase in **New Age movements** since the 1980s can be seen as proof that the **sacred** is becoming **important** again — this is called **resacrilisation**, by the way.
2) It can be argued that Pluralism is evidence of religion being **transformed**. It shows a trend towards **individuation** — people being free to search for their **own religious meanings** (to become "**spiritual shoppers**").

Other sociologists use pluralism as supporting evidence for secularisation

1) Pluralism gives people **choice**. People might feel freer to choose to **reject religion altogether**.
2) Although some people in modern society have joined **new religious movements**, they are still a **small proportion** of the population. Some sociologists claim the **growth** in NRMs has been **overestimated**.

Desacrilisation is Where the **Supernatural** is **Less** of a **Force in Society**

1) Weber **predicted desacrilisation** (see glossary) in his idea of **disenchantment**. He thought that magic and myth were less important in modern society. Similarly, **Bruce (1995)** sees **science** and rational explanations as **undermining religion**.
2) Instead of turning to the supernatural or religion to **explain our problems** we might turn to **science**. We demand pills when we are ill and we use science to explain natural disasters.
3) However, the **death** of a loved one, **injustice**, **natural disasters** and **terrorist atrocities** still sometimes lead people to prayer and faith in the supernatural. Modern science **can't explain everything** to everyone's satisfaction.
4) **Postmodernists** claim that we've moved **beyond scientific** rationality and we now **mistrust science**.
5) Belief in **astrology** and **lucky charms** and **fanatical interest** in magical fantasy like **Harry Potter** and **Lord of the Rings** demonstrates that people still have an interest in **magic**, **myth** and the **irrational**.

The Influence of Religion: Secularisation

Some **Religious Institutions** have Become **Secularised**

1) **Secularisation** of **religious institutions** is when the church becomes **less religious** in its beliefs to **fit in** with the rest of **society**. For example, many churches will now allow divorced people to marry.
2) American sociologist **Herberg (1956)** thinks church attendance shows **commitment to community** and not religion — people go to church to **meet up with friends** and feel like **part of something**.
3) Remember that **not all religious institutions** have become more **secular**. The **New Christian Right** don't compromise their beliefs to fit in with society — they're against divorce, homosexuality and pre-marital sex. The more extreme end of the religious right are also against women working outside the home.

The **Church** May have **Lost Some Functions** and Become **Disengaged**

Differentiation is where **society becomes more specialised** so each **institution** in society has **fewer functions** than in the past. For example, the **church** used to have an important **educational** function. But since the 19th Century more separate institutions have developed for this role and state involvement has increased. Religion becomes less important in society as some of its previous functions are taken over.

Disengagement is when the church becomes **separated from the State**. As a result, it has **less influence**.

1) Although the church may have lost its functions and become disengaged from the State and politics, religion can still be **significant in everyday life** and encourage **shared values** in society.
2) Religion is still closely linked to **politics** in the **Middle East** and **Northern Ireland**.

Secularisation is Very **Difficult to Measure**

There's more about sociological research methods in Section 10.

1) There are lots of different **measures of secularisation**. Some are more valid and reliable than others. **Surveys** show **high levels of religiosity**, but **quantitative measurements** of **church attendance** are **low**. **Different religious groups** measure membership in **different ways**, anyhow.
2) The term **secularisation** is a general term that's sometimes applied just to Christianity. It's important to know **what's being measured** — the decline of **religion in general** or the decline in **Christianity** in particular.
3) It's difficult to measure the significance of religion and make comparisons because sociologists use **different definitions of religion**. Some sociologists use **substantive definitions** which say **what religion is** — e.g. "religion is belief in the sacred". Some sociologists use **functional definitions** saying **what religion is for** — e.g. "religion is for creating value consensus".
4) To measure whether society has become **more secular** you have to compare it to **the past**. Some sociologists argue that we see the past as a **golden age** of religion where **everyone** believed and **no one** was sceptical. This is **far too simplified**.
5) Research into secularisation can also be rather **ethno-centric** — focusing on **Christianity** and what the **predominantly white British mainstream** does. Islam, Hinduism and Sikhism are also changing and developing in different ways.

Practice Questions

Q1 How did Bryan Wilson define secularisation?

Q2 How does religious pluralism support secularisation?

Q3 What is meant by desacrilisation?

Q4 Using the measure of church attendance, give one piece of evidence to support secularisation.

Q5 Define the term disengagement.

Q6 Give one reason why it can be difficult to measure the importance of religion.

Exam Questions

Q1 (a) Identify and briefly explain two problems of measuring secularisation. (15 marks)

(b) Outline and discuss the view that the influence of religion is in decline. (30 marks)

...that's me in the spotlight, losing my religion...

There are lots of different sides to secularisation, and lots of ways to measure it. There's some clear evidence for and against the secularisation thesis — which you need to learn. Oh, and by the way, the Bryan Wilson with the theory on secularisation isn't the same Brian Wilson who was in the Beach Boys. Not that you thought he was. I'm just saying, like.

The Influence of Religion

Many sociologists say religion still has a major impact on our identity.

Fundamentalism Provides *Meaning* and *Certainty* in Periods of *Uncertainty*

Fundamentalism is the return to the **fundamental, literal interpretation** of religious texts. Fundamentalist groups **strictly** and **fervently** follow their beliefs. These groups often have **charismatic leaders**.

In both of the following examples, **fundamentalism** provides **certainty** and **meaning** in periods of **uncertainty**.

1) Islamic Fundamentalism in Iran

Iran was a **traditional** society that **quickly modernised** under the **Shah**. **Women** wore **Western clothes**, alcohol was freely available and there was **secular education**. There was also **inequality** in society — the upper class were **very rich**, and working class areas were **neglected**.
Traditional Muslims were **unhappy** about the direction that Iranian society had taken, and saw the Shah as **corrupt**. They started to oppose the Shah, led by a **fundamentalist** religious leader called **Ayatollah Khomeini**. There was a revolution in 1979 and the Ayatollah came to power. He established a society based on **Islamic Sharia law** — alcohol was banned, there were harsh punishments for crime and women were required to cover their bodies in public.

2) Christian Fundamentalism

The **New Christian Right** in **America** argues that American society is in **decline** and in a state of **moral crisis**. They think this is caused by **liberal reforms** — e.g. easy **divorce**, legalised **abortion**, **gay rights** and **secular education**. The Christian Right **oppose** the teaching of **Evolution** in schools, because it disagrees with their fundamentalist interpretation of the Bible. They started some **universities** that offer not only degrees, but also a strict **Christian education**. They promote their views through **mass communication** — TV and Christian publishing.

The heartlands of the Christian Right are sometimes called the "Bible Belt".

The **uncertainty** of **postmodernism** may generate a need for **order** and **stability**. Postmodernism argues in favour of **relativism** — the belief that there are **many truths**. People may rebel against relativism and decide they only want **one absolute truth** — which **fundamentalism** provides.

Feminists Say *Religion* Passes On *Patriarchal Ideologies*

Feminists claim that religion acts as an **institution** of **social control**. They say religion is an agency of socialisation that reproduces **gender divisions**.

1) Religion passes on **ideologies** that **maintain patriarchy**.
2) The **conventional family ideology** that's expressed in many religions traps women into traditional roles.
3) Patriarchal ideologies maintain **conformity** and the **submission** of women.
4) Women are **excluded from power** in many religious organisations.

Patriarchy = male domination of society

Radical feminist **Mary Daly (1973)** claims that Christianity acts as an ideological force in different ways:

1) **Religious images** — God is the **father**, women are **created from a man's body** and all the **apostles** in the New Testament are **men**.
2) **Religious teachings** — St Paul's letter to the Ephesians says "Wives **submit to your husbands** as to the Lord. For a **husband has authority over his wife**" (Ephesians 5:22-23).
3) **Church hierarchy** — women seem to be **excluded from the top positions**. In 1992 the Church of England allowed **women priests**. In the **Catholic Church** women **can't be priests**.

Some sociologists claim that women are subordinated in **other religious faiths**.
The oppression of women in **Afghanistan** under the previous **Taleban regime** is an example.

Remember, the Taleban aren't representative of Islam as a whole.

There Are *Problems* with *Feminist Anti-Religious Views*

1) Women are not necessarily **passive victims** of religious oppression. Women may **actively resist** oppression. In **Afghanistan** under the Taleban it was forbidden for girls to go to school. Women educated girls in secret.
2) Religion **isn't necessarily patriarchal**. For example, **veiling** can have **positive functions** for Muslim women. The veil can **affirm Muslim identity** and **protect** women from sexual harrassment in public.
3) Some religions affirm the **equality of the sexes** as part of their beliefs — e.g. **Sikhism**.

The Influence of Religion

Religion Passes On Ideologies that Control Sexuality

Religion is an **agent of control** — it promotes a **dominant norm** of **heterosexuality** and **marriage**.

1) Many religions **forbid sex outside of marriage** and **homosexuality**.
2) **Fundamentalist** groups have **rigid views** of **sexuality**. For example, Muslim societies in the Middle East often **segregate** men and women, e.g. in education. In fundamentalist Muslim society, **women cover their bodies** in public. **Homosexuality** and **adultery** are heavily **punished** by Islamic Sharia law.
3) **Feminists** argue that religion **oppresses female sexuality** by imposing a strict norm of staying a **virgin** until **marriage**, only having sex to have **babies**, and being **sexually passive**.
4) **Functionalists** think that the **control** and channelling of **sexuality** is crucial to the **continuation** of **society**. They think it's important to have a **stable family** for kids to be born into, and a monogamous sexual relationship between husband and wife to keep society stable.
5) The **New Right** claim that a **moral decline** caused by secularisation has encouraged **homosexuality**, **abortion** and **pornography**. They say these are all **threats to social order**.

Postmodernists think this is all old hat and that religion doesn't have that big an influence on sexuality any more. They say individuals have **choice** in the **construction** of their **identity**. (But they're maybe not thinking of the Bible Belt).

Religion is Closely Linked to Ethnicity in the Creation of Identity

Ethnicity is about shared cultural traditions and history which are distinct from other groups in society. Modern Britain is said to be a **multi-cultural** society made up of many **different ethnic groups**.

Here are **two examples** of how ethnicity and religion can link together in creating identity.

When **Hindu**, **Muslim** and **Sikh** immigrants from South Asia came to the UK in the 1960s, they found **few opportunities** to practise their faith. They **quickly established religious organisations** which allowed these groups to **maintain their cultural identity** in a new social setting. See page 8 — **Ballard and Ballard (1977)**. Steve Bruce calls this **Cultural Transition** — adapting to new situations and recreating old communities.

Rastafarianism is both a **religious** movement and a **political** movement. It started in the early 20th century, and became popular in the **1970s**.

Racial identity is absolutely **key** for Rastafarianism — it's based around **black resistance to racism** by whites. Many Rastafarians see whites as **inferior**, and white people are excluded from becoming members.

In Rastafarianism, **Old Testament** beliefs are mixed with the "**back to Africa**" beliefs of activist Marcus Garvey. Rastafarians believe that they are the **lost tribe of Israel**. They claim **Ethiopia** as their **homeland**, and believe that God will one day lead them there.

Rastafarianism has been considered **deviant** by **mainstream society** because many members smoke **cannabis** as part of religious meditation.

Practice Questions

Q1 Define fundamentalism.

Q2 Give two examples of problems with religion, according to feminists.

Q3 Give an example of how religion acts as a form of social control in terms of sexuality.

Q4 Why did Sikh immigrants to the UK set up new Sikh temples?

Exam Questions

Q1 a) Identify and briefly explain two ways in which religion has a negative impact upon women. (15 marks)

b) Identify and discuss the view that religion has a large impact on the identity of ethnic minorities. (30 marks)

Unfortunately, no religion can give you certainty of an A grade...

Just like everything in sociology, there are a whole bunch of different views here. Fundamentalism gets a bad press, but it can serve people's needs for some kind of certainty and justice in the world. The same religion can oppress women and liberate them, depending on how it's practised. Remember too, that religion can help people express their ethnic identity.

Religion and Sociological Theory

The old "founding fathers" of sociology were all interested in the role of religion in society. Marx and Durkheim thought that religion stopped social change. Weber thought that religion could start social change.

Marx Said Religion Inhibits Social Change and Helps to Oppress Workers

1) Karl Marx said that in **capitalist** society there was **conflict** between the **ruling class** and the **working class** because the ruling class **exploit** the working class to get the most profit out of them.
2) But — there's **something stopping** the working class from **uniting** and **overthrowing** the ruling class. Marx says the working class are in a state of **false consciousness**. This means they're **not aware** of **how unfair** society is.
3) This is where **religion** comes in. Marx is **very critical** of religion. He says it **keeps** the working class in a state of **false consciousness**. He said, "**Religion is the opium of the people**". This means that it **dulls the pain** of oppression like **opium** — a **drug** which kills pain. It doesn't take the oppression away, though.

Marx says that religion justifies social inequality

1) People have **heaven** to **look forward** to if they're **good**, so they **don't break the rules** and don't challenge the capitalist system.
2) Religion **consoles** people with the **promise of life after death** and so they **put up** with their **suffering** here **on Earth** more easily.
3) Religion often tells people that their **position is decided by God**. This encourages false consciousness by blaming God instead of **blaming capitalism**.
4) If **God is all powerful** he could **do something** about the suffering **if he wanted to**. He **doesn't** do anything — so this must be **how society is meant to be**.

So, Marxism says that religion **passes on beliefs** that **oppress the working class**. Religion is a **conservative** force which prevents revolution. The **rich stay rich** and the **poor** keep on working. It's a **neat social control**.

But... there are problems with applying this Marxist view to today's society

Fewer people go to church than in the past. The idea that religion is an **ideological device** just doesn't seem **relevant** in Britain today. If people **don't go to church**, it's **hard** for them to be duped by church ideology.

There's Evidence that Religion is a Conservative and Oppressive Force

1) **Hymns** like *All Things Bright and Beautiful* contain **really clear ideologies** like "the rich man in his castle, the poor man at his gate, **God made them high and lowly** and **ordered their estate**". Blimey.
2) Monarchs in medieval Europe ruled by **divine right**. People believed they had the **God-given right** to rule — so they had total power. No one could challenge them.
3) **Halevy (1927)** claimed that **Methodism** prevented revolution in the 19th Century. Dissatisfied workers turned away from the established state church to find enlightenment with the Methodists. Although they **changed denomination**, they **kept on working**.
4) **Sidney Hook (1990)** points out that the **Catholic Church** has a **conservative** view on contraception, abortion and homosexuality.

"This church has always been made of mud! You can keep your newfangled bricks and mortar".

But in Some Cases Religion can Encourage Social Change

1) Marx's good pal **Engels** reckoned that in **some circumstances** religion could actually be a **revolutionary** force. Sometimes **religion** is the **only means of change** because all other routes have been blocked.
2) **Early Christian sects** opposed Roman rule and brought about change. **Jesus** encouraged social change.
3) Neo-Marxist **Otto Maduro (1982)** also claimed that religion isn't always a conservative force. In the 1960s and 1970s, **Catholic priests** in **Latin America** criticised the bourgeoisie and preached **Liberation Theology** — using religion to free people from their oppression. This led to **resistance** and **social change** — in 1979, Catholic revolutionaries threw out the oppressive government in **Nicaragua**. Maduro said religion is "often one of the main available channels to bring about a social revolution".
4) Reverend **Martin Luther King** and the **Southern Baptist Church** resisted oppression and segregation, bringing about **political** and **social rights** for black people in **1960s America**.

Religion and Sociological Theory

Functionalists *see Religion as* ***Maintaining Harmony*** *and* ***Social Cohesion***

Functionalists see religion as something that **inhibits change** and helps **keep society as it is**. They think this is a positive role, which creates **social order** based on **value consensus**. Here's those key functionalist's views:

1) **Durkheim** studied **Aboriginal** society and found that the **sacred worship of totems** was equivalent to **worshipping society itself**. Durkheim said that sacred religious worship encourages shared values.
2) **Malinowski (1954)** looked at how religion deals with situations of **emotional stress** that **threaten social order**. Unpredictable or stressful events like births and deaths create **disruption**. Religion **manages these tensions** and recreates stability.
3) **Parsons** wrote in the 1930s and 1940s that religion provides **guidelines** for human action in terms of "**core values**". Religion helps to **integrate** people into a value consensus and allows them to **make sense of their lives**.

There's also a Functionalist idea of **Civil Religion**, which is when secular (non-religious) symbols and rituals create **social cohesion** in a similar way to religion. **Flags**, famous **political figures** and even **royal deaths** bring about some kind of **collective feeling** that generates **order** and **stability**.

> Functionalism ignores **dysfunctional** aspects of religion. There are **religious conflicts** all over the world. Religion can be a source of **oppression**.
> Religion can also bring about **change**, and Functionalism ignores that as well.

Weber *said that* ***Religion*** *can* ***Indirectly*** *Cause* ***Social Change***

Weber's book *The Protestant Work Ethic and Spirit of Capitalism* looked at how the **religious** ideas of **Calvinism** brought about social change. Weber spotted **two important things** in Calvinism:

> 1) **Predestination**: Early Calvinists believed in **predestination**, which says your **life** and whether you have a place in heaven is **predetermined** by **God**. Only a **specific few** were **chosen** for heaven. This created **anxiety** — you didn't know if you'd been chosen.
> 2) **Ascetic Ideal**: **Working hard** in your job was a **solution** to this anxiety. Success might be a sign that you were chosen for heaven. Early Calvinists lived a **strict** and **disciplined** life of hard work and simple pleasures.

Weber claimed that the ascetic ideal created an ethic of **disciplined hard work**. This is the **spirit of capitalism**. Not only was there a build-up of **capital** and **business**, there was the right **work ethic** for capitalism. Religion **indirectly** brought about change.

However — **Eisenstadt (1967)** contradicts Weber's theory by claiming that capitalism occurred in **Catholic** countries like Italy **before** the **Protestant Reformation happened** and before the ideas of **Calvin ever came out**.

Practice Questions

Q1 What role did Marx think religion played in the capitalist system?

Q2 Give two pieces of evidence to support Marx.

Q3 How does the work of Otto Maduro on Liberation Theology challenge traditional Marxism?

Q4 What did Malinowski and Parsons say were the social functions of religion?

Q5 Give an example of a problem with the Functionalist view of religion.

Q6 What did Weber claim was indirectly brought about by Calvinism?

Exam Questions

Q1 a) Identify and explain two ways in which religion acts as a conservative force in society. (15 marks)

b) Outline and discuss the Marxist view that religion is an inhibitor of change. (30 marks)

Learn the different theories – don't lose Marx...

Traditional Marxism sees religion as a conservative force that inhibits change and keeps the working man down. Engels and Maduro see religion as sometimes being the only way you can have social change. Weber suggests that religion indirectly brought about change and Functionalists see religion as something that keeps order and stability. Confusing or what...

Culture, Youth Culture, Subculture

This section is for OCR, so skip it if you're doing AQA. *It's only during the last 60 years that we've started thinking of young people as having a different culture from their parents' generation. Youth culture and subcultures are now considered an important aspect of society. Sociologists have given this new phenomenon quite a bit of attention.*

Youth Culture is a Different Thing from Culture...

Culture means **language**, **beliefs**, **values and norms**, **customs**, **roles**, **knowledge** and **skills** — the "**way of life**" of a **whole social group** or **society**. Culture is **socially transmitted**. That means it's passed on through socialisation from one generation to the next.

See Pages 4 and 5 for a more detailed look at the ideas of Culture and Socialisation.

Youth Culture is different because it often **opposes mainstream society**. It **rejects** the norms and values passed on by previous generations. Rejecting society's values can range from **minor differences** to **total rebellion**.

Sociologists say youth culture is "oppositional".

1) The idea of a **youth culture** first appeared in the **early 1950s**. At the time teenagers seemed to have a **rebellious spirit**.
2) The **school leaving age went up in the 1940s**, so people stayed as "youth" into their **late teens** and didn't have to get jobs.
3) The post-war period was **relatively affluent**. Young people had **disposable income** to spend on **leisure activities**. A **youth culture** based around **popular music** and **fashion** started to develop.

...But There Isn't Just One Youth Culture

Sociologists say that young people form **lots of different subcultures**.

A **subculture** is an **identifiable group** whose members **share values** and **behaviour patterns** which are **different** from **mainstream norms**.

Sociologists Have Tended to Focus on "Spectacular Subcultures"

These are **dramatic subcultures** that attract the **attention** of the public and the **mass media**. They dress **flamboyantly** and **distinctively**, and often appear to **behave** in ways that **break the norms** of society. Examples include **Teddy boys** (1950s), **Mods** and **Rockers** (1960s) and **Punks** (1970s).

Stan Cohen (1972) examined the way the media encouraged spectacular subcultures in the mid 1960s.

1) His research looked at a number of disturbances in English seaside towns involving **Mods** and **Rockers**.
2) **Exaggerated media reporting** of fairly **minor** incidents encouraged an **exaggerated reaction**. The **police** and **court** responses to the fights grew stronger.
3) More young people were **encouraged to join in** the fights. This **seemed** to **justify the fear** that the media had expressed.
4) Cohen called this a **moral panic**.

A moral panic is a strong public reaction to a particular group of people or a social phenomenon. Cohen reckons that these moral panics come from deliberate media exaggeration. For more on moral panics, see page 43.

Some Say this Distorts the Truth about Most Young People

1) Spectacular subcultures are **interesting** to sociologists because they're **dramatic** and **kind of fun to study**. Some sociologists have said that it's a **mistake** to focus on these groups.
2) The term "**ordinary youth**" is used to describe young people who **generally accept mainstream norms** and **values** and don't belong to any identifiable subcultures.
3) According to a **1990** study by **Paul Willis**, only **13%** of young people claim to belong to a **spectacular youth subculture**. This means most young people are "ordinary youth".

Culture, Youth Culture, Subculture

Subcultural Groups *Aren't Just for* **Working Class White Boys**

Many sociologists see spectacular youth subcultures as white, male, and working class. (There's more about that on page 94, by the way). This isn't always true.

> **Hippies** in the 1960s and 70s were often from **middle class** backgrounds. This subculture, with its deliberately **scruffy dress**, **anti-work values**, **anti-authority values**, **drug taking** and **sexual freedom** was **opposed** to the **middle class values** its members had been socialised into.

McRobbie *Says* **Girls** *Have Been Involved in* **Youth Subcultures**

There aren't as many girls in subcultures, and their role is often as **girlfriend** to a male in the group. This is linked to the **social control** of girls, who have generally been given **less freedom** than boys.

Angela McRobbie and Jenny Garber (1976) write about the **bedroom subculture**. This is where girls spend a lot of time in their bedrooms with friends, listening to music, experimenting with make-up and discussing pop music. This means that girls **accept social control** but still have a **private space**. This is **not spectacular**, but **it is a subculture**.

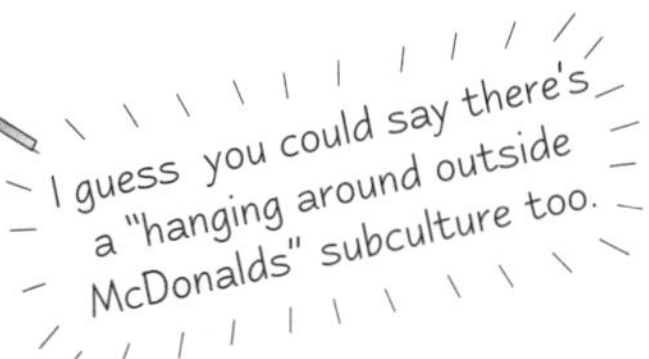

On the other hand, there were **plenty of girls** in the 1980s and 1990s **Goth** subculture. Some elements within the Goth subculture are **particularly feminised** — e.g. both male and female **Romantic Goths** wear lace clothing and lots of eye make-up.

Sociologists have Often **Ignored Ethnic Minority Subcultures**

1) Sociologists have often seen the **whole ethnic group** as a **subculture** — that means if you're a young Asian, sociologists have tended to focus on the "Asian" part and ignore the fact that you're young.
2) There are Asian youth subcultures, but they **haven't had as much attention** from sociologists as say, Punk.
3) Some sociologists like **Maria Gillespie (1995)** (see p.42) have started looking at "**hybrid identities**" which bring together influences from **various cultures** and media.

Rastafarianism *is an* **Important Black Subculture**

Although Rastafarianism is a **religion**, it does have several of the **characteristics** of a **spectacular youth subculture**.

1) It's **oppositional**. Rastafarians rejoice in being black and believe **mainstream white society** is **corrupt**.
2) It requires **illegal activity**. Smoking **marijuana** is a part of Rastafarian **religious meditation ritual**.
3) It has a **spectacular style**. Some Rastafarians wear **dreadlocks**, often with a cap in red, green, gold and black.
4) It's associated closely with a **distinctive music**. Reggae and Dub are strongly linked to Rastafarianism.

Because the **stylistic elements** of Rastafarianism are so **strong**, they've sometimes been taken up by **non-Rastafarian black youth** in a more **subcultural** way. They've also **attracted** young people from **other ethnic groups**.

Practice Questions

Q1 How is youth culture different from culture?

Q2 What is a subculture?

Q3 What do sociologists mean by 'spectacular youth subcultures'?

Q4 What is 'ordinary youth'?

Q5 What is the 'bedroom subculture' of girls, and whose research used this term?

Exam Questions

Q1 (a) Identify and explain two reasons for the development of youth subcultures in Britain during the past 60 years. (15 marks)

(b) Many sociologists see spectacular youth subcultures as mainly white, male and working class. Explain whether or not you think they are right to do so. (30 marks)

Das Boot — a great German sub culture film...

...cos it's set on a submarine. Ha ha ha. Ha ha. Ha... Er, anyway, you've got your mainstream culture, your youth culture and your subculture. These pages really aren't that hard to get your head around. It's fairly likely that you've already got a working idea of what a subculture is. We've all seen a punk, a hippie, a goth etc.

Theories of Subculture

So now you know what a subculture is, the next thing to look at is why young people join them. Sociologists have worked out various reasons. A big point of difference is between the Functionalists, who think everything in society exists for a good reason, and the Marxists, who think that everything is a reaction to the oppression of capitalism.

Functionalists Think that Society Needs Subcultures

1) Pre-industrial societies often used **Rites of Passage** — "growing up" ceremonies to guide children from the **norms and values of childhood** into **adult life**. **Talcott Parsons (1956)** reckoned that youth subcultures are like rites of passage in modern society, acting as a **bridge** between childhood and adulthood. According to Parsons, belonging to a subculture is a **temporary** experience in a person's life.

2) **Eisenstadt (1956)** said subcultures are to do with **ascribed** and **achieved status**. In pre-industrial society every individual's status was **ascribed** from birth. In today's society, people have to **achieve** their status for themselves. **Adolescence** is the time when young people are often **uncertain** about what their status is going to be in the **future**. Eisenstadt believed that **subcultures help young people to cope** with this uncertainty by giving them a **nice, clear status**. You know where you are in a subculture.

3) **Albert Cohen (1955)** was influenced by **Functionalist** ideas, but he added a **new twist**. He says working class boys join subcultures to overcome **status frustration**. In **school** they might feel like **failures**, but in a subculture they can have **high status**. They can **feel superior** to less important members of their own group and to people who aren't members of the subculture.

Fuzzy about the difference between Functionalist and Marxist perspectives? Check out pages 2 and 3. Need to know about ascribed and achieved status — it's on page 5.

Marxists Believe that Subcultures are Caused by Class Conflict

1) **Young, working class males** are at the **lowest level** of society and often have **little to look forward to** in life. It's quite likely that they'll end up in **dead-end jobs** and be tied down by families.
2) According to Marxist Sociologists, this **explains** why **spectacular subcultures** attract working class male youth. The subculture gives them **status** and **independence** which they wouldn't get anywhere else.

Tony Jefferson (1976) researched **1950s Teddy Boys**. Teddy boys wore **Edwardian style jackets**, **suede shoes** and **bootlace ties**. Jefferson reckoned that the **bootlace ties** were from characters in **Western** films who had to **live off their wits** — the sort of character who **working class lads** would **admire**. He thought that the Teddy Boys wore clothes that they felt would give them **higher status**.

Phil Cohen (1972) studied **skinheads**. Cohen thought skinhead style was a **reaction** to the **decline of working class communities**. He said **skinheads** tried to **recreate working class culture** by dressing in grandad shirts, work boots and braces, and by acting in a way that valued **masculinity** and **aggression**.

Dick Hebdige (1979) studied Punk

Hebdige looked for the meanings behind the **clothes** that **punks** wore. He says that Punk was a form of resistance to the dominant cultural values of British society in the late 1970s. The symbolism and style of punk, such as safety pins stuck in the nose, and bin liners for clothes stood for a **rejection** of **common norms** and **values**. Rather than trying to look attractive, punks went out of their way to shock.

Hebdige believes that Punk was a rejection of available **identities**. Instead of accepting the patterns of behaviour, dress and future career that were expected by society, punks chose a different path. They dressed and acted in a way that told the world they wouldn't conform.

Hebdige also looked at how punks mucked about with style and tried to throw away the meaning of objects and symbols — for example they'd use a swastika but they'd try to take away all the Nazi meaning from it.

Feminist Sociologists criticise the above approaches for **ignoring** the role of **gender** in subcultures. They argue that this is because **Sociology as a whole** is **male-dominated**, and subcultures have been of particular interest to **male** researchers. There's more about the relationship between gender and subcultures on page 93.

Theories of Subculture

Postmodernists Say There's **No Such Thing** as Subcultures Any More

Spectacular subcultures seem to be a **thing of the past**. In the 1980s and onwards, youth subcultures **fragmented** into lots of small movements and trends, like rave and hip-hop. They didn't seem to involve huge numbers of young people in the same **spectacular** way as the old subcultures. Maybe there are **no real subcultures** any more. Or perhaps there are **so many subcultures** that it's **hard to tell them all apart**.

> **Hetherington (1998)** believes that the fashions and musical styles of the 1980s were **too bitty and too varied** to be described as subcultures.

1) **Paul Willis (1990)** says there are now a wide range of "style and taste cultures" so young people have lots of different ways to define their identity. There's **too much diversity** these days for any **single youth subculture** to **dominate** society.
2) He says that most young people don't want to join uniformed subcultures like Teddy Boys or Punks any more. Instead, they have a much **more individualistic** approach.
3) Willis believes that the **old spectacular subcultures** were quite **passive** — members accepted norms and styles of the group as a whole. Young people today are **active** and **create** their own **individual styles** by **mixing up** whatever's available. Willis calls this "**symbolic creativity**".

> Examples of symbolic creativity include:
>
> 1) **Mixing up clothing** from **high street stores** and **charity shops**.
> 2) **Sampling** and **scratching** existing music to create **new music**.
> 3) Using **religious iconography** such as **crosses** or rosary beads as **fashion items**.

Bennett Said *"Young People Don't Form Subcultures"*

Bennett says we **shouldn't talk about subcultures** any more. He invented the term **neo-tribes**. This means a loose group based around **fashion** and **lifestyle**, but **without** the **shared values** that members of a **traditional subculture** would share.

Bennett (1999) researched clubs in Newcastle

Bennett found that young people formed brief, **temporary associations**, instead of subcultures. Friendship groups included people with a **wide range of class backgrounds** and musical tastes. This was unlike the mostly working class subcultures of earlier generations.

Individuals **mixed and matched fashion influences** and didn't feel they belonged to any definable group. They didn't identify with just one lifestyle and set of ideas. Bennett concluded that **youth identity** is now very **fluid** and doesn't involve fixed commitments or norms and values.

Practice Questions

Q1 Who thought that youth subcultures were Rites of Passage?
Q2 According to Albert Cohen, why did working class boys join subcultures?
Q3 Give two examples of the symbolism and style of Punk.
Q4 What type of sociologists think that subcultures have died out?
Q5 Who introduced the idea of 'Neo-tribes'?

Exam Questions

Q1 (a) Identify and explain two ways that youth subcultures changed after 1980. (15 marks)

(b) Outline and discuss the view that youth subcultures are a reaction to economic and social conditions. (30 marks)

No future...

All these spectacular subcultures must be a bit like ancient history. I mean, your parents are probably in the right age bracket for Punk. Here's a test to see if your dad was a punk. Put an old Sex Pistols track on, and see if he starts singing along. Then ask him why he was a punk, if it was a working class thing or not — bingo, you'll have learnt something.

Youth and Deviance

Young people's behaviour sometimes breaks the rules. Sociological theory and research has tried to explain why this is and what sorts of deviant behaviour are typical of the young.

Deviance is Behaviour which Goes Against the Norm

OK, remember the idea of **social norms** from page 4. Norms are **ways of thinking and behaving** that are **shared** by most people in **society**. **Normative** behaviour **follows** these "rules", **deviant** behaviour **breaks** them.

Juvenile crime is where young people break the law

Some types of crime such as **vandalism** and **joyriding** are more likely to be committed by the **young**.

Juvenile delinquency is all disruption caused by young people

This includes **serious crimes**, such as rioting or burglary, **less serious crimes** like graffiti and public drunkenness and **non-criminal misbehaviour** like being cheeky or truanting from school.

Official statistics show a **pattern** of **crime** and **delinquency**.
It seems that **most criminals** are:
1) male 2) adolescent (young) 3) working-class 4) urban

Some Functionalists link Youth Crime to Subcultures

Quite a few **functionalist sociologists** tried to explain why crime tended to be committed by young working class men. Many based their ideas on **Robert Merton's work** from the 1950s and 1960s. They thought that crime and delinquency occur because **society seems to expect more** from **young men** than they can ever **achieve**. They called this "an **imbalance** between **culturally prescribed goals** and **opportunity structures**". Here's what it means:

1) **Young working class males** are **taught** through primary and secondary socialisation that **hard work** brings **material rewards**. →

2) They're bombarded with **images of success** — through advertising, for example. →

3) They **realise** they **don't have** any **real opportunity** to **achieve** this success. →

4) They **rebel** against social norms and look for status from delinquent peers.

1) **Albert Cohen (1955)** saw that young people often committed delinquent acts in **groups** or **gangs**. He called these groups "**delinquent subcultures**".
2) Cohen believed that **working class youth** were **judged** according to **middle class goals** and **values**, which made them **frustrated** with their **status** and gave them a sense of failure.
3) Delinquent subcultures gave these young people a **different source** of **status**. In **delinquent subcultures**, individuals **get status** from their **peers** for doing **deviant** acts like vandalism and shoplifting.
4) **Miller (1962) disagreed**. He said delinquents **weren't rejecting middle class values** — they were **accepting working class ones**. According to Miller, working class communities value masculinity, toughness and thrill-seeking.

Status frustration is the feeling that you can never achieve a position of respect in society. Functionalist sociology says that status frustration happens when a person is given a set of goals, that they know they can't reach.

Left Realism Tries to Explain Causes and Consequences of Delinquency

Left Realism is a viewpoint in sociology which tries to focus on the real world and **not be too theoretical**. Left realist sociologists **Lea and Young (1984)** say inner city **youth crime** is a big problem which damages working class communities. They say crime happens because **working class** and **black** youth **interpret** their situation **negatively**.

1) These groups feel **relatively deprived** because their job potential, income, standard of living and status are all **lower** than **middle class** and **white** youth.
2) They feel **marginalised** (pushed to the outside of society), believing that **nobody listens** to them, the police **harass** them, there are **no places** designed for them, teachers **label** them and so on.

This leads some youths to **look for status** in **subcultures**. **Positive subcultures** such as **sports clubs** offer **status** for **normative** (socially acceptable) behaviour. **Negative** ones give **status** for **delinquent** behaviour, including crime.

Youth and Deviance

Hirschi Says People **Weigh Up** the **Pros** and **Cons** of **Crime**

1) **Travis Hirschi (1969)** is a conservative criminologist.
2) Hirschi **rejects sociological ideas**. Instead of looking at **social causes**, he links youth crime to **individual responsibility**.
3) He says that people **choose** to commit crime after **weighing up** the **benefits and costs**.
4) In Hirschi's view, **older people** commit **fewer crimes** because they usually have **controls** in their lives. When you have family commitments and a career, the **costs of crime** such as prison far **outweigh the benefits**.
5) Youths have **fewer controls** and less to lose — so for them the **benefits** of crime are more likely to **outweigh the risks**.

Labelling Theory Says it's All About ... **Labelling**

Some studies suggest that certain young people are **labelled as delinquent** by the **media** and the **police** — for example, young black men. This means they're **more likely** to be **stopped**, **searched** or **arrested**.

Some sociologists argue that **deviant values** and behaviour appear **throughout society**, but **working class** youth is more likely to be **negatively labelled**. They get **more media attention** and more arrests, though maybe they don't actually commit any more crime than other social groups.

Labelling theory says "**deviance**" is a **master status**. Once you're labelled as delinquent, that becomes the most **important aspect** of your identity. **Everyone** sees you as a **delinquent**, and that's how you **see yourself** too. So, you **behave like a delinquent**. It ends up as a **self-fulfilling prophecy**.

Feminists Point Out That These Theories **Don't Refer** to **Women**

Feminists also say that the studies, which are mostly **just of male youth**, are presented as studies of **all youth**. **Merton's theories** about **expectation** and **failure** would suggest that **young, working class women** would commit a lot of crime — but they **don't**.

1) **Some sociologists** think that **women** have a **civilising influence** on men. When they want to develop **stable relationships** with **women**, young men often have to **give up delinquent activity**.
2) This is because **young women** are more likely to have **normative goals** — in other words their goals and aims are more likely to be in line with the norms of mainstream society.
3) This argument says that although **delinquency** is mostly a **male** activity, you can't understand it properly without looking at **gender relations**.

Practice Questions

1) What is the difference between normative behaviour and deviant behaviour?
2) What is juvenile delinquency?
3) What four characteristics do most criminals have, according to official statistics?
4) According to Hirschi (1969), what leads people to commit crime?
5) Which group in society does Matza (1964) argue are more likely to be negatively labelled?

Exam Questions

Q1 (a) Outline and explain two differences between youth crime and adult crime. (15 marks)

(b) Outline and discuss the view that youth crime is the result of a rational choice by the criminal. (30 marks)

All this talk of deviance is making me feel positively... dirty...

As usual, there are several different explanations of why people do naughty things which society doesn't like. Some sociologists say that people feel they can't measure up to society's standards, so they kick against society — maybe out of some kind of spite. Others say it's about self-fulfilling prophecies — give a dog a bad name. Others say it's personal choice. Hmm...

Youth and Deviance, Gender and Ethnicity

Lots of the sociology on youth crime has (no big surprise here) looked at social class, gender and ethnicity. Page 96 was all about social class. So that leaves... dun dun daaaaahhh...

Statistics Show That Females are Less Involved in Crime

1) **Frances Heidensohn (1986)** says that **gender socialisation** explains why females do less crime.
2) **Male gender roles** include things like **toughness**, **aggressiveness** and **physical strength**. These qualities are associated with **delinquency**.
3) **Female gender roles** include elements like **prettiness**, **softness**, **emotion** and **domesticity**. These aren't the sort of qualities that go with delinquent behaviour.
4) To make sure that girls are **successfully socialised** into female gender roles, they're given **far less freedom** than **boys** are. During adolescence, for example, they're more likely to be **confined** to the **home** by their parents — not allowed to go out.
5) **Sue Lees (1986)** showed that adolescent girls also learn that they have to **control their own behaviour**, especially their contact with boys — so they don't get a **bad reputation**.
6) This **social control** often leads to girls developing a "bedroom subculture" where **girls visit each other** to **play records**, **practise dance moves**, share **teen magazines** and chat. Unlike male adolescent subcultures, this all happens **indoors**, not out on the streets where there are opportunities for delinquent behaviour.

One result of **socialisation** is that girls are **less interested** in committing crime.
One result of **social controls** is that girls have **fewer chances** to get involved in crime.

Some Sociologists Say Females Commit More Crime than People Realise

Anne Campbell (1981) asked males and females to fill in a **self-report survey** by ticking which deviant activities they'd done. She found that **official statistics** show **less female crime** than **actually happens**.

In recent years, statistics have shown that the **female crime rate** has **increased**. **Ann Hagell (1998)** says one explanation is a **reduction in social control**. Girls are **supervised less** than they were in the past.

Statistics Suggesting Links Between Ethnicity and Crime are Criticised

1) According to official statistics from 2000, **Afro-Caribbean** people are **four times as likely to be arrested** as other ethnic groups. Based on the UK population, you'd expect 8% of prisoners to be from ethnic minorities. In fact it's 18%.
2) Sociologists such as **Stuart Hall**, **Paul Gilroy (both 1982)** and **John Solomos (1993)** have all said that **racism** in the **police**, the **media** and the **white population** means that black criminality is exaggerated.
3) **Afro-Caribbean** and **Asian** youths are much **more likely** than white youths to get **stopped** or **arrested**. Some say this shows that the police deliberately **target ethnic minorities**. The **MacPherson report (1999)** stated that the (London) Metropolitan Police were "**institutionally racist**".
4) In 1981, Lord Scarman's **report on the Brixton Riots** discussed the police tactic of **stop and search.** Because they had a **strong street culture**, and were out on the streets more than other ethnic groups, **Afro-Caribbeans** were **more likely** to be **stopped and searched**. Stop and search was **racially discriminatory**.

Some Sociologists Say There are Social Reasons for Black Crime

Paul Gilroy (1982) thinks that black street crime reflects young black people's **anger at white society**. He says it's a **rational political response** to **prejudice** and **discrimination**, especially **police harassment**. He also links it to black people's anger at the **history of slavery** and colonialism.

Left Realists (look at page 96 for more on them) say black youth commit more crime because they're suffering from **relative deprivation** and a feeling of being **marginalised**.

1) Sociologists like Lea and Young also say that youth crime often **damages its own community** or **other underprivileged communities**.
2) Data shows that people from Afro-Caribbean backgrounds are **twice as likely** to be **victims of burglary**. They're also **more likely to be assaulted** than the white population.
3) *But* the **mass media** (see section 4) tends to portray black people as more likely to commit crime, not more likely to have a crime committed against them.

Youth and Deviance, Gender and Ethnicity

Sociologists** have been **Very Interested** in **Gang Culture

Youth gangs are **subcultural groups** who aim to **control a geographical area** called a "**territory**".
They're usually involved in **delinquent** behaviour, such as **crime** and **violence**.
Everything you've learned so far about **deviant youth subcultures** can be applied to gangs.

1) Most gangs are **male**.
2) Mostly, gangs are formed in **poorer urban communities** where there aren't many **opportunities** for young men to get **status** through **education** or a **career**.
3) Gangs are often **linked to boredom**. Gangs form because kids feel there's "**nothing to do**".
4) Gangs often start off with **low-level delinquency** such as **vandalism** and **fighting**. As they get **more organised** and **older**, gangs can move into more **serious criminal activities** like rape and gun crime.
5) Gangs often have very **strict rules** and **status systems**. Sociologists of subculture and deviance see this as a way young people can **replace the norms and values of mainstream society** with their **own**.

Most Sociological Work** on Gangs Comes From the **USA

1) In big American cities, there's often been a strong gang culture.
2) In the **1920s**, **Frederick Thrasher** said that gangs were an important **part of socialisation** in all **poor communities**, helping young people to learn about "**group awareness**", and giving them a **sense of belonging**.
3) By the **1970s**, US sociologists like **Malcolm Klein** were looking at it in a different way. They saw gangs as basically **criminal groups** which are often **tied in** with **specific ethnic groups** — Italian, black, Mexican, Puerto Rican etc.
4) In Britain, **Bullock and Tilley (2002)** did research which backed up this idea of **ethnic selection** in gangs. They found that known members of four main South Manchester gangs were mostly **male** and **black**.

Because **gang members** are mostly from **specific ethnic groups**, a lot of the sociology of **ethnicity** and **youth crime** applies, and you can use it in your answers. Also, since gangs appear in **poorer** communities, all the stuff on **social class** is relevant too.

Gangs** Aren't Just **Male

Mary Celeste Kearney (1998) looked at the recent growth in the numbers of **girl gangs**. She says this reflects wider **changes in gender roles**.

Anne Campbell (1986) studied **New York gangs**. She found that **females** were **full members of gangs** and that they were involved in a wide range of delinquent activities — **violence**, **drug dealing** etc.

Don't mess with the Rollerblade Crew. They'll, uh, nick your water bottle.

Practice Questions

Q1 How did Frances Heidensohn explain the fact that statistics show fewer female criminals than male criminals?

Q2 What did Ann Campbell's self-report survey show?

Q3 According to the Scarman Report (1981), why were African-Caribbean youths more likely to be stopped and searched by the police?

Q4 What did Bullock and Tilley (2002) find about the sex and ethnicity of most known South Manchester gang members?

Exam Questions

Q1 (a) Identify and explain two reasons why young people join gangs. (15 marks)

(b) Outline and discuss the view that females are less deviant than males. (30 marks)

So what's Cell Block H full of then — blokes?...

This link between gender and delinquency isn't as clear cut as you might think. Seems that girls don't tend to go off the rails, but when they do, they can go as far as the guys and get involved in gang violence. Ethnicity and crime is a biiig hot button topic in society. It's all tied up with the relationship between the police, black communities and the media.

Youth and Education

These two pages are for OCR — but they're useful for AQA as well, although they repeat bits of the Education section. *Young people all respond differently to schooling — some pupils accept the rules and the authority of teachers, but some don't. Many sociologists think it's all to do with which subculture you belong to.*

There are *Pro-school Subcultures* and *Anti-school Subcultures*

Pro-school subcultures are **positive** about school. They **accept school rules** and **conform**. They gain **status** from the **school**, from **adults** and from their **friends** by working hard and **achieving highly**. They tend to be **middle class**.

And, guess what... **Anti-school subcultures** are **negative** about school. They **reject school rules** and don't conform in school. They get **status** from their **friends** by **not conforming**. These pupils tend to be **working class**.

These are all common forms of nonconformity in schools:

1) **Truancy** — skipping school
2) **Resistance** — not doing school work
3) **Challenging teachers' authority**
4) **Damaging school buildings** or **property**
5) **Fighting**

Research Suggests *Anti-school Subcultures* are *Working Class* and *Male*

David Hargreaves (1967) says that **working class** pupils are **more likely** to be placed in **lower sets** and feel **labelled** as **failures**. Because of this they **reject the school's values** and follow their own set of **delinquent values** instead. This gives them a chance to **feel successful** in the eyes of their **peers**.

Cecile Wright (1992) found that teachers tended to **label** boys from an **Afro-Caribbean** background as "likely to misbehave". These boys often **felt they'd been unfairly treated** and quickly started to **resent school**. **David Gillborn's research (1990)** revealed similar patterns.

Paul Willis researched lad subcultures in the 1970s

He found that **working class boys rejected** the **values of school** because they associated being a "good pupil" with being "**girly**". The working class lads thought that education offered them nothing. Middle class pupils expected to stay on at school and get higher qualifications. Willis reckoned that because the working class boys didn't achieve in school they got **trapped** into **working class jobs** when they left.

Máirtín Mac an Ghaill (1994) studied low achieving boys

He looked at a group of low-achieving white working class boys, who he called the **"macho lads"** because they were very keen to seem masculine. They were in bottom sets for all subjects, and their behaviour was difficult and aggressive. Mac an Ghaill said they were suffering from a **crisis of masculinity**. They knew that their failure at school meant their future wasn't looking great. They decided all the values of school were effeminate. They linked successful, pro-school boys with homosexuality and called them "dickhead achievers". Which was nice.

On *Average*, *Girls* do Much *Better* than *Boys* at School

Eirene Mitsos and **Ken Browne (1998)** suggest a number of reasons for this — all connected to each other.

1) **Teachers expect less** from **boys**. Because of this, boys are under **less pressure** to **achieve**. Boys are allowed to get distracted and to miss deadlines more than girls are. This is a **self-fulfilling prophecy**.
2) Boys seem to **gain status** from their **peers** by **not doing school work**.
3) There's been a **decline** in **traditional male jobs**. This can make boys feel like education won't lead to a secure future, so some boys see no point in trying at school.
4) Boys can suffer from a **lack of self-esteem**. They may try to build up a **positive self-image** and feel cool about themselves through "**laddish behaviour**".
5) Schools are **pretty darn feminine**. There **aren't very many male teachers** in primary school. **Reading** is really important in education, but boys tend to think reading is "**girly**".
6) A lot of work kids do in school is based on **language skills** as well as **long-term concentration** and **organisation skills**. In general, girls seem to be better at these skills at a younger age than boys.

Youth and Education

Boys and **Girls** Choose **Different Subjects** at School

Girls are **more likely** to take **arts subjects**, like English literature, foreign languages and sociology. More boys choose **scientific** and **technological** subjects. This starts at **GCSE** and gets **more obvious** at **A-Level**.

Some Scientists Say It's Because Of **Biology...**

Some **scientists** believe that boys and girls choose different subjects because their **brains work in different ways**.

The idea of "**biologically programmed**" gender differences has been connected with the fact that **girls** now tend to do **better** than boys at school (see previous page).

Boys are "biologically programmed" for:	Girls are "biologically programmed" for:
Competition	Co-operation
Physical Construction	Language
Factual knowledge	Conceptual knowledge

...But Sociologists Say It's Because Of **Socialisation**

Sociologists reckon that **gender socialisation** is a **much better explanation** for these differences.

It starts with primary socialisation

For example, boys and girls are **encouraged** to play with **gendered toys** — Lego and Meccano sets for boys, dressing-up and dolls for girls. This encourages boys to become interested in technical and science subjects.

Secondary socialisation in school carries on gender stereotypes

1) The **advice** teachers give about **choosing GCSE options** may **reflect gender stereotypes**.
2) **Science** and the science classroom have a **masculine** image. According to **Alison Kelly (1987)** boys dominate science classrooms, **grabbing equipment** and answering questions first.
3) **Anne Colley (1998)** found that **girls did better at science** and technology in **single-sex classes**. Her research showed that many subjects **still** have **gendered images**. For example, ICT is seen as more **masculine** because there's **not much discussion**, students **work in isolation** on machines and the teaching is very **formal**. **Sociology** is seen as **more feminine** — lots of talking.

Gender might be **Less Important** than **People Think**

You can **criticise** this **whole debate**. Gender is an **important issue**, but it **can be overemphasised** — it's **only one** of the factors which affect children's education, after all. In lots of ways, boys and girls have **very similar experiences** at school — same teachers, same classrooms, same National Curriculum, same tests.

Practice Questions

Q1 How do members of anti-school subcultures gain status?

Q2 What is the usual social class and gender of members of anti-school subcultures?

Q3 Why did the boys Willis (1977) studied feel that education offered them nothing?

Q4 Why did Mac an Ghaill (1994) call the boys he studied "the macho lads"?

Q5 Give four reasons, according to Mitsos and Browne (1998), why girls outperform boys in school.

Exam Questions

Q1 (a) Identify and explain two differences between pro-school and anti-school subcultures. (15 marks)

(b) Outline and discuss the view that boys and girls have different experiences of school. (30 marks)

Hide this book behind a magazine, they'll never know you're studying...

Kids have different reasons for thinking it's good to fail at school. The thing is that they don't decide based on what parents or teachers say, but based on what their own peer group will think. Sociologists haven't decided which comes first — boys anti- school subcultures or boys feeling useless at school. Check out the AQA Education section if you like.

Key Issues in Research and Methods

This section is for OCR and AQA. *Sociologists do research to get evidence which helps them understand society. Unfortunately, it's not all that straightforward to study human behaviour. If only we were ants in an ant farm.*

Sociologists** Have **Three Aims** When **Collecting** and **Using Data

1) Sociologists try to make their research **valid** and **reliable**. Research is **valid** when it gives a **true picture** of what's being measured. Research is **reliable** if other sociologists using the **same methods** get the **same data**.

2) You can't research the whole population. You have to take a **sample**. Sociologists try to make sure that their **sample represents the population** — it needs similar proportions of different ages, gender, class and ethnic groups.

3) Sociologists aim to be **objective** and **avoid bias**.

If a study focuses on a particular group, e.g. teenagers or working class people, researchers must still ensure that their sample is representative of that particular group.

Sociologists get data from different sources

1) **Primary sources of data** involve **first hand research** — things like interviews, focus groups, questionnaires or observations.
2) **Secondary** data includes things like **official statistics**.

Data can be either quantitative or qualitative

1) **Quantitative data** is **numbers** and **statistics**. You can easily put quantitative data into a graph or a chart.
2) **Qualitative** data gives a detailed picture of what people do, think and feel. It's **subjective** — it involves **opinions, meanings** and **interpretations**. You can't turn qualitative data into a list of numbers or a graph.

Positivists** Use **Reliable Methods** That Give **Quantitative Data

1) **Positivists** say behaviour is influenced by **external social factors**.
2) They think sociology should be **scientific** and **analyse social facts**. Social facts are things that **affect behaviour** and can be **easily measured**. They're **external** things like laws, **not internal** things like people's opinions.
3) Positivists look for **cause and effect relationships**. They investigate questions like, "Does poverty **cause** underachievement in schools?"
4) They use methods like **questionnaires** and **official statistics**. These are **objective** and **reliable**. They produce **quantitative** data.

Interactionists** Use **Valid Methods** That Give **Qualitative Data

1) **Interactionist sociologists** (also called **interpretivists**) use methods that let them discover the **meanings**, **motives** and **reasons** behind **human behaviour** and **social interaction**.
2) Interactionists reckon that the **scientific** methods used in **positivist** research **don't tell you much** about how **individual people** act in society.
3) Interactionists say you can't count meanings and opinions and turn them into statistical charts. They reckon **sociology isn't scientific** because **humans can't be measured** like ants in an ant farm. People don't always understand questions in questionnaires and they don't always tell the truth to researchers.
4) Interactionists like to use methods that produce **qualitative** data — they try to understand human behaviour from the point of view of the **individual person**. They use methods like **participant observation** and **unstructured interviews** that give a valid and detailed picture of what individual people think.
5) **Max Weber** said it's important to use **empathy** to **get inside a person's head** to figure out **why** they're doing what they're doing. He called this **"verstehen"**. Interactionists take this idea of Weber's very seriously — they're big on empathy.

Participant observation means being actively involved in the research as both participant and observer.

Positivism looks at the **institutions** in society. It's called **macro sociology**.
Interactionist sociology looks at the **individual**. It's called **micro sociology**.

Key Issues in Research and Methods

Theoretical Background *Affects Your* ***Choice*** *of* ***Method***

Theoretical background	Positivism	Interactionism
Explanation of behaviour	It's determined by **social forces beyond people's control**.	Humans actively **make sense** of **social situations** during human interaction.
Aims of sociology	Sociology should discover **what causes what.**	It should **describe** and **explain** how people **make sense** of situations — using **empathy**.
Research methods	**Questionnaires** and **structured interviews** — they give **quantitative data** and they're **reliable** and **objective.**	**Observations** and **unstructured interviews** — they give **qualitative data** and a more **valid insight** into society.

Ethical Factors *Affect Your* ***Choice*** *of* ***Method***

The **British Sociological Association** gives **ethical guidelines** for research. Researchers should use **informed consent** — people should know who's doing the research, why they're doing it and what it's about. **Covert participant observation**, where people don't know a sociologist is watching them, should only be used when there's **absolutely no other way** of getting data.

> Researchers studying **sensitive issues** like domestic violence often choose to use **informal interviews** to put the person answering the questions **at ease**.

Practical Factors *Affect Your* ***Choice*** *of* ***Method***

1) **Time** — Some methods need more time. **Covert participant observation** takes a **long time**. The researcher has to get into the group they're studying and win their trust before starting the actual research. A **social survey** doesn't need the researcher to participate all the time and the **workload can be shared** in a team.
2) **Money** — This affects the **length** and **method** of the research. Money is needed to **pay the researcher**, for **transportation** to interviews and pay for **resources** like computers. **Large scale social surveys** are **expensive**. The 1991 Census cost £135 million. A small focus group will cost a lot less.
3) **Characteristics and skills of the researcher** — It'd be difficult for a **female** researcher to be involved in a participant observation of **monks** in a monastery. Some researchers may be OK with **dangerous situations** and others may prefer to **stay at their desk** and do **detailed analysis** of statistics.
4) **Access and opportunity** — If researchers **don't have access** to certain groups to carry out interviews or observations they have to turn to **secondary sources**.

Practice Questions

Q1 Why do sociologists carry out social research?

Q2 What is the difference between quantitative and qualitative data?

Q3 Name two characteristics of positivism.

Q4 What type of data do interactionists prefer?

Q5 Briefly explain how practical factors affect your choice of method.

Exam Questions

Q1 (a) What is meant by the term validity? (2 marks)
(b) Identify three criticism positivists would make of interactionists. (6 marks)
(c) Examine the different factors that influence the sociologist's choice of research method. (20 marks)

Ready, aim, research...

Sociologists use different methods to produce different types of data. Positivists and interactionists prefer different research methods. There are also ethical and practical factors which influence which method you choose. Remember that funding is a huge factor — sociologists don't work for nowt, y'know.

Surveys

Sociologists choose to use different research methods when they carry out social research. Some methods produce quantitative data. Others produce qualitative data. There are lots of different methods and lots of different problems.

Before You Can Start — You Need a Sample

1) It is **too expensive** and **time consuming** for sociologists to involve the **whole population** in their research. They select a **sample**. Only the census includes everyone.
2) When they select the sample they usually try to make it **represent the population** — with similar proportions of people in terms of age, class, ethnicity and gender.
3) If the population is **homogenous** (all the same) the sample needs to be homogenous. If the population is **heterogeneous** (all different), the sample needs to be heterogeneous.
4) **Random sampling** is where names are selected at random from a list of names called a **sampling frame**. Random sampling is often more representative than non-random sampling.

How to do random sampling

1) **Simple random sample** — Pick names **randomly** from a list. Everyone has an **equal chance** of being selected.
2) **Stratified sample** — Divide the population into groups and make a **random selection** with the **right proportions** (if 60% of the population is male, 60% of the sample must be male).

How to do non-random sampling

1) **Snowball sample** — Find an **initial contact** and get them to **give you more names** for your research.
2) **Quota sample** — Pick people who fit into a certain **category** (say 15 people between 30 and 40).

A Pilot Study Lets You Have a Practice Run

1) A pilot study is a **small-scale** piece of research used as a **practice run**. You might want to **test** the **accuracy** of your **questions**, or **check** to see if there are any **technical problems** in your research design. You do this to make the study **more valid** and **more reliable**.
2) You can also **test how long** the research will take, **train** your **interviewers** and get **research funding** — once you show your project is useful.
3) Pilot studies are **time consuming** and **expensive** and they create a **lot of work**.

Social Surveys Give Quantitative Data

1) **Social surveys** collect information about a large population, using **standardised questionnaires** or **structured interviews**.
2) Social surveys tend to be used by **positivists** as a **primary source** of **quantitative data**.
3) Standard questionnaires and structured interviews are **reliable**. They're used by **Government agencies** and **research companies**.

Townsend used a 39 page questionnaire in his 1979 research on poverty.

Longitudinal Studies are Social Surveys Over a Period of Time

Longitudinal studies are done at **regular intervals** over a **long period of time**. They're often **large scale quantitative** surveys, and they tend to be used by **positivists**. Some TV programmes like *Seven Up* are more **qualitative**.

Seven Up was a TV documentary that asked 14 kids aged 7 what they thought about life, and what they wanted to be when they grew up. The programme makers came back to interview the children every seven years. The latest instalment was *Forty-Two Up*.

Strengths of longitudinal studies

1) You can **analyse changes** and **make comparisons** over time.
2) You can study how the **attitudes** of the sample **change** with time.

Limitations of longitudinal studies

1) It's **hard** to recruit a **committed sample** who'll want to **stay** with the study.
2) It's **hard to keep contact** with the sample, which may make the study less valid.
3) You need **long-term funding** and you need to **keep the research team together**.
4) Longitudinal studies rely on **interviews** and **questionnaires** which might not be **valid** or **reliable**.

Surveys

Questionnaires *Mainly Give* ***Quantitative Data***

Questionnaires mainly use **closed questions** and standardised **multiple choice answers** — e.g. "What's your favourite fish? Tick *cod, haddock, salmon, sea bass, tuna* or *other*". Don't forget though that some questionnaires use **open-ended** questions.

Questionnaires mainly give you **quantitative** data which positivists like. **Standardised questions** make them **reliable**. A questionnaire with **open-ended questions** can give you some insight into **meanings** and **motives**. They give you **qualitative** data. The **reliability** and **validity** of a questionnaire depends on **how it's designed**.

Questionnaires should...

1) Use **clear, simple questions** which are **easy to understand.**
2) Give **clear instructions** and make it **easy** for the respondent.
3) Have a nice **clear layout** that doesn't **intimidate** people.
4) Give a **range of options** on **multiple choice** questions.
5) **Measure** what **you want to measure.**

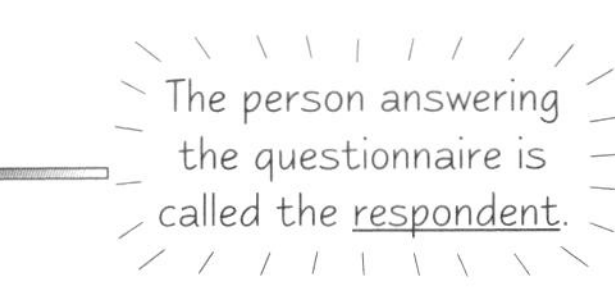

Questionnaires shouldn't...

1) Ask **embarrassing, threatening** or **complex** questions.
2) Ask **two questions instead of one.**
3) Be **too long.**
4) Use **sociological** terms that **no one understands.**
5) **Lead** the respondent to **answer a question** in a **particular way.**

Strengths of questionnaires

1) They're **quick, cheap** and they can reach lots of respondents.
2) They're **reliable** because the questions are **standardised.**
3) They're **easy to analyse** with computer programmes.
4) There's **no interviewer** to **affect** people's answers.
5) You can **spot patterns** in the answers and **make comparisons.**

Limitations of questionnaires

1) Respondents **may not tell the truth.**
2) Questions may be **misleading** or **mean different things** to **different people.** They may not measure what you actually **want to measure.**
3) Postal questionnaires have a **low response rate.** If it's **too low** it won't be a **representative** sample.
4) **Open ended questions** make it **hard to quantify the data** into nice neat **numbers.**
5) No one can **explain** the questions if the respondent doesn't understand them.

Practice Questions

Q1 Why do sociologists select a sample?

Q2 Briefly explain two types of sampling procedures.

Q3 What is a social survey?

Q4 What are the benefits of carrying out a pilot study?

Q5 Name two problems with questionnaires.

Q6 What type of data do questionnaires mainly produce?

Exam Questions

Q1 (a) What is meant by a longitudinal survey? (2 marks)
(b) Identify three problems with longitudinal surveys. (6 marks)
(c) Assess the usefulness of questionnaires in sociological research. (20 marks)

I had to give a sample at the doctor's, don't say I need one here as well...

Pick your sample first, then do a pilot study. Check what you're doing is really as valid and reliable as you'd like it to be. Questionnaires are harder to work out than you might think — you've got to give sensible options for multiple choice questions, and you've got to make the questions really clear and easy to understand.

Interviews and Observations

These pages are about getting primary data from interviews and observation.

An **Interview** is a **Conversation** Between a **Researcher** and a **Respondent**

1) An **interview** is a **conversation** between a **researcher** and an **interviewee** where the researcher asks a set of questions.
2) You have to pick the **sample**, organise an **interview**, select / train your **interviewers**, **ask the questions** and **record the answers**. **Bias** can get in the way in each step. An interviewer should create a **friendly relaxed atmosphere**.
3) An **interview effect** is when the **response** given isn't what the interviewee **really thinks**. This can be caused by the **gender**, **age**, **class** or **personality** of the interviewer. The **opinions** of the **researcher** and **interviewer** can **influence** the interviewee.

Structured Interviews = Quantitative Data, Unstructured ones = Qualitative Data

1) **Structured interviews** ask the **same standardised questions** each time. The questions are closed questions, with set **multiple choice answers**.
2) They give **quantitative data** and they're very **reliable**.
3) They're used in **large-scale social surveys**.
4) The interviewer can **explain** and **clarify** the questions.
5) Structured interviews can ask the **same questions** as a questionnaire, but they get a much **higher response rate**. People tend to agree to be interviewed.
6) They're **more expensive** than questionnaires — you need to **pay for the interviewer**.
7) The interviewer has to **follow the list of questions** so they **can't ask for more detail** if the respondent says something **particularly interesting**.

1) **Unstructured interviews** are **informal**, with **no rigid structure**.
2) They're good for researching **sensitive issues** where the interviewer has to gain the respondent's **trust** — for example sexuality, domestic violence, crime.
3) They use **open ended questions** and give **qualitative** data. They're quite **valid**.
4) The interviewer needs to have **skill** so they can **probe** to **find out more detail** about the interviewee's **beliefs** and **opinions**.
5) They're used with **smaller samples**, which means they're **not very representative**.
6) There are a lot of **interviewer effects** in an unstructured interview. The interviewee may say what they **think** the **researcher wants to hear**.
7) It takes a **long time** to write up an **unstructured interview** — you have to write down a **whole conversation**, not just the **codes** for particular **multiple choice answers**.

Ethnography Studies the **Way of Life** of a Group

1) **Ethnography** was first used by **anthropologists** to study **traditional societies**. They joined the community, learnt the language and noted their observations.

Anthropology is the study of humans.

2) It's small scale field work that tends to produce **qualitative** data. It's **valid** because you can study behaviour in **natural settings**.
3) You can use all sorts of methods to get **primary data**. You can use **unstructured interviews**. You can **observe** a community and see what they get up to.
4) **Case studies** are in-depth studies of **particular events** like **demonstrations**.
5) You can find out an **individual's life history** with **interviews** and **observations**.
6) **Time budgeting** is where you ask people to keep a **detailed diary** of their activities during a specified time. This can create **qualitative** and **quantitative** data.
7) Researchers may also analyse **diaries** and **letters**, which are **secondary data**.

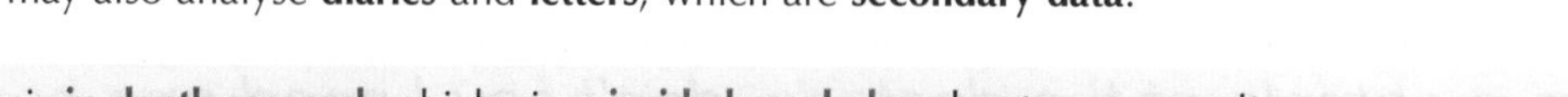

- Ethnography is **in-depth research** which gives **inside knowledge** about a community.
- You get a **valid** picture from ethnography, but it relies on the **researcher's interpretations** of what people do and say.
- It's **difficult** to **make generalisations** from small scale research.

Interviews and Observations

Observation is Watching Behaviour in Real-Life Settings

1) In **covert observation**, the researcher **doesn't tell the group** they're being observed. The BSA advise that you should only use covert participant observation when there's **no other way** of obtaining the data.
2) **Overt observation** (direct observation) is when the group is aware of the research and they know who the researcher is.
3) **Participant observation** is when the researcher **actively involves themselves in the group**.
4) **Non-participant observation** is when the researcher **observes** the group but isn't actively a part of the group.

Interactionists prefer observation because the researcher can get to the action.
It tends to produce **qualitative** data that's more **valid** than questionnaires.

Participant and *Non-Participant Observation* Have Pros and Cons

Participant observation

1) Participant observation gets the researcher **right to where the action** is — so they can **check out the dynamics of a group** from **close up**.
2) **Participant observation** allows you to research the workings of deviant groups.
3) The researcher gets **first hand insight** of people in **natural real life settings**.
4) If it's **covert**, people **can't mislead** the researcher.

But...

1) The researcher may get too involved and find it **hard to stand back** and **objectively observe** the group.
2) **Overt research** may **influence** the behaviour of the group.
3) The researcher in a **covert observation** may join in with illegal acts if they're in a deviant group.
4) You **can't repeat the research**. It **lacks reliability**. A covert observer may find it difficult to remember all the events and accurately record them.
5) There are **ethical** and **practical** problems in **getting in**, **staying in** and **getting out** of the group.
6) The research usually includes a **small group** so it's not **representative** of the population.
7) It is **hard work**, **time-consuming** and **expensive**.

Non-participant observation

1) In **non-participant** observation, the researcher **isn't drawn into the group** so they can be more **objective** about the group's behaviour.
2) If you want to observe **deviant** groups, you have to be very **inconspicuous**.

But...

1) **Observing from the outside** stops you from getting to where the **action** is.
2) **Overt research** may **influence** the **behaviour** of the group.

Practice Questions

Q1 What is ethnography?

Q2 What research methods could you use to carry out ethnographic research?

Q3 What is the difference between covert and overt observation?

Q4 Briefly explain two strengths of participant observation.

Q5 Give two differences between structured and unstructured interviews.

Exam Question

Q1 Assess the usefulness of unstructured interviews to the sociologist. (20 marks)

Sociologists could be everywhere, watching us... shhhh...

It's annoying, this tendency people have to say what they think the researcher wants to hear. Can you really trust anything someone says in an interview...? I dunno. Participant observation gives access to people, but it's difficult to do and you won't necessarily get the same results twice. I don't think I'd want to do a participant observation of serial killers.

Experiments

You can use experiments to give you quantitative primary data.
You can get quantitative secondary data from statistics, and qualitative secondary data from documents.

Experiments Let You Find Cause and Effect

Testing a hypothesis with an experiment is called the Hypothetico-deductive model.

1) Experiments are used by **natural scientists** — biologists, chemists etc.
2) The researcher starts with a **hypothesis** and they use the experiment to **test** it out.
3) All the variables are kept constant, apart from the one you're interested in — the **independent variable**. Scientists **change the independent variable** and observe the effects on the **dependent variable**. If you were testing the effects of temperature on electrical resistance, **temperature** would be the **independent variable** which **you control** and **electrical resistance** would be the **dependent variable** which you **measure**.
4) The results are **turned into numbers** — the scientist looks for **patterns** and **cause and effect** relationships.
5) This method has been developed and used by **social scientists** to look for **social** causes and effects.

There are Three Kinds of Experiment

1) **Lab experiments** are done in a **controlled environment**. The researcher **changes** the **independent variable**. The researcher observes the effect on the **dependent variable**. The researcher usually uses a **control group**, which is **left alone** to see what happens if you **don't do anything** to the **independent variable**. This method is often used by psychologists.
2) **Field experiments** are a response to the criticisms of lab experiments. They take place outside of the lab in **real social settings** and those involved are often **unaware**. This method is used by **interactionist** sociologists.
3) **Natural experiments** are not set up artificially. An example would be **twin studies**, but these are quite rare.

Twin studies are where you study identical twins (who are genetically identical) in different situations, to see whether something's caused by genetics or if it's caused by socialisation.

Strengths of lab experiments

1) The **researcher** has **control** over the experiment.
2) You get **quantitative** data.
3) You can **replicate** the research.

Limitations of lab experiments

1) It's **hard to reproduce real social situations** in a lab — lab experiments are **artificial**.
2) It is **difficult to isolate single variables**. **Social behaviour** is influenced by **many factors**.
3) There are often **moral** and **ethical** issues in lab experiments.
4) People may feel **intimidated** or **act differently** in the lab.

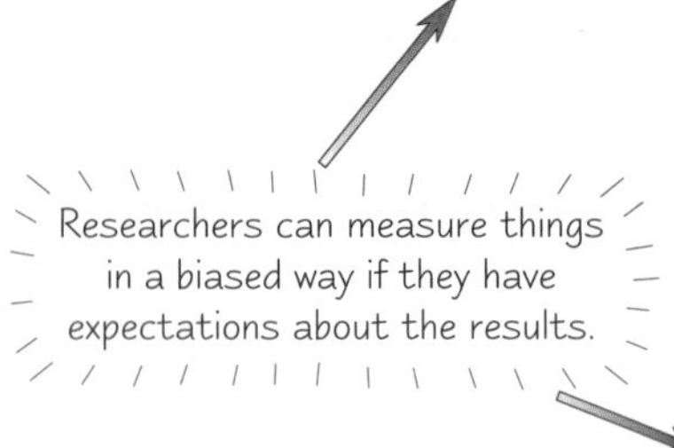

Strengths of field experiments

1) They're done in **natural social settings** and are more like **real life**.
2) They can show the **hidden meanings** of **everyday social interaction**.

Limitations of field experiments

1) You **can't control the variables** like you can in lab experiments.
2) If people **know they're being studied** they may **change** their **behaviour**.
3) There's an **ethical problem** in carrying out experiments when the subjects **aren't aware** that they are taking part in an experiment.

When People Know They're Being Studied, They Sometimes Act Differently

1) When people are **interested** in something, they **try harder**. They may try harder at what they're doing to get a **positive response** from the researchers. This is called the **Hawthorne Effect**.
2) People try to **figure out** what kind of **response** the **researchers want**. People often either give the researchers the **response they think they want** or the **exact opposite** — depending on whether they want to please the researchers or whether they want to be stubborn.
3) People usually try to show themselves in the **best possible light**. They may say they **wouldn't commit crime** when **really they would**. They may say they **recycle all their rubbish** when **really they don't**.
4) These effects mean data from experiments may not be **valid**.

Secondary Data

Official Statistics are a Source of *Secondary Data*

1) **Official statistics** are a source of secondary data. They're produced by local governments, central government and government agencies.
2) **Hard statistics** are **objective**. Politicians can't fiddle with them. Statistics on births and marriages are hard statistics.
3) **Soft statistics** are more **subjective**. Politicians can fiddle with them. Statistics on **crime**, **poverty** and **unemployment** are soft statistics. In the 1980s and 1990s, the government **changed the method** used to **measure unemployment** over 20 times.
4) **Social Trends** is a collection of **regular government surveys** published every year. It's a **great source** of **secondary data**.
5) The **Census** is a survey of every household every 10 years. Every household has to fill in the form **by law**.
6) The **British Crime Survey** looks at victims of crime. The data is collected by a questionnaire.

Documents and *Mass Media* are a Source of *Secondary Data*

1) A document is **written text**. Documents can be **personal** — like **letters**, **diaries**, **autobiographies**, **memoirs** and **suicide notes**. Documents can also be **official**, like **school records**, **health** records, **church** records and **social work** records.
2) Documents can be **expressive** — more to do with **meanings**, like a **suicide note**. Documents can be **formal** — like **official documents**. **Interpretivists** prefer **expressive** documents because they're a big source of **qualitative data**.
3) **Max Weber** used **historical documents** when he was studying how the **religious** beliefs of Calvinism brought about a **social change**. **Michel Foucault** used **historical documents** to analyse changes in **social control** and **punishment**.
4) There are **problems** with documents. They can be **difficult to understand** if they're old. They might be **fakes**. They might contain **lies** — especially personal documents.
5) The **mass media** is another source of **secondary data** about people and society.
6) Sociologists analyse **documents and the media** by looking at **content**, **themes** and **style of language** used.

Sociologists Compare Different Secondary Documents

1) Sociologists look for **similarities** and **differences** between different secondary documents. They can compare different **times**, different **cultures** and different **groups** within society by looking at secondary data.
2) Researchers can analyse real social behaviour and make comparisons without having to set up artificial experiments.
3) Durkheim used this **comparative method** in his famous 1897 study of suicide. He looked at the rates of suicide in different European societies. He found that the suicide rate was **consistent over time**, **but varied between societies** and varied for **different groups** within society.

Practice Questions

Q1 What's meant by an independent variable?

Q2 Name two advantages of the field experiments over laboratory experiments.

Q3 What is the Hawthorne effect?

Q4 What is the difference between hard and soft statistics?

Exam Questions

Q1 (a) What is meant by social variables? (2 marks)

(b) Identify and briefly explain two sources of secondary data. (8 marks)

(c) Assess the usefulness of experiments to the social scientist. (20 marks)

Anyone up for an experiment on how people cope with being millionaires...

If you're not really into science, this business about dependent and independent variables might seem a tadge confusing. Don't be too confused — just remember that the dependent variable is the one you measure to see how it's changed. All the stuff on secondary data is fairly straightfoward, I reckon — it's about what kind of secondary data sociologists use.

Interpreting Data

You can interpret, analyse and evaluate data in lots of different ways.

Check Data's **Reliable, Valid** and **Representative**

Valid = data is a **true picture** of **what you're measuring.**
Reliable = you can use the **same method again** under the **same conditions** and get the **same results.**
Representative = the **sample** has the **same proportions** as the **population.**

Look for **Correlations** and Patterns in **Quantitative** Data

Correlation is where one variable is related to another.

GCSE attainment by parents' socio-economic classification, 2002

	5 GCSE grades A*-C	1-4 GCSE grades A*-C	5 GCSE grades D-G	1-4 GCSE grades D-G	None reported
Higher professional	77	13	6	...	3
Lower professional	64	21	11	2	2
Intermediate	52	25	17	2	4
Lower supervisory	35	30	27	4	4
Routine	32	32	25	5	6
Other	32	29	26	4	9

Published in *Social Trends 34*. Source — Youth Cohort Study.

The appendix of *Social Trends*, tells you that the Youth Cohort study had 35 000 respondents.

If you were **analysing this data**, you would have to:

1) See **what the table's about**. The **title** tells you that this table is about how **educational achievement** is related to **parents' socio-economic position**.
2) Find out **where it's from**. It says ***Social Trends***. This is a collection of government research. It's possible that there could be political **bias** here.
3) Look for a **correlation** between the variables. In this table, high socio-economic class seems to go with lots of GCSEs at grades A*-C.
4) See what it **tells** you. It says that children with parents in higher socio-economic positions achieve a **higher percentage** of top grades. Children with parents in **routine** occupations achieve a **higher percentage** of **grades D-G**.
5) Ask if the data is **valid**. The **cause and effect** relationship you can **see** might not be the **only one** there. There's a **correlation**, but it might not be the **cause**. Some sociologists would say that **material deprivation** is the cause but there might be **other causes** that the table just doesn't show.
6) Find out about the **sample**. It's from the **Youth Cohort** study, which has a **large** sample — so you could make **generalisations** about the **population** as a **whole**.
7) Find out about **how** the data was collected. The Youth Cohort study gets its data from school records. You could repeat this study again and get the same results.

If you've got a hypothesis about educational achievement and class, you can use the figures to test it out.

Question the **Method** and the **Sample** with **Qualitative** Data

"I always leave the quiet ones to just get on with their work. Girls are OK in the class too. It's the boys you have to be tough on. They are usually the trouble makers."

Imagine you got this quote from an **unstructured interview** with a teacher. You would have to:

1) Ask yourself whether the interviewee might have said it because of something to do with the **method**. A **different method** might produce a **different response**, so it might not be very **reliable**.
2) Ask yourself if it's **really what the interviewee believes** or whether they said what they **thought** the **interviewer wanted to hear**. This quote might not be a **true reflection** of how this teacher really acts.
3) See if the sample is **representative**. The research might use a **small** or **untypical sample** — which doesn't tell you much about **teachers in general**.
4) Find out **who carried out the research**. A researcher might have a particular **political** or **sociological point of view**. They can present the research in a way that suits their theories. This is **bias**.
5) Figure out what it **means**. The item tells us something about processes like **labelling** that go on in schools.

Interpreting Data

Analyse **Official Statistics** — They're Not as **Objective** as they First Seem

Official statistics are a **really useful** source of **existing information**. Some sociologists love them because they're **cheap** and **available** (fnar, fnar...). With **official statistics**, you can look at **trends** over **time**. The sample sizes tend to be **huge**, so at least you know they're **representative**. Official stats are sometimes your **only source of information**. There are some **problems** with official statistics, though — they don't always **measure** what they **say** they measure.

1) **Positivists** like official stats — they think official stats are a source of **objective**, **reliable** data. They **analyse** the relationship between social **variables** and look for **correlations** and **cause and effect relationships**.
2) **Marxists** say that **official statistics** are **Government statistics**. They think all official stats are **politically biased** to serve the **interests of the ruling class**, and **designed** to **avoid political embarrassment**.
3) **Interactionists** say that **official statistics** are **not hard facts**. They are **not as objective** as they **first seem**. Interpretivists say **statistics** are **social constructions** and don't tell you about **meanings** and **motives**.

Example — crime statistics don't tell you an **objective figure** of how many **crimes** are committed.

The police **don't know about all crimes** that are committed. Some criminals get **let off**. Some people **don't trust the police** enough to **tell** them about a crime. Some people might not **realise** they're a victim of crime. So — there's crime that we **plain don't know about** if we use **official statistics**.

Analyse Content of **Documents** and the **Mass Media** — but **Take Care...**

1) Traditional **quantitative content analysis** produces **statistical data**.
2) For example, you can **count** the **number of times something happens** in a **TV programme** — like the number of times girls are in a passive role.
3) The research is **reliable**, **easy to obtain** and you can **make comparisons**.
4) The problem is that the **researchers' interpretations** may be **biased**. Researchers **might not agree** on exactly what counts as a "passive role" for example.
5) You still have a lot of **explaining** to do even if you have a **clear result** like "ethnic minorities are under-represented in TV programmes". You have to explain **how** and **why**.

Qualitative content analysis looks for **themes** and **meanings** in media and documents. **Interpretivists** prefer this method because it **uncovers hidden meanings**. It's more **valid** than quantitative analysis. The down side is that the researcher can **interpret** the sources in **different ways**. It's not very **reliable**.

John Scott (1990) thinks sociologists should be **really careful** when **analysing secondary sources**.

1) Documents might **not** be **authentic** — they might be **fakes**.
2) They might **not** be **credible** — the author might not be telling the **truth**.
3) They might **not** be **representative**.
4) They might be **difficult to understand** — full of **old fashioned** meanings.

Practice Questions

Q1 How are the methods used to analyse quantitative data different to those used for qualitative data?

Q2 Name a strength of official statistics.

Q3 How would interactionists criticise official statistics?

Q4 What does John Scott (1990) say about analysing documents?

Exam Questions

Q1 a) What is meant by the term reliability? (2 marks)
b) Suggest three problems when using documents. (6 marks)
c) Examine the advantages and disadvantages of official statistics as a source of data for the sociologist. (20 marks)

I'm looking for patterns in an Argyle jumper...

In the OCR exam, you can get given a set of data to make sense of. Make sure you go through it like these pages tell you to, and you'll be fine. Always look at how data's collected, the sample size, bias, validity and reliability. Don't get validity and reliability confused, will you. People seem to get them mixed up in the exam, and it'll lose you marks.

Limitations of Research

Research has its limits — it can't tell you everything. Here are all the pros and cons of different kinds of data.

Primary Data is Collected First Hand — it has Good Points and Bad Points

The researcher collects primary information first hand — they find it themselves. You could use methods like **interviews**, **questionnaires**, **observations**, **ethnography** or **experiments**. You gather the quantitative or qualitative data.

1) Primary data is **first-hand research**. It doesn't rely on **another sociologist's research** and you can carefully **choose your method** to make your data as valid and reliable as possible.
2) Primary data is always **brand new** and **bang up to date**.
3) **Some methods** of getting primary data can be **expensive** and **time-consuming**.
4) **Some methods** may put the researcher in a **dangerous situation**.
5) **Some methods** may be **unethical** if you don't give **informed consent**.
6) The **researcher's own values** may mess with the research process. This creates **bias**.
7) You **can't always get access** to the group you want to study.

Secondary Data is Existing Information — it has Pros and Cons

Secondary data includes **official statistics**, **diaries**, **letters**, **memoirs**, **emails**, **TV documentaries** and **newspapers** as sources. You gather the data together and analyse it, but you don't generate the data.

1) You can **quickly** and easily collect secondary data.
2) You can **easily** use **secondary data** to **compare different societies**.
3) With secondary data you can study **past events and societies**. You can **compare past** and **present**.
4) You don't have to worry about **informed consent**.
5) The **existing data** may not be **valid** or **reliable** — you're **stuck** with the way the research was **originally done**.
6) Documents may not be **authentic**, **representative** or **credible**. Official statistics can be **biased**.
7) You **might not be able to find** the information that you need from existing data.
8) **Your values** don't influence the **collection** of the data, but the **researcher's values** might have ruined the validity of the **original research**. **Your values** can get in the way in **how you analyse** the data.

Quantitative Data Can be Reliable but Not Very Valid

1) With quantitative data, you can **test your hypothesis** and look for **cause and effect** relationships.
2) You can **compare** your statistics against existing statistics, and look for **trends over time** and between societies.
3) It's **easy** to **analyse tables**, **charts** and **graphs** — especially line charts, bar graphs and pie charts.
4) You can **repeat** questionnaires and structured interviews to **test reliability**.
5) Quantitative methods allow **large samples** so the findings **represent** the **general population**.
6) **Statistics** can **hide reality**. **Categories** in **interviews** or **questionnaires** can **distort** the truth.
7) They don't tell you anything about the **meanings** and **motives** and **reasons** behind behaviour — there's not much **depth** and **insight** into **social interaction**.
8) They can be **politically biased**. The method may have been chosen in order to get the "right" data.

Qualitative Data can be Valid but Not Very Reliable

1) **Qualitative data** gives **insight** into **social interaction**. It's a **detailed description** of social behaviour.
2) Qualitative data lets you find out the **meanings** and **motives** behind behaviour.
3) You don't have to **force** people into **artificial categories** like in questionnaires.
4) Qualitative methods let you build up **trust** and research **sensitive topics**.
5) Qualitative methods are **difficult to repeat** — they **aren't very reliable**.
6) The research is often on a **small scale** — so the findings might not **represent** the whole population.
7) **Positivists** say qualitative results **lack credibility** because they're **subjective** and open to interpretation.
8) The **researcher** can get the **wrong end of the stick** and **misinterpret** the group or individual they're studying.

Limitations of Research

Triangulation *is When You* ***Combine Methods*** *or* ***Data***

Triangulation is when sociologists try to combine different methods or data to **get the best out of all of them**.

1) **Triangulation** gives a more **detailed picture** than when you only use **one method**, so it's more **valid**.
2) When you triangulate, you can **check different sets of data against each other**, so it's more **reliable**.
3) Triangulation combines the **strengths** and the **weaknesses** of different types of data
4) It can be **expensive** and **time consuming** to do the same research with lots of methods.
5) Sometimes, it's **not possible** to use triangulation — you might only be able to use **one method**, or there might not be very many **different kinds of data** for what you're studying.

Eileen Barker (1984) studied the Moonies

The Moonies are a religious organisation, also known as the Unification Church. Barker used **in-depth interviews**, **overt participant observation** and **questionnaires**. She used questionnaires to test out hypotheses that she'd thought of after doing the interviews and observations.

Mac an Ghaill (1994) studied masculinity

He used **overt participant observation** and **interviews** with young straight men and young gay men.
He **discussed ideas** about what made a man masculine.
He didn't just observe the young men and try to figure out what they thought.

Research Results *can be Reported in* ***Books*** *and* ***Journals***

Sociological research is published in **books** or in **journals** like the *British Journal of Sociology* (**BJS**). Journals give very specific **guidelines** on how to write the report. The BJS has **rules** about spelling, grammar, length and **avoiding sexist** and **racist language**. There are also **ethical** guidelines to follow.

All journal articles tend to follow a **similar pattern**:

1) **Abstract** — a **small paragraph** which **briefly** describes **intentions**, **results** and **conclusion**.
2) **Introduction** — explains what's being investigated and why.
3) **Methods** — describes the **methods** used and **why they were chosen**.
4) **Results** — presented with tables, charts, quotes etc.
5) **Discussion** — the **significance** of the results, any **methodological problems**, any **suggestions** of **new social policy**.
6) **References** — a list of the books, journals, websites and newspapers that were used.

Quantitative data is reported in the form of **tables**, **figures**, **pie charts**, **line graphs** and **bar charts**.

Qualitative data is reported in the form of **quotes**. If you were researching bullying with **unstructured interviews** you might **quote** different people's **feelings** about being bullied. You can stick the whole **interview transcripts** at the end in the **appendix**.

Practice Questions

Q1 Give an example of a method that produces quantitative data.

Q2 Name a strength of quantitative data.

Q3 What is secondary data?

Q4 Name a limitation of secondary data.

Q5 What is triangulation?

Q6 What pattern do journal articles usually follow?

Exam Question

Q1 Assess the usefulness of unstructured interview to the sociologist. (20 marks)

Oops, my revision's just done some Bermuda triangulation...

Eee by 'eck there's a lot on these two pages. Thing is, you can be asked to assess and evaluate any kind of method or data, so you really do need to know all the pros and cons. If you've got your head around the section as a whole, you'll know where you are with structured interviews, primary data, secondary data etc.

Do Well in Your AQA Exam

These two pages are all about how to do well in AQA exams. So don't bother reading them if you're not doing AQA.

Units 1 and 2 each have 3 Core Areas

1) **Units 1 and 2** each have **three core areas.** Unit 1 has 'Families and Households', 'Health', and 'Mass Media'. Unit 2 has 'Education', 'Wealth, Poverty and Welfare' and 'Work and Leisure'. You will have been taught at least **one core area for each unit.**
2) The exam papers for units 1 and 2 are worth **60 marks** each and are each **1 hour 15 minutes** long.
3) In the exam, there's **one large question** about **each core area** in the unit. You only have to do **one** of these large questions. Make sure you **choose** the **unit** which you have been **taught and revised.**
4) Each large question has **six parts** to it — (a) to (f). There's always a **source** or two to read at the start.
   - **Part (a)** is worth **2 marks,** and asks you to define a term or phrase from the sources.
   - **Parts (b)-(d)** are worth **4, 6** and **8 marks** respectively — they ask you to give **examples** of something, give **reasons** for something, or **briefly explain something.**
   - **Parts (e)** and **(f)** are **essay questions,** worth **20 marks each.** In part **(f)**, you have to **refer to one of the sources.**

Unit 3 is about Sociological Methods

1) **Unit 3** is 'Sociological Methods'. This exam is worth **60 marks** too but you only get an **hour** to do it.
2) There's **one big question** which you have to answer — you don't get any choice on this paper.
3) The question has a similar layout to units 1 and 2:
   - You get **two sources** to read, which can be **descriptions** of a **sociological study** or **articles** about **sociological methods.**
   - You get asked **four simple questions** worth between **2 marks** and **10 marks** — you have to define something or write about the problems with a particular method.
   - Then you get two long essay questions worth **20 marks** each. In one of them, you **have to refer** to **one of the sources** you've been given.

You Get Marks For...

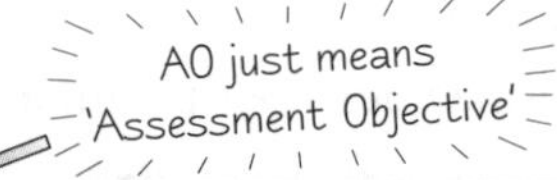

You Get Marks for AO1 — Knowledge and Understanding and AO2 — Identification, Analysis, Interpretation and Evaluation

Part (a)-(d) questions mainly ask you to demonstrate your **knowledge and understanding (AO1)** of the theories, studies and concepts of the module that you have studied. You'll be asked to explain terms, identify reasons and explain key ideas. You might also be asked to identify criticisms of a theory or idea.

Part (e) and (f) questions test **AO1 skills** *and* **AO2 skills.** Part **(e)** has **14 marks** for AO1 and **6 marks** for AO2. Part **(f)** has **6 marks** for AO1 and **14 marks** for AO2. So it's **most important** to **demonstrate your AO2 skills in part (f).**

For AO2 marks you need to do things like:

1) **Choose relevant information / studies** for answering the question.
2) Present the **strengths and weaknesses** of a theory / study.
3) Present **alternative** explanations / interpretations of findings.
4) Use the material to provide a **commentary** — a well-argued essay.

Oh... and don't forget **the basics.**

The AQA examiners really care about stuff like being able to read your handwriting — they're always going on about it in their examiners' reports.

- Write as **neatly** as you can.
- Use good **grammar** and **punctuation.**
- Check your **spelling** — especially of words to do with sociology.
- Make sure you **answer the question.**

Here are some Hints for Short Answer Questions

1) If you're asked for **two** things, give **two** things. **Not one.** Not three. Or four. Five is right out.
2) If you're asked for two things, spend **equal time and effort** on **both.** You **won't** get as many marks for a **lopsided** answer.
3) Give **examples** from **sociological studies** and from **statistics** to **back up** your points.
4) Refer to **sociological theories** like Marxism, Functionalism, Interactionism — but **only** if they're **relevant.**
5) Use the **number of marks** as a **guide** for **how long you should spend on each question.** The more marks a question is worth, the longer you should spend answering it.

Do Well in Your AQA Exam

An **Example Essay** to Show You What to Aim at:

(e) Examine the ways that the mass media portrays men and women. (20 marks)

Don't waffle at the start. Get straight in there with some facts.

Men appear in the media far more often than women. For example, Cumberbatch found that 90% of advertising voiceovers are male. It can be argued that, by not representing women, the mass media marginalises them.

Women's roles in the mass media are often stereotyped. Cumberbatch's study found that women in advertising are unlikely to appear in a workplace setting, which suggests an ideology of women not belonging in paid work. Women who appeared in advertisements were likely to be young and blonde, suggesting an ideology of the importance of youth and beauty. Tuchman thought that there were only two roles for women on television: a domestic housewife role and a young, attractive "babe" role. These two stereotypes are still recognisable in 2004 — women are used as "eye candy" in tabloid newspapers, in men's hobby magazines and on TV gameshows. The Marxist feminist idea of a "double burden" is often apparent in the mass media portrayal of women. Women in advertisements and sitcoms are still often portrayed as responsible for domestic work — even though representations have changed to show them also working outside the home.

Bring in sociological theory.

Ferguson's study of women's magazines concluded that they passed on an ideology which reinforced stereotypes of women as domestic and romantically sexual. She found that the magazines trained women to be feminine, to conform to an ideology of femininity. The idea that magazines pass on an ideology of femininity is also seen in McRobbie's study of magazines for teenage girls. Her study of 'Jackie' magazine concluded that the main theme of the magazine was how to get and keep a boyfriend. The study of teenage magazines raises two key points. The first is that the media is part of the socialisation of young women. Girls are taught to conform to a norm of femininity. The second key point is the importance of being attractive to men — the idea that women are to be looked at by men.

Write about men as well as women.

Societal stereotypes about men are also reflected in the mass media. Men are portrayed as breadwinners in the workplace. They are portrayed as "fix it" guys in ads for DIY products. Male stereotypes in advertising can have the effect of limiting women. For example, in advertisements for cleaning products, men are often portrayed as hapless idiots. This reinforces gender stereotypes: the message is that men do not belong as househusbands, domestic labour is a woman's job. Not all portrayals of men in the media are positive. For example, men are portrayed as less emotional than women. Aggressors and criminals in the media are almost entirely men. Shock is expressed in the media when women are connected with violent crime.

Interpret and analyse data.

The control which men have over the media can be seen as hegemonic and patriarchal. The people who select and control media content are largely men. Croteau and Haynes found that only 6% of newspaper managers were women and 20% of TV managers were women. The theory of hegemonic control says that the ideas of those who run the media are presented as if they were the most natural and obvious things to believe.

Back up your points with evidence.

Put in a conclusion.

In conclusion, the way the media portrays men and women often conforms to gender stereotypes. Men are often portrayed in the role of strong, capable breadwinner. Women are often shown in more domestic roles, or as 'eye-candy'. These roles are fairly limiting for both men and women. However, the stereotypes are more constricting for women, as they tend to be typecast in more passive, submissive roles, while men are typecast in more active, powerful roles.

Here's an Example of a **Unit 3 Question** and **Answer**:

(f) Assess the uses of different kinds of secondary data in sociological research. (20 marks)

Secondary data is data which is not generated first hand by the researcher. It includes official statistics, personal documents, mass media and research generated by other sociologists. Secondary data can be quick and easy to collect, and allows researchers to make comparisons between past and present.

Official statistics present quantitive data, and appear to be objective and reliable. They are readily available, and easy to understand. Official surveys with large sample sizes are representative and can be easily generalised to apply to the whole population. One type of official statistics are called hard statistics, e.g. the number of births, marriages and deaths. These are registered when they occur by law, so these statistics are entirely objective. Another type of official statistics are called soft statistics (e.g. crime statistics and unemployment figures) and these might not be as objective as they first seem. They are open to manipulation for political ends, and can be considered to have a political use. For example, the methods used to measure unemployment have been changed several times: not everyone without a job counts as unemployed. The picture that statistics give can depend on how they were collected, and on what "counts" — they do not always present a valid picture of society.

Give examples.

Statistics appeal to positivists. It is easy to look for correlations and cause /effect relationships in statistics. Unfortunately, the cause and effect that a particular set of statistics shows may not in fact be the most important factor. To compare two variables is to ignore all other sets of variables. Furthermore, to analyse figures on a table or chart is to ignore all the subjective and individual factors which interactionist sociologists focus on.

Discuss theoretical viewpoints.

Interactionists use qualitative secondary data such as diaries and letters. These give an insight into individual opinions and motivations in a society. However, John Scott has pointed out that the subjective nature of this kind of data is a problem — the researcher can misinterpret documents or find them hard to understand, especially if they are old. Documentary data may also be faked or unrepresentative. It may not be credible; the author of the document may have skirted around the truth or lied.

Discuss both strengths and weaknesses.

Mention theorists and studies.

The mass media is a huge source of secondary data which can be analysed with quantitative and qualitative methods. Quantitative content analysis can involve counting the number of times a member of a particular group appears in the media — for example Van Dijk's statistical analysis of newspaper headlines involving members of ethnic minorities. Qualitative content analysis looks for hidden meanings in media texts. It has validity, but it is highly subjective. It is low on reliability because two different researchers could interpret the same text in two different ways — and their interpretation is likely to be covered by their theoretical background. A Marxist is guaranteed to focus on issues of class and is likely to perceive the transmission of an ideology that serves capitalism.

Discuss bias.

In conclusion, the main point in favour of secondary data in general is that the researcher doesn't have to do all the leg work. Gathering primary data by means of surveys, questionnaires and interviews can take up a lot of time, effort and money. The responsibility is with the researcher to collect data with a reliable and repeatable method. However, when using secondary data, the researcher has a responsibility to interpret and analyse the data in an unbiased way.

Put in a conclusion for full marks.

Do Well in Your OCR Exam

This page is all about how to do well in OCR exams. So don't bother reading it if you're not doing OCR.
You have to do exams for the 'Individual and Society' unit and the 'Culture and Socialisation' unit. You might also do an exam on the 'Sociological Research Skills' unit — or you might do coursework instead (depends on your school).

You'll have an Exam on the ***'Individual and Society'*** *Unit*

1) There are two questions on this exam paper, and you **choose one** of them.
2) Each question has a **source** to read at the start and **four parts (a) to (d)**.
3) **Parts (a) and (b)** are worth **8 marks each**. They ask you to give **examples** of something, give **reasons** for something, or **explain the difference** between two things.
4) **Part (c)** is worth **18 marks**. It asks you to **outline and evaluate two things**. It's **part way** between a **long essay question** and a **short question**.
5) **Part (d)** is a long **essay question**, worth **26 marks**. It asks you to discuss a **sociological view**.

You get 1 hour for this 60 mark exam — a minute for each mark.

You'll have Another Exam about the ***'Culture and Socialisation'*** *Unit*

1) The **Culture and Socialisation** unit covers 4 topics: **Family**, **Mass Media**, **Religion** and **Youth and Culture**.
2) There are **eight questions** — two on each topic. **Chose two questions** on topics you have been taught and have revised. **Each question** has **two parts**: **(a)** and **(b)**.
3) **Part (a)** is worth **15 marks**. You have to **identify** and **explain** two sociological trends, or two reasons for a social fact, or two ways that something happens in society.
4) **Part (b)** is worth a honking **30 marks**. It asks you to **outline and discuss** a sociological view.
5) You can do **both questions** on the **same topic** if you like.

You get 1½ hours for this 90 mark exam — again, a mark a minute.

You'll ***Either*** *have an* ***Exam*** *on* ***'Sociological Research Skills'*** *or* ***Coursework***

If you choose to do the **exam unit**, then you'll be faced with **one exam question** which has **four parts (a)** to **(d)**.
There are two sources at the start of the question, which can be **sociological data**, **descriptions** of a **sociological study** or **articles** about **sociological methods**.
1) **Part (a)** is worth **6 marks**. You have to **explain** a **concept** of **sociological research**.
2) **Part (b)** is worth **8 marks**. You have to look at the **sources** and **identify trends or differences**.
3) **Part (c)** is worth **16 marks**. You have to point out the **strengths** and **weaknesses** of a research design.
4) **Parts (d)** is a long **essay question**, worth **30 marks**. It asks you to pick a method for a sociological study, and evaluate it.

You get 1 hour for this 60 mark exam.

You Get Marks For...

AO just means 'Assessment Objective'

You Get Marks for ***AO1 — Knowledge and Understanding*** *and* ***AO2 — Identification, Analysis, Interpretation and Evaluation***

The **shorter answer questions** in each unit which ask you to **give examples** or **explain terms** are for **AO1** marks. You have to show your **knowledge and understanding** of sociological theories, studies, methods etc.

The **shorter answer questions** in each unit which ask you how a data source is related to a sociological concept are **AO2** marks. You have to **interpret** the source and give **examples** or other information relating to it.

Essay questions test **AO1** and **AO2**. You get **AO1** marks for **knowing what you're talking about**, and AO2 marks for **choosing data** to **prove your point**, and for **evaluating** the **ideas you've described**.

Oh... and don't forget **the basics**.

You get marks for the **quality of your writing** on the long answer questions.

- Write in **proper sentences** and **paragraphs**.
- **Structure your essay** — remember the introduction and conclusion.
- **Explain ideas** as **clearly** as possible.
- Use good **grammar**, **spelling** and **punctuation**.

Here are some ***Hints*** *for* ***Short Answer Questions***

1) If you're asked for **two** things, give **two** things. **Not one**. Not three. Or four. Five is **right out**.
2) If you're asked for two things, spend **equal time and effort** on **both**. You **won't** get as many marks for a **lopsided** answer.
3) Give **examples** from **sociological studies** and from **statistics** to **back up** your points.
4) Refer to **sociological theories** like Marxism, Functionalism, Interactionism — but **only** if they're **relevant**.
5) Use the **number of marks** as a **guide** for **how long you should spend on each question**. The more marks a question is worth, the longer you should spend answering it.

Do Well in Your OCR Exam

A Short Example Essay to Show You What to Aim at:

This one is the kind of thing you'd get for a 15 mark question in the Culture and Socialisation paper.

(a) Identify and explain two ways in which religion affects contemporary society. (15 marks)

Refer back to the question in your answer.

Religion can affect contemporary society by influencing peoples' sexuality and by influencing gender roles.

Some religious groups promote a dominant norm of heterosexuality and marriage, which limits and regulates peoples' sexuality. For example, the New Christian Right in America argue, from a fundamentalist Christian viewpoint, that liberal reforms allowing people more freedom and control over their sexuality (for example gay rights) are causing a moral decline in society. They believe people shouldn't have sex before marriage and promote abstinence to young people. They promote their views to society through mass communication, for example television and Christian publishing.

Give examples to support your point.

Other fundamentalist religious viewpoints also try to influence and regulate the sexuality of their believers. For example, under traditional Islamic Sharia law, homosexuality and adultery are heavily punished. In some modern Middle Eastern societies, for example in Saudi Arabia, Sharia law is still used, and has a strong influence on society.

Give TWO ways.

Another way that religion can be argued to affect contemporary society is through influencing gender roles. Many feminists argue that religion acts as an agent of social control, passing on patriarchal ideologies which reinforce the male domination of society. Many churches support and promote conventional family values with traditional roles for women as wife and mother. This encourages women into a passive role. The radical feminist Mary Daly argues that Christian teachings, imagery and hierarchy contribute to this. For example, St. Paul's letter to the Ephesians says, "Wives submit to your husbands" and the central female image in Christianity is of Mary the mother. Modern church hierarchy often excludes women, for example women can't become Catholic priests.

Put in a short conclusion.

In conclusion, some religions directly and indirectly try to influence the social norms of what is acceptable in society in terms of individuals' gender and sexuality. This influence is perhaps strongest in more religious households and communities within society as a whole.

A Longer Example Essay to Show You What to Aim at:

This one is the kind of thing you'd get for an essay question in the Individual and Society paper.

(d) Discuss the view that primary socialisation is responsible for the construction of gender identity. (26 marks)

Primary socialisation takes place in the family, during the child's early years. It is a major force in the social construction of gender, but it is by no means the only important force.

Gender identities are ideas of what it is to be a man and what it is to be a woman. Along with gender identities go gendered norms of what behaviours count as masculine and what behaviours count as feminine. Most sociologists agree that gender is socially constructed: a product of socialisation.

A01 marks for knowledge of a debate about socialisation.

There is evidence that children are gendered by their family from birth. This is their primary socialisation. Studies comparing adult reaction to a baby dressed in blue and introduced as a boy and the same baby dressed in pink and introduced as a girl show very different reactions. The "boy" was described as "big", "strong" and "lively" and the "girl" was described as "sweet" "beautiful" "quiet" and "good".

A02 marks for choosing a study to support your argument.

Ann Oakley (1974) described four ways in which primary socialisation constructs gender. 1) Manipulation — girls are put in pretty dresses and boys are allowed to get more mucky when they play outside. 2) Canalisation — children are directed to play with toys that the parents consider gender-appropriate, e.g. dolls and toy hoovers, building bricks and toy planes. 3) Verbal appellations — girls are called "pretty" and "good", boys are called "cheeky" and "strong". 4) Boys and girls are exposed to different activities. For example, boys often help out with gardening and DIY, girls often help mum with the housework and childcare. This teaches children what men's work is and what women's work is. Oakley said that by the age of five most children have a good idea of what appropriate behaviour for their gender is.

A02 marks for analysing and interpreting the study.

On the other hand, there are other ways, apart from primary socialisation, in which gender identity is constructed. By the age of five, the groundwork of gender socialisation is done, but the process isn't over — secondary socialisation also has a big effect on children. Education treats girls and boys differently. Labelling theory says that labels given to an individual by others affect their behaviour, and can turn out to be self-fulfilling prophecies. Girls are usually labelled as more studious and more compliant than boys. Boys are labelled as disruptive, and often prove to be so. However, boys' disruptive behaviour is likely to be not solely due to negative labelling by teachers. Primary socialisation may have already directed boys to be boisterous and girls to be calm.

Some sociologists also say the hidden curriculum in education passes on gender stereotypes. Girls tend to choose more arts subjects and boys tend to choose more science subjects. The advice that teachers give about subject options may transmit gender stereotypes.

A02 marks for choosing a study to support your argument.

Peer groups in school also have a big effect on gender socialisation. Children are ready to criticise behaviour they consider deviant — insufficiently masculine or insufficiently feminine. Mac an Ghaill found that young men were extremely concerned about masculinity to gain status in their peer groups. He also found that they saw academic achievement as effeminate. Mitsos and Browne thought that this was because education is highly feminised, and therefore does not provide role models for boys. However, if primary socialisation had not already irreversibly socialised children into genders, the fact that the teacher is a woman would not impact upon a male pupil in the least.

A02 marks for giving alternative explanations.

Another factor which affects children's view of gender is the media. The media have a huge effect on the transmission of ideologies about gender. Advertising perpetuates an image of women as concerned with their attractiveness, and her ability as a homemaker. Many films portray women as in need of rescuing by men. Children see media images and are affected by them.

Evaluate — give alternative explanations.

In conclusion, primary socialisation is very significant in the construction of gender identity, and is the first influence on children's ideas about gender. However, as the child grows older, other factors are also important in shaping their gender identity, for example the media, their peer group and their education.

References

These are details of studies which are discussed in the Revision Guide.

Anderson, B. (1983) *Imagined Communities: Reflections on the Origin and Spread of Nationalism* (New York: Verso)

Anderson, M. (1971) 'Family, Household and the Industrial Revolution' in Anderson, M. (ed.) *Sociology of the Family* (Harmondsworth: Penguin)

Ansley (1972) quoted in Bernard (1976) *The Future of Marriage* (Harmondsworth: Penguin)

Aries, P. (1962) *Centuries of Childhood* (New York: Vintage Books)

Atkinson, J. (1986) 'The Changing Corporation' in Clutterbuck (ed.) *New Patterns of Work* (Aldershot: Gower)

Bagdikian, B. (1997) *The Media Monopoly* (Boston: Beacon Press)

Ball, S.J. (1981) *Beachside Comprehensive: A Case Study of Secondary Schooling* (Cambridge: CUP)

Ballard, R. and Ballard, C. (1977) 'The Sikhs' in Watson (ed.) *Between Two Cultures* (Oxford: Blackwell)

Ballard, R. (1994) *Desh Pardesh: The South Asian Presence in Britain* (London: C Hurst)

Bandura, Ross and Ross (1963) 'The Imitation of Film Mediated Aggressive Models' (*Journal of Abnormal and Social Psychology* vol. 66 no. 1)

Barker, E. (1984) *The Making of a Moonie: Choice or Brainwashing* (Blackwell: Oxford)

Baudrillard, J. (1988) *Selected Writings* ed. M Poster (Cambridge: Polity Press)

Becker, H. (1971) 'Social Class Variations in the Teacher Pupil Relationship' in Cosin, B.R. et al. *School and Society* (London: Routledge & Kegan Paul)

Bennett, A. (1999) 'Subcultures or Neo-tribes: Rethinking the Relationship Between Youth, Style and Musical Taste' (*Sociology*, vol. 33 no. 3)

Benston, M. (1969) 'The Political Economy of Women's Liberation' (*Monthly Review* 21, vol. 4)

Bernstein, B. (1970) 'Elaborated and Restricted Codes: Their Social Origins and Social Consequences' in Danziger, K. (ed.) *Readings in Child Socialisation* (Oxford: Pergamon)

Biggs, S. (1993) *Understanding Ageism* (Milton Keynes: Open University Press)

Blauner, R. (1964) *Alienation and Freedom* (Chicago: University of Chicago Press)

Bott, E. (1957) *Family and Social Networks* (London: Tavistock Press)

Boulton, M. G. (1983) *On Being A Mother* (London: Tavistock Press)

Bourdieu, P. (1997) 'The Forms of Capitalism' in Halsy, Lauder, Brown, Wells (eds.) *Education, Culture, Economy and Society* eds. (Oxford: OUP)

Bourdieu, P. (1984) *Distinction: A Social Critique of the Judgement of Taste* (London: Routledge & Kegan Paul)

Bowles, S. and Gintis, H. (1976) *Schooling in Capitalist America* (London: Routledge & Kegan Paul)

Braverman, H. (1974) *Labour and Monopoly Capitalism* (New York: Monthly Review Press)

Bruce, S. (1995) *Religion in Modern Britain* (Oxford: OUP)

Buckingham, D. (1993) *Children Talking Television* (Lewes: Taylor and Francis)

Bullock and Tilley (2002) *Shootings, Gangs and Violent Incidents in Manchester: Developing a Crime Reduction Strategy* (London: Home Office)

Busfield, J. (2001) *Rethinking the Sociology of Mental Health* (Oxford: Blackwell)

Campbell, A. (1981) *Delinquent Girls* (Oxford: Blackwell)

Campbell, A. (1986) *The Girls in The Gang* (Oxford: Blackwell)

Cantril, H. (1940) *The Invasion from Mars: A Study of the Psychology of Panic* (Princeton, N.J.: Princeton University Press.)

Cartwright and O'Brien (1976) *Social Class Variations in Health Care and in the Nature of General Practitioner Consultations* (Sociology Review: Monograph)

Cashmore and Troyna (1990) *Introduction to Race Relations* (London: Routledge)

Clark, J., McLoughlin, I., Rose, H. and King, R. (1988) *The Process of Technological Change* (Cambridge: Cambridge University Press)

Clarke, J. and Critcher, C. (1985) *The Devil Makes Work: Leisure in Capitalist Britain* (London: Macmillan)

Coard, B. (1971) *How the West Indian Child is Made Educationally Subnormal in the British School System* (London: New Beacon Books)

Coates, K. and Silburn, R. (1970) *Poverty: The Forgotten Englishmen* (Harmondsworth: Penguin)

Cohen, A. F. S. (1955) *Delinquent Boys* (Glencoe, Illinois: The Free Press)

Cohen, P. (1972) *Subcultural Conflict and Working Class Community* (CCCS)

Cohen, S. (1973) *Folk Devils and Moral Panics* (London: Paladin)

Cohen, S. and Young, J. (1981) *The Manufacture of News: Social Problems, Deviance and Mass Media* (London: Constable)

Colley, A. (1998) 'Gender and Subject Choice in Secondary Education' in Radford, J. (ed.) *Gender and Choice in Education and Occupation* (London: Routledge)

Comte, A. (1853) *The Positive Philosophy of Auguste Comte* (ed. Harriet Martineau), (London: Chapman)

Condon, T. and Graham, A. et al. (1995) *The Cross Media Revolution: ownership and control* (London: John Libbey)

Croteau and Hoynes (2000) *Media Society: Industry Images and Audiences* (London: Pine Forge)

Cumberbatch, G. (1990) *Sexual Stereotyping in Advertising* (Broadcasting Standards Council)

Cumberbatch and Negrine (1992) *Images of Disability on Television* (London: Routledge)

Daly, M. (1973) *Beyond God the Father* (Boston: Mass Beacon Press)

Davies and Moore (1945) 'Some Principles of Stratification' (*American Sociological Review* Vol 10)

Dean, H. and Taylor-Gooby, P. P. (1992) *Dependency Culture: The Explosion of a Myth* (Hemel Hempstead: Harvester Wheatsheaf)

Delphy and Leonard (1992) *Familiar Exploitation* (Cambridge: Polity Press)

Dobash and Dobash (1979) *Violence Against Wives* (New York: The Free Press)

Dobash and Dobash (1992) *Women, Violence and Social Change* (London: Routledge)

Douglas, J. (1964) *The Home and School* (London: MacGibbon and Kee)

Douglas, Ross, and Simpson, (1968) *All Our Future* (London: Panther)

Doyal and Pennell (1979) *The Political Economy of Health* (London: Pluto Press)

Drewnowski, J. and Scott, W. (1966) *The Level of Living Index* (Geneva: UN Research Institute for Social Development)

Driver, G. and Ballard, R. (1981) 'Contemporary Performance in Multiracial Schools: South Asian Pupils at 16+' in James, A. and Jeffcoate, R. (eds.) *The School in the Multicultural Society* (London: Harper and Row)

Durkheim, E. (1897; translated 1951) *Suicide: A Study in Sociology* (London: Routledge & Kegan Paul)

Dutton, B. (1986) *The Media* (London: Longman)

Edgell (1980) *Middle-class Couples* (London: Allen & Unwin)

Edwards and Scullion (1982) *The Social Organisation of Industrial Conflict. Control and Resistance in the Workplace* (Oxford: Blackwell)

References

These are details of studies which are discussed in the Revision Guide.

Eisenstadt (1956) *From Generation to Generation* (New York: The Free Press)

Eisenstadt (1967) 'The Protestant Ethic Thesis' (*Diogenes* 59)

Engels, F. (1884) *The Origin of the Family, Private Property and the State* (New York: International Publishers)

Eversley, D. and Bonnerjea, L. (1982) 'Social Change and Indications of Diversity' in Rapoport et al. *Families in Britain* (London: Routledge and Kegan Paul)

Eysenck, H. (1971) *Race, Intelligence and Education* (London: Temple Smith)

Featherstone, M. and Hepworth, M. (1995) *Images of Positive Ageing* in M. Fetherstone and A. Wernick (eds.) *Images of Ageing* (London: Routledge)

Ferguson (1983) *Forever Feminine: Women's Magazines and the Cult of Femininity* (London: Heinemann)

Ferri, E. and Smith, K. (1996) *Parenting in the 1990s* (London: Family Policy Studies Centre)

Feshbach, S. and Singer, R. (1971) *Television and Aggression: An Experimental Field Study* (San Francisco: Jossey-Bass)

Fiske, J. (1988) *Television Culture* (London: Methuen)

Friedmann, A. (1977) *Industry and Labour: Class Struggle at Work and Monopoly Capitalism* (London: Macmillan)

Fuller, M. (1980) 'Black Girls in a London Comprehensive School' in Deem, R. (ed.) *Schooling for Women's Work* (London: Routledge & Kegan Paul)

Gans, H. (1974) *Popular Culture and High Culture* (New York: Basic Books)

Gershuny, J. (1992) 'Changes in the Domestic Division of Labour in the UK 1975-1987' in Abercrombie, A. and Warde, A. (eds) *Sociology and Policy Change in Contemporary Britain* (Cambridge: Polity Press)

Ghaill, M. Mac an (1994) *The Making of Men: Masculinities, Sexualities and Schooling* (Milton Keynes: Open University Press)

Giddens, A. (1992) *The Transformation of Intimacy: Sexuality, Love and Eroticism in Modern Societies* (Cambridge: Polity Press)

Gillborn, D. (1990) *Racism, Ethnicity and Education* (London: Routledge)

Gillespie, M. (1995) *Television, Ethnicity and Cultural Change* (London: Routledge)

Gilroy, P. (1982) in Hall et al. *The Empire Strikes Back* (London: Hutchison)

Gilroy, P. (1987) *There Ain't No Black in the Union Jack* (London: Hutchinson)

Gittins, D. (1993) *The Family in Question (2nd ed.)* (Basingstoke: Macmillan)

Glasgow University Media Group (1976) *Bad News* (London: Routledge & Kegan Paul)

Glasgow University Media Group (1980) *More Bad News* (London: Routledge and Kegan Paul)

Glasgow University Media Group (1982) *Really Bad News* (London: Writers and Readers)

Glennon and Butsch (1982) 'The Family as Portrayed in Television 1946-1978' in Pearl, D. et al. (eds.) *Television and Behaviour* (National Institute of Mental Health).

Goffman, E. (1961) *Asylums: Essays on the Social Situation of Mental Patients* (Harmondsworth: Penguin)

Goffman, E. (1970) *Stigma: Notes on the Mismanagement of Spoiled Identity* (Harmondsworth: Penguin)

Goldthorpe, J.H., Lockwood, D., Bechhofer, F., and Platt, J. (1969) *The Affluent Worker in the Class Structure* (Cambridge: CUP)

Gough, I. (1979) *The Political Economy of the Welfare state* (London: Macmillan)

Gray, A. (1992) *Video Playtime* (London: Routledge)

Greenberg, B. et al. (1983) *Life on Television: Content Analysis of US TV Drama* (Norwood, N.J.: Abblex)

Grint, K. (1991) *The Sociology of Work: An Introduction* (Cambridge: Polity Press)

Grint, K. and Woolgar, S. (1992) 'Computers, Guns and Roses: What's Social About Being Shot?' (*Science, Technology and Human Values* vol. 17 no. 3)

Grossberg et al. (1998) *Media Making: Mass Media in a Popular Culture* (London: Sage)

Guibernau, M. (1996) *Nationalism: the Nation-state and Nationalism in the Twentieth Century* (Cambridge: Polity Press)

Guibernau and Goldblatt (2000) 'Identity and Nation' in Woodward, K. (ed.) *Questioning Identity: Gender, Class, Nation* (Routledge)

Hagell, A. (1998) in Rutter, Giller and Hagell (eds.) *Antisocial Behaviour in Young People* (Cambridge: CUP)

Halevy, E. (1927) *A History of the English People in 1815* (London: Unwin)

Hall, S. et al. (1982) *The Empire Strikes Back* (London: Hutchinson)

Hall, S. (1992) 'The Question of Cultural Identity' in Hall, Held and McGrew (eds.) *Modernity and its Futures* (Cambridge: Polity Press)

Hall, S. (1996) 'New Ethnicities' in Morley and Chen (eds.) *Stuart Hall: Critical Dialogues in Cultural Studies* (London: Routledge)

Halsey, A. H., Heath, A. F., and Ridge, J. M. (1980) *Origins and Destinations* (Oxford: Clarendon)

Hargreaves, D., Hester, S. and Mellor, F. (1975) *Deviance in Classrooms* (London: Routledge & Kegan Paul)

Hargreaves, D. (1967) *Social Relations in Secondary School* (London: Routledge and Kegan Paul)

Hart, N. (1985) *The Sociology of Health and Medicine* (Ormskirk: Causeway Press)

Hartmann and Husband (1974) *Racism and the Mass Media* (London: Davis-Poynter)

Hebdige, D. (1979) *Subculture: The Meaning of Style* (London: Routledge)

Heelas, P. (1996) *The New Age Movement* (Oxford: Blackwell)

Heidensohn, F. (1986) *Women and Crime* (London: Macmillan)

Herberg, W. (1956) *Protestant – Catholic – Jew* (New York: Doubleday)

Hermes (1995) *Reading Women's Magazines* (Cambridge: Polity Press)

Hetherington (1998) *Expressions of identity: Space, Performance, Politics* (London: Sage)

Hides, S. (1995) 'Consuming Identities' (*Sociology Review* vol. 5 no. 2)

Hill, R. (1987) *The Housing Characteristics and Aspirations of Leicester's Inner City Asian Community* (unpublished PhD: University of Leicester)

Hirschi, T. (1969) *Causes of Delinquency* (Berkeley: University of California Press)

Hobson, D. (1990) 'Women Audiences and the Workplace' in Brown, M. (ed.) *Television and Women's Culture: The Politics of the Popular* (London: Sage)

Hook, S. (1990) *Convictions* (New York: Prometheus Books)

Hyman, H. H. (1967) *The Value Systems of Different Classes* in Bendix, R. and Lipset (eds.) *Class, Status and Power* (London: Routledge & Kegan Paul)

Illich (1971) *The Deschooling Society* (Harmondsworth: Penguin)

Illich (1975) *Medical Nemesis* (London: Calder and Boyars)

Jefferson, T. (1976) 'Cultural Responses of the Teds' in Hall, S. and Jefferson, T. (eds.) *Resistance through Rituals: Youth Subcultures in Post-war Britain* (London: Hutchinson University Library)

Jones, N. (1986) *Strikes and the Media* (Oxford: Blackwell)

Katz and Lazarsfeld (1955) *Personal Influence: The Part Played by People in the Flow of Mass Communication* (Glencoe, Illinois: The Free Press)

References

These are details of studies which are discussed in the Revision Guide.

Kearney, M.C. (1998) 'Don't Need You: Rethinking Identity Politics and Separatism from a Grrrl Perspective' in Epstein (ed.) *Youth Culture in a Postmodern World* (Oxford: Blackwell)

Keddie, N. (1971) 'Classroom Knowledge' in Young, M.F.D. (ed.) *Knowledge and Central* (London: Collier and Macmillan)

Kelly, A. (1987) *Science for Girls* (Milton Keynes: Open University Press)

Kerr, C. and Siegel, K. (1954) 'The Inter-industry Propensity to Strike' in Kornhauser, Dubin and Ross (eds.) *Industrial Conflict* (New York: McGraw Hill)

Kincaid, J. C. (1973) *Poverty and Equality in Britain: A Study of Social Security and Taxation* (Harmondsworth: Penguin)

Klein, M. (1997) *The American Street Gang: its Nature, Prevalence and Control* (Oxford: OUP)

Kling, R. (1991) 'Computerisations and Social Transformations' (*Science, Technology and Human Values* vol. 16 no. 3)

Labov, W. (1973) 'The Logic of Nonstandard English' in *Tinker, Tailor, The Myth of Cultural Deprivation* (Harmondsworth: Penguin)

Lane, T. and Roberts, K. (1971) *Strike at Pilkingtons* (London: Fontana)

Lash, S. and Urry, J. (1993) *Economies of Signs and Space* (London: Sage)

Laslett, P. (1972) 'Mean Household Size in England Since the Sixteenth Century' in Laslett (ed.) *Household and Family in Past Time* (Cambridge: CUP)

Lea, J. and Young, J. (1984) *What Is To Be Done About Law and Order?* (Harmondsworth: Penguin)

Le Grand, J. (2003) *Motivation, Agency and Public Policy: Of Knights and Knaves, Pawns and Queens* (Oxford: Oxford University Press)

Le Grand, J. (1982) *Strategy and Equality: Redistribution and the Social Services* (London: Allen and Unwin)

Lees, S. (1986) *Losing Out: Sexuality and Adolescent Girls* (London: Hutchinson)

Lewis, O. (1959) *Five Families* (New York: Basic Books)

Lewis, O. (1961) *The Children of Sanchez* (New York: Random House)

Lewis, O. (1966) *La Vida* (New York: Random House)

Lull (1990) *Inside Family Viewing: Ethnographic Research on Television Audiences* (London: Routledge)

McKeown, T. (1976) *The Role of Medicine: Dream, Mirage or Nemesis* (London: Nuffield Provincial Hospitals Trust)

McQuail (1972) *The Sociology of Mass Communications* (Harmondsworth: Penguin)

McRobbie, A. (1991) 'Working Class Girls and the Culture of Femininity' in *Contemporary Cultural Studies Part II: Women Take Issue* (London: Hutchinson)

McRobbie, A. and Garber, J. (1976) 'Girls and Subcultures' in Hall and Jefferson (eds.) *Resistance through Rituals* (London: Hutchinson)

Mack, J. and Lansley, S. (1985) *Poor Britain* (London: Allen & Unwin)

Mack, J. and Lansley, S. (1992) *Breadline Britain 1990s: The Findings of the Television Series* (London: London Weekend Television)

Macpherson of Cluny, Sir William (1999) *The Stephen Lawrence Inquiry: Report of an Inquiry by Sir William Macpherson of Cluny* (London: The Stationery Office)

Malinowski, B. (1954) *Magic, Science, Religion and Other Essays* (New York: Anchor Books)

Matza, D. (1964) *Delinquency and Drift* (New York: Wiley)

Maduro, O. (1982) *Religion and Social Conflicts* (Maryknoll, New York: Orbis Books)

Marcuse, H. (1964) *One Dimensional Man* (London: Routledge & Kegan Paul)

Marsland, D. (1989) 'Universal Welfare Provision Creates a Dependent Population: The Case For' (*Social Studies Review*, Nov. 1989)

Meehan (1983) *Ladies of the Evening* (New York: Scarecrow Press)

Melton, G. 'Another Look at New Religions' (*The Annals of the American Academy of Political and Social Science* vol. 527)

Merton, R. (1968) *Social Theory and Social Structure* (New York: Free Press)

Miliband, R. (1969) *The State in Capitalist Society* (London: Weidenfeld and Nicolson)

Miller (1962) 'Lower Class Culture as a Generating Milieu of Gang Delinquency' in M.E. Wolfgang et al (eds.) *The Sociology of Crime and Delinquency* (New York: John Wiley and Sons)

Mirza, H. (1992) *Young, Female and Black* (London: Routledge)

Mitsos, E. and Browne, K. (1998) 'Gender Differences in Education: The Underachievement of Boys' (*Sociology Review* vol. 8 no. 1)

Modood, T. et al. (1997) *Fourth National Survey of Ethnic Minorities* (Policy Studies Institute)

Morgan, D. H. J. (1975) *Social Theory and the Family* (London: Routledge and Kegan Paul)

Morley (1980) *The Nationwide Audience* (London:BFI)

Morrison, D. (1999) *Defining Violence: The Search for Understanding* (Luton: University of Luton Press)

Murdock (1949) *Social Structure* (New York: Macmillan)

Murray, C. with Heinstein, R. (1993) *The Bell Curve* (Free Press)

Murray, C. (1995) 'The Next British Revolution' (*The Public Interest Journal*, 1st January)

Murray, C. (1989) *Underclass* (Sunday Times Magazine, 26 Nov. 1989)

Navarro, V. (1976) *Medicine Under Capitalism* (New York: Neale Watson)

Nicolson, P. (1998) *Post-Natal Depression: Psychology, Science and the Transition to Motherhood* (Chichester: Wiley)

Oakley, A. (1972) *Sex, Gender and Society* (London: Temple Smith)

Oakley, A. (1974) *The Sociology of Housework* (Oxford: Martin Robertson)

Oakley, A. (1984) *The Captured Womb: A History of the Medical Care of Pregnant Women* (Oxford: Blackwell)

O'Brien, M. and Jones, D. (1996) 'Revisiting Family and Kinship' (*Sociology Review* Feb. 1996)

Orbach, S. (1991) *Fat is a Feminist Issue* (Berkeley: Berkeley Publishing Group)

Pahl, R. (1984) *Divisions of Labour* (Oxford: Blackwell)

Pahl, R. (1989) *Money and Marriage* (Basingstoke: Macmillan)

Pahl, R. (1993) Money, Marriage and Ideology: Holding the Purse Strings (*Sociology Review*) Sep. 1993

Parker, S. (1976) 'Work and Leisure' in Butterworth, E. and Weir, D. (eds.) *The Sociology of Leisure* (London: Allen & Unwin)

Parsons, T. (1951) *The Social System* (New York: The Free Press)

Parsons, T. (1956) *Family, Socialisation and the Interaction Process* (London: Routledge & Kegan Paul)

Phillips, M. (2003) 'The Tyranny of Victim Culture' (*The Daily Mail*, 3rd Dec.)

Piachaud, D. (1981) 'Peter Townsend and the Holy Grail' (*New Society*, 10 Sep.)

Piachaud, D. (1987) 'Problems in the Definition and Measurement of Poverty' (*Journal of Social Policy* 16, no 2)

Pollert, A. (1988) Dismantling Flexibility (*Capital and Class* vol. 34)

Pollock, L. (1983) *Forgotten Children: Parent:Child Relations From 1500 to 1800* (Cambridge, C.U.P)

Roberts, K. (1978) *Contemporary Society and the Growth of Leisure* (New York: Longman)

Rowntree, S. (1901) *Poverty: A Study of Town Life* (London: Macmillan)

References

These are details of studies which are discussed in the Revision Guide.

Rowntree, S. (1941) *Poverty and Progress* (London: Longman)

Rowntree, S. and Lavers, G. (1951) *Poverty and the Welfare State* (London: Longman)

Rutherford (1998) *Male Order: Unwrapping Masculinity* Chapman and Rutherford (eds.) (London: Lawrence and Wishart)

Saunders (1990) *Social Class and Stratification* (London: Routledge)

Rt. Hon. The Lord Scarman *The Brixton Disorders, April 10-12, 1981: Inquiry Report. Chmn. Lord Scarman (Command Paper)* (London: The Stationery Office Books)

Schudson, M. (1994) *Culture and the Integration of National Societies* (Oxford: Blackwell)

Schwartz, A.J. (1975) 'A Further Look at the Culture of Poverty: Ten Caracas Barrios' (*Sociology and Social Research*, Vol. 59, no. 4)

Scott, J. (1980) *The Upper Classes: Property and Privilege in Britain* (London: Macmillan)

Scott, J. (1990) 'Documents in Social Research' (*Social Studies Review*, September)

Scraton, S. (1994) 'The Changing World of Women and Leisure: Feminism, Postfeminism and Leisure' (*Leisure Studies* vol. 13, no. 4)

Sharpe, S. (1976 and 1994) *Just like a Girl: How Girls Learn to be Women* (Harmondsworth: Penguin)

Signorelli (1989) 'Television and Conceptions about Sex Roles' (*Sex Roles* vol. 21)

Smith, J. (1987) *Different for Girls: How Culture Creates Women* (London: Chatto and Windus)

Solomos, J. (1993) *Race and Racism in Britain* (London: Macmillan)

Spender, D. (1983) *Invisible Women: Schooling and Scandal* (London: Women's Press)

Stacey, J. (1990) *Brave New Families: Stories of Domestic Upheaval in Late Twentieth Century America* (New York: Basic Books)

Stanworth, M. (1983) *Gender and Schooling: A Study of Sexual Divisions in the Classroom* (London: Hutchinson)

Stark and Bainbridge (1985) *The Future of Religion* (Berkeley: University of California Press)

Sugarman, B. (1970) 'Social Class, Values and Behaviour in Schools' in Craft, M. (ed.) *Family, Class and Education* (London: Longman)

Swann Report (1985) *Education for All* (London: HMSO)

Szasz, T. (1971) *The Manufacture of Madness* (London: Routledge & Kegan Paul)

Thompson, E.P. (1967) 'Time, Work Discipline and Industrial Capitalism' (*Past and Present* no. 38)

Thompson, P. (1989) 'The End of Bureaucracy' in Haralambos, M. (ed.) *The Labour Process: Changing Theory and Changing Practice* (London)

Thrasher, F. (1927) *The Gang* (Chicago: Chicago University Press)

Townsend, P. (1970) *The Concept of Poverty* (London: Heinemann)

Townsend, P. (1979) *Poverty in the United Kingdom* (Harmondsworth: Penguin)

Troeltsch, E. (1931 and 1956, originally 1912) *The Social Teachings of the Christian Churches* (New York: Macmillan)

Tuchman (1978) *Hearth and Home: Images of Women in the Mass Media* (New York: Oxford University Press)

Tudor Hart, J. (1971) 'The Inverse Care Law' (*The Lancet* Saturday 27th Feb.)

Tumin, M. M. (1967) 'Some Principles of Stratification: A Critical Analysis' in Bendix and Lipset (eds.) *Social Stratification: The Forms and Functions of Social Inequality* (Englewood Cliffs, NJ: Prentice Hall)

Turkle (1996) *Life on the Screen: Identity in the Age of the Internet.* (London: Weidenfeld and Nicholson)

Van Dijk (1991) *Racism and the Press* (London: Routledge & Kegan Paul)

Walker, A. (1990) 'Blaming the Victims' in Murray, C. *The Emerging British Underclass* (London: IEA)

Walker, C. and Walker, A. (1994) 'Poverty and the Poor' in Haralambos (ed.) *Developments in Sociology Vol. 10*

Wallis, R. (1984) *The Elementary Forms of the New Religious Life* (London: Routledge & Kegan Paul)

Weber, M. (1958) *The Protestant Work Ethic and the Spirit of Capitalism* (New York: Scribner's Sons)

Wedderburn, D. (1974) *Poverty, Inequality and Class Structure* (Cambridge: CUP)

Westergaard, J. and Resler, H. (1976) *Class in a Capitalist Society* (Harmondsworth: Penguin)

Willis, P. (1977) *Learning to Labour: How Working Class Kids Get Working Class Jobs* (London: Saxon House)

Willis, P. (1990) *Common Culture* (Buckingham: Open University Press)

Wilmott, P. (1988) 'Urban Kinship Past and Present' (*Social Studies Review*, Nov.)

Wilmott and Young (1960) *Family and Class in a London Suburb* (London: Routledge & Kegan Paul)

Wilmott and Young (1973) *The Symmetrical Family* (Harmondsworth: Penguin)

Wilson, B. (1966) *Religion in a Secular Society* (London: CA Watts)

Woods, P. (1983) *Sociology and the School: An Interactionist Viewpoint* (London: Routledge & Kegan Paul)

Woolf, N. (1990) *The Beauty Myth* (Chatto and Windus)

Wright, C. (1992) 'Early Education: Multiracial Primary School Classrooms' in Gill, Mayor and Blair (eds.) *Racism and Education* (London: Sage)

Wright Mills, C. (1951) *White Collar: The American Middle Classes* (New York: Oxford University Press)

Zaretsky, E. (1976) *Capitalism, The Family and Professional Life* (London: Pluto Press)

Zimbalist, A. (1979) *Case Studies on the Labour Process* (London: Monthly Review Press)

Zuboff, S. (1988) *In the Age of the Smart Machine* (New York: Basic Books)

Every effort has been made to ensure these references are as accurate and comprehensive as possible. For those studies where it has been difficult to obtain full details, we would be grateful for information. Please contact the publisher if you notice any inaccuracies or omissions, and we will gladly update the book at the next reprint. Thank you.

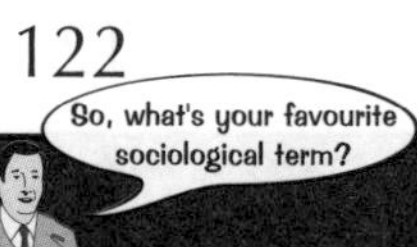

Glossary

absolute poverty Not having the essentials needed for life — food, warmth and shelter.

achieved status Status you get by working for it.

affluent workers Workers who do boring jobs that pay well so they can have a nice life outside work.

alienated labour Work that's turned into a lot of boring meaningless tasks, where workers have no say in what they do, and not enough share of the profits.

allocation function Sorting people out into appropriate jobs depending on their skills.

anomie A state of confusion where the norms of society break down.

ascribed status Status you have from birth.

Bourdieu, Pierre French sociologist who came up with the idea of cultural capital.

bourgeoisie What Marx called the capitalist class.

capitalism Where employers buy workers' labour in return for wages, and sell the things the workers make for profit.

censorship Controlling what can and can't be printed and broadcast.

class Division of society based on how people earn money.

collective consciousness The shared values and norms that hold society together.

communism A system of government which is theoretically based on a classless society and where private ownership has been abolished.

conform To go along with society's norms and values.

conjugal roles Husband and wife roles — who does the paid work, who does the washing up etc.

consensus A shared agreement.

cultural capital The skills and cultural know-how that children learn from their parents.

cultural deprivation theory This theory says working class culture makes people disadvantaged.

culture A way of life, a set of norms and values.

deferred gratification Working and waiting for a while until you get your reward.

delinquency Bad behaviour and social disruption. Includes criminal behaviour and plain annoying behaviour.

desacrilisation Religious and spiritual beliefs ceasing to have a place in society.

deskilled labour Where a job used to need skill, but doesn't any more.

deviant Something that goes against society's norms and values. Deviant behaviour is behaviour that society doesn't approve of.

discourse Any kind of discussion or talk about something.

Durkheim, Emile (1858-1917) French founding father of sociology. He thought that different parts of society had different roles, like the organs of the body.

ethnic group A group of people with a common culture — language, religion and way of life.

ethnocentric Centred around the values and interests of one particular ethnic group.

ethnography Studying the way of life of people by observation, interviews, case studies etc

extended family Three or more generations all living together — grandparents, aunts, uncles, etc.

false consciousness Marxism says that workers are in a state of false consciousness about their place in society. Workers don't realise how unfair it is. If they did, they'd start a revolution.

false needs Herbert Marcuse said that workers are fed the idea that they "need" fancy goods that they don't really need at all.

feminism Belief that women are disadvantaged in society, and that women and men should have equal rights. Feminist sociologists think that mainstream sociology has ignored the lives of women.

folk devil A scapegoat for things going wrong in society.

Functionalism The belief that everything in society exists for a reason.

gender Masculinity and femininity. Sociologists say that gender is a social construction. Being male or female is the biological sex you're born with, while masculinity and femininity are identities you're socialised into.

globalisation The breaking down of traditional national boundaries. This happens due to factors such as the growth of multinational companies, increased migration of people between societies, and the global marketing of culture products.

Hall, Stuart (b.1932) British sociologist, big on studying ethnicity and popular culture.

hegemony The domination of one group of people over another, or of one set of ideas over another.

hidden curriculum The social norms and values that are taught at school, but not as part of the regular curriculum. Includes conformity, respect for authority and other cultural values.

hierarchy A system which ranks people according to status. Any system where you have a boss in charge of people is a hierarchy.

household A group of people who live together. They needn't be related.

hypothetico-deductive model Where you come up with an idea (a hypothesis) and do experiments to test if it's true or not.

iatrogenesis Health problems caused by the medical system.

identity An individual's concept of themselves. This can be related to class, gender, ethnicity.

ideology A set of ideas and beliefs.

industrial action Action that workers take in disputes with their bosses — includes strike, sabotage, work to rule, absenteeism.

infrastructure The economic structure of society.

institutional racism When the policies, attitudes and actions of an institution discriminate against ethnic minorities — sometimes unintentionally.

institutions of society Things like the family, religion, the education system, the healthcare system.

Interactionism A sociological approach which focuses on the actions and the thoughts of individuals. Also called **interpretivism**.

Glossary

internalised norms and values Norms and values that have become part of who you are and the way you think.

interpretivism See interactionism.

labelling theory This theory says that labelling someone as deviant will make them more deviant.

longitudinal study A study done over a period of time.

Marcuse, Herbert (1898-1979) German Neo-Marxist sociologist who had the idea of false needs.

Marx, Karl (1818-1883) German social theorist who wrote *Das Capital* and came up with the somewhat influential theory about power being the control of the means of production.

Marxism The belief that society is divided into the bourgeoisie, who own the "means of production", and the proletariat, who do the work. The bourgeoisie or capitalist class exploit the workers, and arrange society to keep the workers down. Most of the profit from the work that the working class do is kept by the bourgeoisie.

mass media Newspapers, TV, magazines, radio, Internet — media that lots of people use and consume.

master status A label has master status when it's the most important thing about you and it rules how other people view you and how you behave.

means tested benefit A benefit that you can only get if you can prove you're poor enough.

meritocracy A system where the best (most talented and hard-working) people rise to the top.

moral panic A fear of a moral crisis in society. Moral panics are usually linked to "folk devils". The mass media have a big role in stirring up moral panics in modern society.

Murray, Charles American New Right sociologist who believes that there's an underclass who are too dependent on benefits.

nonconformity Not going along with society's norms and values.

norm A behaviour that's considered normal in a particular society, e.g. queuing, wearing clothes, making some eye contact when talking to someone.

nuclear family Mum, dad and children living together.

Oakley, Ann Feminist sociologist who studied housework and gender socialisation.

Parsons, Talcott (1902-1979) American Functionalist sociologist who wrote about the structure and functions of society.

patriarchy A society where men are dominant. Feminists often describe male-dominated societies and institutions as "patriarchal."

peer groups Groups of people who all have the same status in society.

pluralism The belief that society is made of lots of different parts, and that each of those parts gets their say, via democracy and a free market.

positivism A theoretical point of view which concentrates on social facts, scientific method and quantitate data (facts and figures).

post-Fordism A new type of flexible work and management.

postmodernism A movement that emphasises a mix-and-match approach to values, and which says there isn't a single objective truth.

postmodernity The world after the modern age — with flexible working, individual responsibility and people constructing their own identity.

qualitative methods of research Methods like unstructured interviews and participant observation that give results which tell a story about individual's lives.

quantitive methods of research Methods like surveys and structured interviews that give results which you can easily put into a graph or table.

reliability Data is reliable if you can do the same research again and get the same results.

rite of passage A growing up ceremony that young people do to prove they aren't kids any more.

sanction To sanction means to punish.

secularisation When religion becomes less important.

self-fulfilling prophecy When people behave in the way that they know others have predicted.

social construct An idea or belief that's created in society, and doesn't come from a scientific fact.

social democrats People who think the state should redistribute wealth, and that there should be a strong welfare state paid for out of taxes.

social policy Things that governments do that affect society, e.g. raising taxes, having a free healthcare system, allowing schools to run their own budgets, changing divorce laws.

stereotype A generalisation about a social group — often inaccurate and insulting.

stratification The way society is divided up into layers or classes.

stratified sample A sample with the same proportions of gender or class or age as the population you're studying.

subculture A group who share values and norms which are different from mainstream ones.

superstructure The cultural structure of society.

symmetrical family A family structure where conjugal (husband and wife) roles are shared.

text Any piece of media — a book, a TV programme, an advert, a photo.

third way politics A political viewpoint that combines elements of right wing self-sufficiency and left wing social democracy.

triangulation Combining different methods and data to get the best results.

universal benefit Benefit that everyone gets, whether they're rich or poor.

validity Data is valid if it gives an accurate picture.

values Beliefs or standards shared in a society.

vocational education Education to do with work.

Weber, Max (1864-1920) German academic, considered father of modern sociology.

Willis, Paul (b. 1945) Sociologist who studied working class boys and their anti-school subcultures.

Index

Index

Index